Casino Gambling For Dummies®

Safer Bets: Go Ahead, Make Your Day

A casino is a stormy ocean of bad bets, lousy payouts, and unfair odds. But four games do offer a safe harbor. If you made one hundred $1 bets at these recommended games, your average loss would only be about a buck. These odds aren't good enough to retire on, but they stretch your bankroll as far as possible, even if you're on a limited budget. However, remember that life and gambling don't offer any guarantees, and your actual daily results may be far different than your theoretical loss, so plan accordingly.

Jacks or Better Video Poker (the 9/6 Version)

- Make sure you're playing a full-pay 9/6 version by looking at the Full House/Flush payouts for one coin.
- Because of the increased payouts for a royal flush, always play the maximum coins to get the best odds — even if that means finding nickel or quarter machines to stay within your bankroll.
- Never keep a *kicker* (a high card along with a pair).
- Throw away a *small pair* (tens or lower) if you have four cards to a flush or three cards to a royal flush.

Craps (the pass line or don't pass with odds)

The smartest strategy is to stick to the following bets in craps:

- Pass line bet with odds bet
- Come bet with odds
- Don't pass bet with odds
- Don't come bet with odds

Blackjack

- Play the table with the least number of decks.
- Stay away from gimmick games like 6-5 blackjack, Spanish 21, or Super Fun blackjack.
- Remember the following important tips:
    - Double down on 10 or 11 when the dealer shows 2 to 9.
    - Stand on 13 to 16 when the dealer shows 2 to 6.
    - Hit on 12 to 16 when the dealer shows 7 or higher.
    - Never take insurance.

Baccarat

You may be intimidated by baccarat with its glitz, glamour, and European aura, but behind the stiff exterior lies a decent game for the average bettor.

- Always bet on the banker (house edge is 1.06 percent, meaning if you made a hundred bets of $1, your average loss would be about a buck).
- You can also bet on the player's hand. (The house edge is only slightly worse than the banker's hand at 1.24 percent.)

Worst Games: Stay Away at All Costs

Most games have a high *house edge* (percentage advantage the casino has on each bet). Here are some games that I suggest you avoid, unless you want to go home with a lighter wallet:

- Three-Card poker
- Let it Ride
- Red Dog
- Roulette
- Caribbean Stud poker
- Big Six Wheel
- Keno

Casino Gambling For Dummies®

Cheat Sheet

"Disguised as Safe, but Stay Away" Bets

Although the four games in the "Safer Bets: Go Ahead, Make Your Day" section on this Cheat Sheet offer some of the smartest bets in a casino, they also offer bets that can drain your wallet.

- **Jacks or Better Video Poker (6/5 Version):** The payouts are much worse on some versions of video poker. For example, when you make a full house on a 6/5 machine, you get paid only six coins instead of nine.
- **Blackjack — the insurance bet:** This side bet pays back 2 to 1 when the dealer has a blackjack, but the true odds are closer to 2.2 to 1, making this a losing bet over time.
- **Craps — the field and proposition bets:** The house edge can be as high as 16 percent for these seductive bad bets. (Can you say *ouch?*)
- **Baccarat — tie bets:** If you want to keep your money, steer clear of this bet; the house has an edge of 14.36 percent on tie bets.

Managing Your Money

A successful gambler must understand the math and odds behind the games, but staying disciplined is also critical. Losing control is easy after you're inside the casino, so here are a few tips to keep you in the *safe zone.*

- **Never borrow money while gambling.** Chances are good that you'll lose it, making a bad situation even worse.
- **Only bet what you can afford to lose.** Gambling with *scared money,* any portion of your gambling stake you can't afford to lose, is neither enjoyable nor wise.
- **Set and stick to a budget.** Write it on your forehead if you have to, but no matter what, when you hit that number, leave the casino.
- **Avoid ATM machines or lines of credit.** Using credit is a real easy way to get financially overextended while gambling.
- **Limit your playing time.** Taking a break keeps your mind sharp.
- **Hotel rooms have beds — use them.** When you only gamble a few times a year, it's tempting to play marathon sessions. But your body and your bankroll aren't built to handle the casino's pulsating 24/7 schedule, so make sure you sleep and rest.
- **Don't drink and gamble.** If the casinos serve drinks for free, you should be very suspicious.
- **Remember the law of gravity — what goes up must come down.** Casino profits soar when players get greedy. Quitting with a small win is far better than losing the farm.
- **Don't play any game you don't understand.** One of the fastest ways to burn through your cash is to jump into a game where the rules or strategies confuse you.
- **Never lie about your wins or losses.** If you find yourself deluding a person or several people in your life about your gambling, take pause and reevaluate your gambling.

For Dummies: Bestselling Book Series for Beginners

2–

12
/23

Casino Gambling

FOR DUMMIES®

Casino Gambling

FOR

DUMMIES®

by Kevin Blackwood

Foreword by Max Rubin
Author of *Comp City: A Guide to Free Casino Vacations*

WILEY

Wiley Publishing, Inc.

Casino Gambling For Dummies®

Published by
Wiley Publishing, Inc.
111 River St.
Hoboken, NJ 07030-5774
www.wiley.com

Copyright © 2006 by Wiley Publishing, Inc., Indianapolis, Indiana

Published by Wiley Publishing, Inc., Indianapolis, Indiana

Published simultaneously in Canada

For general information on our other products and services, please contact our Customer Care Department within the U.S. at 800-762-2974, outside the U.S. at 317-572-3993, or fax 317-572-4002.

For technical support, please visit www.wiley.com/techsupport.

Wiley also publishes its books in a variety of electronic formats. Some content that appears in print may not be available in electronic books.

Library of Congress Control Number: 2006926109

ISBN: 978-0-471-75286-8

Manufactured in the United States of America

10 9 8 7 6 5 4

1B/TR/RQ/QY/IN

Dedication

I dedicate this book to my father, Malcolm. He taught me long ago the value of a dollar and how to be a smart gambler — lessons that have served me well in life.

About the Author

Growing up in a conservative small town along the Maine coast, Kevin Blackwood never anticipated visiting Sin City. With aspirations of becoming a college professor, he traveled the usual roads of academia, earning bachelor's and master's degrees in religious education and Biblical history.

His journey took a sudden detour in 1984. While working on his doctorate at the University of Oregon, he learned how to count cards and started playing blackjack on weekends. His studies began to pale in comparison to the exciting world of gambling. And one day, after a futile effort to find a parking spot on the crowded campus, he bagged his plans to teach church history, quit school — and headed to Las Vegas.

Since then, Blackwood has lived what many would consider the American dream, earning big bucks while working only part-time, winning consistently at blackjack tables all over the world. More recently, he has jumped on the Texas Hold'em bandwagon, with several poker tournament wins under his belt.

His unusual life experiences inspired Blackwood to write a novel, *The Counter* (Wooden Pagoda Press). In addition, he is the author of *Play Blackjack Like the Pros* (HarperCollins), the most comprehensive guide to becoming a winning blackjack player. He has also written for magazines, including *Casino Player, Midwest Gaming and Travel, Blackjack Insider,* and *Gambling.com.* His TV appearances include the *World Series of Blackjack* (semifinalist 2005) and the *Ultimate Blackjack Tour* (finalist 2006).

Blackwood lives in Oregon with his wife of 25 years. They have two sons in college and a 22-year-old feline that is the most worshipped cat since the golden era of the pharaohs. You can reach Kevin by e-mail at Kevin@ kevinblackwood.com.

Author's Acknowledgments

Any good book is always a collaborative effort. Several people took time out of their busy schedules to offer tips, suggestions, and insights. These include

- Annie Duke, not only a great poker player but a superb writer.

- Phil Hellmuth, a poker icon and the gold standard for any aspiring tournament player.

- Howard Lederer, perhaps the most admired and respected name in poker.

- Antonio Esfandiari, a flamboyant poker player who let me tag along for a rare peek at how a world-class mind operates.

- Russ Hamilton, the 1994 WSOP champion and a terrific all-around gambler.

- Scott Fischman, one of the brightest young stars in poker.

- Anthony Curtis, publisher of *Las Vegas Advisor*, and a man who always has the answer for any question in the world of gambling.

- Michael Shackleford, gifted mathematician and author of *Gambling 102*, who allowed me to use several examples from his excellent Web site, www.wizardofodds.com.

- Max Rubin, one of the funnier and more colorful people I know, who wrote the foreword and let me adapt ten principles from his book, *Comp City* (Huntington Press) for Chapter 22 of this book.

- Barry Meadow, a great writer who generously loaned me several books to aid in my research. I regret that we've never worked together on a project.

- Michael Traum, public relations manager of John Ascuaga's Nugget Casino, who provided screen shots, illustrations, and several helpful items on keno and bingo.

- Rod Wood, who shared tips on video poker.

- Barney Vinson, a fellow author who contributed a great roulette story for this book.

- Steve C., who reviewed the chapters on slots and video poker.

- Barry Finn, who corrected some mistakes in the poker chapter.

- Tom Grieder, for sharing information from his *research* trips.

- Tim and Justin Wood, who helped set up the book's graphs and charts.

✔ Tony Delise, director of slots at John Ascuagua's Nugget, for helping on keno and bingo.

✔ Mickey, who opened his home to me, and Tiffany Whitney, who helped me start the early chapters.

✔ My agents, Matt Wagner (Fresh Books) and Frank Scatoni and Greg Dinkin (Venture Literary) deserve a big thank-you for making this project happen. Also, Betsy Sheldon, Tracy Boggier, Chad Sievers, and Pam Ruble helped polish this book. Thanks to Larry Barker for doing the technical editing and Stanford Wong for suggesting my name to author this book.

✔ Some excellent writers provided invaluable assistance, including Fara Kearnes, Rusty Fischer, Mark Salley, and Swain Schep. I doubt I could have finished the book without them, and the text is markedly better because of their efforts. Fara worked on several chapters in this book, and Swain contributed some much-needed humor. Mark has now helped me on all three of my books, and I greatly appreciate his long-term friendship.

✔ But the biggest thank-you goes to my wife, who reviewed nearly every chapter and gave great critique and feedback. Though not a gambler, she took a big risk marrying me.

Publisher's Acknowledgments

We're proud of this book; please send us your comments through our Dummies online registration form located at www.dummies.com/register/.

Some of the people who helped bring this book to market include the following:

Acquisitions, Editorial, and Media Development

Project Editor: Chad R. Sievers

Contributor: Betsy Sheldon

Acquisitions Editor: Tracy Boggier

Copy Editors: Melissa Wiley, Pam Ruble

Editorial Program Coordinator: Hanna K. Scott

Technical Editor: Larry Barker

Editorial Manager: Michelle Hacker

Editorial Assistants: Erin Calligan, Nadine Bell

Cover Photos: © Steve Mason/Getty

Cartoons: Rich Tennant
(www.the5thwave.com)

Composition Services

Project Coordinator: Tera Knapp

Layout and Graphics: Carl Byers, Andrea Dahl, Mary J. Gillot, Stephanie D. Jumper, Barbara Moore, Shelley Norris, Barry Offringa, Brent Savage, Lynsey Osborn, Alicia B. South

Proofreaders: John Greenough, Leeann Harney, Aptara

Indexer: Aptara

Special Help: Josh Dials, Kristin DeMint

Publishing and Editorial for Consumer Dummies

Diane Graves Steele, Vice President and Publisher, Consumer Dummies

Joyce Pepple, Acquisitions Director, Consumer Dummies

Kristin A. Cocks, Product Development Director, Consumer Dummies

Michael Spring, Vice President and Publisher, Travel

Kelly Regan, Editorial Director, Travel

Publishing for Technology Dummies

Andy Cummings, Vice President and Publisher, Dummies Technology/General User

Composition Services

Gerry Fahey, Vice President of Production Services

Debbie Stailey, Director of Composition Services

Contents at a Glance

Table of Contents

Foreword

· ·

Do you like to gamble? So do I. And so do the estimated 50 million people who set foot in U.S. casinos each year. In fact, Americans spend more money on gambling than on all sports, movies, music, and even gentleman's clubs combined. Why? Because gambling is *fun!*

Gambling can be even more fun when you know what you're doing. But learning how to do the right thing in a casino normally requires enormous intellectual and emotional investments that most people simply aren't willing to make.

Here's a great example of a play that a novice gambler would normally make: You see a $100 minimum blackjack game at a casino on the Strip in Las Vegas, but the casino across the street is advertising a $10 minimum game. Obviously the $10 game is cheaper to play, right? Wrong. In fact, you'll lose less over time by playing the $100 blackjack game *if* you know a basic strategy.

"How's that?" you ask. The $10 game likely has terrible rules and terrible payoffs that cost the uninformed gambler about 25 cents a hand, while the high roller's game is set to make about 20 cents for every $100 you put in action. And the bonus? When you play the high-dollar game, you also earn spectacular comps.

Which game should you play? That decision depends on your bankroll, your stomach for action, and your availability to control passions on the game. Understanding yourself and the house advantage on every game is the core message in *Casino Gambling For Dummies*.

Kevin Blackwood is one of very few successful professional gamblers who know how to write and teach recreational gamblers — in everyday, common language. He shows how to evaluate the dizzying array of gambling games so that you can lose less money and have more fun, all while you're pursuing this great pastime.

Have fun!

Max Rubin

Author and Blackjack Hall of Famer

Introduction

· ·

*T*he ancient Chinese and Egyptians gambled. Greeks and Romans loved games of chance. Julius Caesar sealed the deal for the biggest risk of his life when he crossed the Rubicon and pronounced, "The die is cast." Even on this side of the pond, gambling has a long history. Native Americans have passed down tribal traditions that sanction betting, and forefathers of the United States funded the nation's birth with lotteries. In fact, Thomas Jefferson allegedly harbored a passion for betting that bordered on the compulsive.

Today's culture accepts gambling, too. Whether in casino resort areas, through state-sponsored lotteries, or in church bingo games, gambling has become a legitimate form of entertainment. But, as popular as it is, gambling has risks, particularly in casinos.

Here's why: The folks who run the casinos are professionals who are astute business people with a successful formula for profit. They have the technology and resources to conduct research and development, to fine-tune their operational strategy, and to grow their business.

The average casino patron, however, isn't a professional. He's the one who thinks he can win his retirement in Atlantic City just because he takes his brother-in-law for a few bucks on card night. Or she's the one on the Caribbean cruise who relies on intuition to pick the lucky slots. And that couple who went to Vegas just for the entertainment? They're suddenly seduced by the roulette wheel before they make it to the next show.

A poorly prepared player — someone who doesn't understand the games or the odds behind them — has virtually no chance to beat the house at its own game. Remember this fact: The Las Vegas Strip is an impressive stretch of elaborate resorts built one brick at a time from the losses of clueless sheep. The same story holds true for the casinos in Atlantic City, Tahoe, and Reno, cruise ships, Indian reservations, and riverboats. Inexperience, intuition, and lucky guesses are poor guides in casino gambling.

But you don't have to follow the flock to slaughter. This book arms you with the knowledge to turn casino odds in your favor. I've won more than $1 million in casinos worldwide, so I know it can be done. Follow my advice, educate yourself, and get ready for a positive — even profitable — gambling experience.

About This Book

If you're heading to Vegas, Atlantic City, your nearest riverboat gambling haven, an ocean cruise, or anywhere casino bets are buzzing, then this is the book for you. From blackjack to baccarat, from sports betting to slot strategies, I give you the essential information to help you succeed on *all* games and broaden your casino experience.

Casino games range in complexity and risk, so it's critical that you understand those games and then choose the best ones for your gambling dollars. For example, you should know that blackjack and poker require skill, while slots and keno typically remove brains from the equation. Feel free to gamble your dollars any way you want inside the casino, but my mission is to steer you toward the best games (and away from gimmicks and bad bets).

In addition to carefully explaining the nuts, bolts, and winning strategies of each casino game, I offer overviews of important concepts, such as probability, money management, and the role of luck in gambling. Too many people neglect these dynamics; by mastering them, you improve your chances of winning.

I don't view casinos as evil empires and dens of sin. However, they have no vested interest in showing you how to win or play smarter. Such information runs contrary to the primary goal of their business: to part you from your money. But in *Casino Gambling For Dummies,* I share the knowledge and tools to increase your chances of coming home a winner.

Conventions Used in This Book

Each game of chance covered in this book comes with its own vocabulary — gambling jargon — that helps you become a successful player. For example, to play craps correctly, you must know what a *field bet* is and why you should avoid it. To make money at blackjack, you want to understand the terms *double down* and *insurance*.

Starting to sound like the first session of a foreign language course? Don't worry; it's much easier than you think. I use the following conventions in this book to help you:

- Each time I introduce a new word, I *italicize* it and then define it.
- I put all Web sites in monofont.
- I use **bold** text to indicate keywords in bulleted lists or to highlight the action parts of numbered lists.

What You're Not to Read

If you only care about the games, you can skip the sidebars (framed in gray boxes) throughout the book. They serve as asides, anecdotes, or examples, but they aren't critical to your understanding of the game. In many cases, however, they clarify the principles and tactics in that chapter.

Foolish Assumptions

Call me psychic, but I'm assuming you picked up this book because you're open to the sport of casino gambling. I make the following assumptions about you, my dear reader:

- You're preparing for an upcoming visit to a casino and want to understand the basics and correct protocol before entering that foreign world.
- You may be familiar with most games, but you simply want some tips to improve your performance and skills.
- You want to win when you gamble in a casino.
- You also want to have fun. (Sure, casino gambling is entertainment, but it's a lot more fun when chips are flowing in your direction.)

Are you an expert who doesn't really identify with these assumptions? Don't worry. I provide a few advanced tidbits for the more experienced gambler as well, so you don't feel left out.

How This Book Is Organized

Like other *For Dummies* books, each chapter is self-contained, so you can read only the chapters that interest you most. This modular feature allows each section to stand alone, without demanding that you read the rest of the book. For example, if you're anxious to throw some dice, feel free to fast-forward to the craps chapter.

That said, the book does have a logical sequence, and the following sections give you a better idea of its five major parts. (You can also check out the table of contents and index to see what interests you.)

Part I: Casino Gambling Basics: Everything You Need to Know to Start

Part I is a quick overview of the fast-paced, adrenalin-pumped world of casino gambling. The first chapter provides the big picture of casino gambling. Chapter 3 looks more closely at odds, probability, luck, and house edge. In Chapter 4, I give important money-management tips, including how to report your winnings (and losses) to Uncle Sam. The last chapter covers gambling etiquette and protocol.

Part II: Conquering the Table Games

This part examines the most popular table games, starting with poker. I explain the rules of several different types of poker and provide some strategy tips from well-known stars, such as Phil Hellmuth and Annie Duke. This part also includes chapters on blackjack, craps, roulette, and other table games.

Part III: Beyond the Tables: Slots, Video Poker, Sports Betting, and More

In Part III, I cover a wide variety of casino topics. First, because slots are the biggest cash cow for casinos, I offer practical, no-nonsense advice on which ones to play and, more importantly, which ones to avoid. I also include a chapter on video poker, where I analyze several games and offer optimal playing strategies. Chapter 14 focuses on two popular games: keno and bingo. Finally, I show first-timers how to navigate the complex, high-tech sports books in order to place bets on your favorite sports team or horse.

Part IV: Taking Casino Gambling to a Different Level

This part is short, but it has valuable information. Although most of the book focuses on casino gambling, I offer a chapter in this part on online casino gambling. The chapter includes guidelines for staying out of trouble in that murky yet potentially profitable arena. I also provide a chapter on the current craze of tournaments, which comes from the explosion of TV poker matches.

Part V: The Part of Tens

Every *For Dummies* book ends with the famous *Part of Tens*. Mine includes — drum roll, please — ten great places to gamble, ten mistakes to avoid when gambling in a casino, and ten really cool ways to score comps.

Part VI: Appendixes

This part includes two helpful appendixes. The first one is a handy glossary to keep all these casino gambling terms straight (or is that *flush?*). The second appendix provides additional resources for delving deeper into casino gambling.

Icons Used in This Book

Icons are a signature feature of *For Dummies* books. They help draw your eye to specific types of information. And after you have read the book, the icons provide a great guide for a final review before hitting the casino.

This bull's-eye denotes a suggestion that can potentially save money, win money, or help you play better. Mastering these tidbits can keep you on the winning road.

Casinos have numerous pitfalls that trap novice gamblers. This icon acts as a caution, a red light that guides you away from an action or aspect of gambling that's potentially harmful.

When you see this sign, look for critical information that you want to take away with you — key concepts that come up repeatedly when you're gambling. Remembering these pointers can help you stay on the road to success.

Information after this icon can help you understand the odds behind casino bets. Educated gamblers choose the best games and bets, greatly increasing their chances of coming home a winner.

Where to Go from Here

The best place to begin is Part I because it sets up the remaining chapters. This section covers the gambling basics, orients you to casinos, and tells you how formidable a foe you are up against.

From there, just pick the chapters that appeal to you. Scan the table of contents or index and find the topics that interest you. Feel free to frolic — there are no rigid road maps to follow in *Casino Gambling For Dummies*.

I can't guarantee you'll hit a jackpot after studying this book. No one wins all the time. But knowledge is power. And I'm guessing you want to find out which games offer the best odds and the best bets. If so, you've come to the right place. And odds are, even if you don't come out a winner, this book can guide you toward a great casino experience.

Part I
Casino Gambling Basics: Everything You Need to Know to Start

The 5th Wave   By Rich Tennant

GAMING TABLES of LAS VEGAS

JD   BLACKJACK   PAI GOW   PAPER·SCISSORS STONE

In this part . . .

This overview introduces the fast-paced, adrenaline-pumping world of casino gambling. The first chapter offers a sneak preview of what to expect in *Casino Gambling For Dummies*. Chapter 2 helps you find your way around a casino and introduces you to the key players. Chapter 3 provides a quick overview on probability, odds, house edge, and luck so you have a strong foundation before you start playing. Chapter 4 focuses on important money-management issues, including essential tax-reporting info. Chapter 5 identifies casino gambling etiquette so you don't make a gambling faux pas.

Chapter 1

Casino Gambling 101: The Inside Scoop

In This Chapter

▶ Entering the world of casino gambling

▶ Tallying up the casino's many offerings

▶ Pinpointing casinos on the gambling map

▶ Testing your gambling aptitude

1 was a big golf fan during the game's golden age, when Jack Nicklaus and Arnold Palmer ruled the links. Yet, despite the presence of those two titans, I idolized Gary Player, a South African whose diminutive size made for a less-than-intimidating physical presence in the tee box. But Player's welter-weight appearance belied a heavy-weight swing. I was always amazed that someone so small could hit the ball so far.

Believe it or not, casino gambling is a lot like golf. And, no, not because both games are about going for the green. Golf is all about technique, skill, and knowledge. And masters of the game are inspiring to watch. With swings as graceful and elegant as a ballet dancer's leap, they make each challenging stroke look effortless. The pros seem to play as smoothly as those on the PGA tour. But, as in golf, the successful player has gathered important knowledge and studied effective strategies to finesse the outcome in his or her favor.

In other words, casino pros aren't winners just because they're lucky, any more than Tiger Woods is a golf god because the angels of the green have smiled upon him. Trust me, the greats of the poker tournament circuit may look like they could take the table in their sleep — but they're skilled, savvy, and have studied the game diligently.

I'm guessing, though, that you're not planning to become the Tiger Woods of blackjack . . . or keno . . . or the slots. Your gambling aspirations are probably similar to my golf ambitions: to play better, win more often, and increase enjoyment of the experience. And you have every reason to believe that you can attain your goal. But success requires knowledge, strategy, and some skill. You've come to the right place. This chapter (and book) can provide the preparation you need to help you find your *swing* in the casino.

Entering the Casino: What You're Up Against

The first secret to gambling success is to understand the inner workings of the casino world before you're seduced by the flash and dazzle. Casinos are sophisticated and highly successful enterprises — and they don't get that way by giving away money. Your best bet, then, is to be aware of basic casino operations so you can manipulate the experience to your advantage.

Marketing their way to your wallet

They see you coming from miles away. They know exactly who you are, how much money you make, what you like and dislike, and whether you're married, single, or divorced. Who are these omniscient watchers who track your secrets? The IRS? CIA? Al-Qaeda?

None of the above. I'm talking about the marketing gurus at modern casinos. They're constantly studying reams of data on millions of gamblers to develop profiles of guests who most willingly spend their discretionary income on a couple hours of distraction.

Nothing is left to chance in a modern casino. Every possible element, from the design of the wallpaper to the thickness of the carpet, is there to draw you in and keep you gambling as long as possible. All the colors, sights, sounds, and sensations serve one purpose: to make you happy — even when you lose.

Accepting the odds: The house rules

The casino's first commandment is "The house shall always win." A couple of games permit sharp players to break even or eke out a small edge occasionally. But casinos are in business to make money, so for most players, winning is a losing proposition.

Why? Three good reasons:

✔ The house charges a *vigorish* (commission) in some games, such as sports betting. (Check out Chapter 15.)

✔ In many games, the casino doesn't pay out *true odds*.

In roulette, for example, there are 37-to-1 odds of guessing the right number. But if you win, the payout is only 35 to 1. This difference may seem small, but that discrepancy actually gives the house one of the biggest edges in the casino. (Refer to Chapter 3 for an explanation of *true odds* and Chapter 9 for more info on roulette.)

✔ The casino has a *house edge* — a mathematical advantage over the player in any game. Throughout the casino, players must overcome odds that aren't favorable to winning. (Read more about the edge in Chapter 3.)

Your goal is to find games where the casino has the lowest edge. Craps is a great example. This fun, exciting game offers great odds — if you stay away from the *bad* bets. I explore craps in Chapter 8.

To get the lowdown on house edge in other games, check out the individual chapters in Parts II and III.

Protecting your money with a plan

For most people, developing a strategy for doling out their gambling bankroll can keep them out of serious trouble. Set a budget and stick to it. Consider contingencies (such as losing your bankroll in the first few minutes of your visit) and know how to respond when your wallet gets whacked.

Your strategy, however, is only as good as your willpower. Nothing jacks up casino profits faster than undisciplined gamblers. If you're an impulsive type, then gambling may leave your bank account looking like it just went 15 rounds with a heavyweight boxing champion. (Refer to Chapter 4, where I discuss important money-management issues.)

Now, it's certainly true that most people can save their money by avoiding casinos altogether. So, the best advice I can give to folks who don't want to lose money is simple: Don't gamble! But the conservative and prudent path in life isn't the only choice (and that would make for a very short book). Gambling can be a great way to spice up a vacation and break out of a boring routine. Gambling is all about taking a risk — exposing yourself to a chance of loss.

However, don't overdo it. Government studies show that as many as 1 in every 25 adults has a problem with compulsive gambling. Think about that the next time you sit down at a blackjack table. Several people in the pit probably shouldn't be there. Could you be one of them? Gambling addiction is a serious matter (refer to Appendix B for some helpful info).

Identifying the colors of the rainbow

Knowledge is power and is your only ally against the formidable forces that threaten to separate you from your hard-earned cash. One piece of knowledge you definitely need, particularly if you're going to wade into the shark-infested waters of table games, is the varying colors and matching denominations of standard casino chips.

The casinos make this bit easy for you because the chips also have a denomination printed on them so that you know the red chip, for instance, is worth $5 and the green chip is worth $25. The following is a comprehensive list of common casino-chip colors, as well as their corresponding values:

- ✔ White: $1
- ✔ Red: $5
- ✔ Green: $25
- ✔ Black: $100
- ✔ Purple: $500
- ✔ Burgundy: $1,000
- ✔ Brown: $5,000

Playing the Games: What's Your Poison?

Casino games are as diverse as the people who play them — and that's part of the fun. You may think of craps as a rough-and-tumble game, played by hustlers and wiseguys, but step into a casino and you're just as likely to spot an angelic-looking nurse rolling dice next to a cursing cowboy from Texas. And, because no game has a precise player profile, don't restrict yourself to the few games that you think suit you. Give each one a try and see where it takes you.

Although the majority of casino visitors prefer slot machines, chances are, if you're reading this book, you're willing to try new ways to gamble. After you read this book and know which games have the best odds, I suggest you take a quick walk around the casino floor to see where you want to start and give several of them a try.

Touring the table games

In a casino, the tables come in all shapes and sizes, from the oval shape of poker tables to the half-round crescent of blackjack to the long rectangle of craps. And the table is just about all they have in common.

Unspoken rules seem to govern the table games. Most casino guests have discovered from experience to avoid the taboos: holding your cards with two hands, touching chips in the betting circle after the cards are dealt, and throwing the dice so wildly that they fly over the rail and end up in some-body's drink. You can discover general casino etiquette in Chapter 5 and more game-specific rules in most chapters. However, before you worry about acting proper, this section includes a brief overview of the main table games that you may encounter in a casino.

Poker: Boosted by Internet and TV tournaments

To say that poker is taking over the world may be only a slight exaggeration. Considering its current popularity explosion, Texas Hold'em could replace war as a way to settle regional conflicts. In truth, many factors have con-tributed to the card game's wide appeal, including the broad reaches of the Internet and television poker tournaments.

But technology is only one factor. The big draw? Poker is one of the few games where good players consistently win. In poker, you compete against other players rather than the house. And with honed skills and intimate knowledge of the game, you can have a significant edge over those other, less-prepared gamblers.

 Hiding your emotions is a requisite skill for successful poker. They don't call it *poker face* for nothin'! So, if you can't control your nervous ticks when you bluff or if your eyes get as big as saucers when you make a full house, either play your poker online or put a bag over your head. (For other tips, read Chapter 6.)

Blackjack: The best odds

Blackjack (also called *21*) has been the most popular table game in casinos for more than 40 years. The card game always draws a loyal crowd because it's easy to understand, provides good camaraderie, and offers great odds. If you memorize basic strategy (that is, the optimal way to play every hand), your chances of winning at blackjack are better than at virtually any other game in the casino.

Blackjack also is intriguing because each hand is like a movie clip — with you as the star. Each game has an opening scene (the deal), the simmering suspense (the dealer's hidden card), the moment of truth when the hero (you!) makes a dramatic choice, and finally the conclusion, where the hero wins or loses. The trick, of course, is to have more happy endings than tragedies. (Chapter 7 provides a thorough look at best blackjack strategies.)

Craps: Backslaps, high-fives, and cheerleaders

This dice game draws a raucous crowd and has many of the best bets in the casino. Some guests find the noise and the complex layout of craps to be a little intimidating. But before you slink back to your comfort zone, consider this fact: The house advantage is low in craps, making this game a great bet. Just be sure you stick with the best craps bets.

Furthermore, craps is like a sporting event, with its dramatic swings of luck, high-fives, backslaps, and noisy cheering section. Every roll has a home team (players who bet with the dice) and an opposing team (wrong-way bettors) that gets dirty looks and ridicules from the hometown fans. Now, if they just had those big foam *We're No. 1* fingers, the experience would be complete (but a little hard to roll the dice). For more on craps, check out Chapter 8.

Roulette: The place for eccentric hunches

The spinning wheel of roulette symbolizes the world of casino gambling. This popular, entry-level game is ideal for novice gamblers because it requires absolutely no skill, concentration, or complex strategies. You simply bet on the number or possible numbers that the ball will land on. A table full of players can be quite sociable, although not as rowdy as a craps game. Roulette gives you a chance to play your eccentric hunches on a single number, a combination of numbers, or on an even-money wager that can just extend your playing session. Refer to Chapter 9 for more on roulette.

Baccarat: More tuxedo than T-shirt

Although blackjack and poker appeal to the masses, baccarat is a card game that draws a far more upscale and refined crowd. You're more likely to see tuxedos than T-shirts playing this game. But everyone is welcome, so even if you don't have a penguin costume in your closet, check out baccarat for a game that's simple to play (just bet on the bank) and has fair odds. For the complete lowdown on baccarat, read Chapter 10.

Let It Ride, Pai Gow, and other table games

Beyond the traditional favorites, several other table games have developed a strong following. Today, most casinos intersperse Caribbean Stud poker, Let It Ride, Pai Gow, and Three Card poker tables throughout their pits.

These games are fun diversions when you need a change of pace, but a word of caution: Don't play too long. These games have odds that may make you wish you'd gotten mugged instead of gone gambling. Unless you have a passion for these games (along with a bottomless bank account), don't make a habit of playing them. I tell you why in Chapter 11.

Turning to machine games

For some folks, the intimidation factor of table games is too much to bear. Excuse me while I dab the tears from my eyes, but I'm touched when I realize that nearly all casino operators — through the goodness of their hearts — thoughtfully accommodate shy gamblers by supplying acres of go-solo gaming machines.

Even the most timid gambler can enjoy a satisfying time at these machines — no bluffing by other players, no angry gamblers if you hit or stand at the wrong time, and no embarrassment about table rules. The lone gambler squares off against a machine (or in the case of the loony gambler, against several machines at once).

Just remember that the best and worst that the casino has to offer are often sitting side by side. This section looks more closely at slot machines and video poker, two entirely different beasts. They have very different rules and very different odds. This section also briefly discusses keno and bingo.

Slot machines: From one-armed bandit to high-tech robotic

At one time, slot machines were simple devices. You put a coin in, you pulled a lever, and the reels spun. When they stopped, you heard the soothing sounds of clinking coins . . . or painful silence. Sure, you spent only a nickel or a quarter, but that silence was so painful that you couldn't help but put in another coin.

If you've been in a casino recently, you know how everything about gaming machines has changed. The humble one-armed bandit is now a sophisticated robotic master thief, with enough computing power to fly the space shuttle. This soulless adversary even plays you a little song while it gleefully sucks up all your coins. Sure, the games still have some reminders from the past (like fruit or bells on the paylines), but the level of sophistication grows every day. And today's slots are the most popular game in the casino, hands down — despite the fact that they offer some of the worst odds in the house.

Slot machines occupy all that space on the casino floor for a good reason — people love to pump money into them, and they're available in practically any denomination — from pennies to dollars. If you're a person who just can't say *no* to their alluring call, make sure you read Chapter 12, so you can pick a worthy game with a better-than-average payout table.

Video poker: Not your Aunt Beatrice's kitchen-table game

Like slots, video poker offers a solo gambling experience, yet the two games are very different. Slots are primarily about luck, but video poker requires a certain amount of skill and technique. And just because you've played some kitchen-table Five Card Draw with your Aunt Beatrice, don't assume you can break the bank at video poker. Several variations confront the casino guest, and you want to master the strategies before you decide whether to hold 'em or fold 'em.

The strategies for video poker can be a little complicated (see Chapter 13), but the reward for that extra work is worth it. Video poker offers perhaps the best odds of any game in the house — at least for those who play correctly.

Keno and bingo: Two old standards

Keno and bingo have many similarities, and both have a long history and a loyal following. Keno is a casino staple and a great way to stay in action while sipping on your soup in the coffee shop. Bingo is less common in casinos, although some clubs still offer this venerable game.

There is not much strategy to playing either game other than hoping to get lucky, but I do cover the basics in Chapter 14 and give a quick overview for anyone unfamiliar with how to play either game.

Betting on ball games and fast horses

Some people travel across the country to a casino in order to do exactly what they do at home: sit in an easy chair and watch sports on TV. The only difference? In a casino, they're viewing sporting events and horse races on the massive projection screens in today's best *race and sports books*. These plush, high-tech rooms draw fans to cheer their favorite teams or horses. So what's the major difference between these rooms and your living room? The casino is ready and willing to take your bet on just about any sporting event.

Sports betting: Thrill of victory, agony of defeat

Currently, only Nevada has casino sports betting. (You can make some sports bets online as well. Read Chapter 17 for more info.) When you're in a Nevada casino, you may notice that the employees in the sports book are strangely unemotional when the crowd cheers for one team or another. Why? Because the house takes a *vigorish* (a small commission) from every wager, virtually ensuring a profit on every bet.

Casino guests can find all kinds of betting opportunities in the wide world of sports, including football, basketball, baseball, hockey, tennis, boxing, golf, and special events. But being a great sports fan doesn't make you a natural winner at the sports book. Why? Point spreads and money lines add complex challenges to the process. But understanding how to handicap and analyze sports statistics can simplify that process — and help you improve the odds of winning. (See Chapter 15 for more on sports betting in a casino.)

Horse racing: A run for your money

If you love a day at the track, the race book is going to feel like home sweet home. After all, through the modern miracle of simulcasting, you can enjoy a day at *several* tracks at once, without leaving your cozy chair. Casinos dedicate luxurious space and resources to keep fans happy: leather seats, private work desks, and stacks of publications full of data on the ponies. And just when you think the experience can't get any better, the cocktail server hands you a double espresso to get your brain into high gear before the race day starts. Comfortable? Good, now you just need to pick some winners.

In both horse racing and sports betting, your understanding of handicapping and external factors can improve your chances of winning. And both kinds of betting favor gamblers who take a *contrarian* view. When you go against the grain — and you're right — you win bigger than when you bet with the crowd. (Read Chapter 16 for more about horse racing.)

Gambling Near and Far: Where to Find Casinos

Formerly quarantined to select areas, today's casinos are nearly everywhere, making gambling possible in almost every state. Only two states (Hawaii and Utah) have no legalized gambling. The main reason for this explosion is that the stigma of gambling has mostly been removed from our society. Although the previous generation generally viewed gambling with moral indignation, today's attitudes are more relaxed, and many people consider casinos fun entertainment rather than one of the seven deadly sins.

This section looks more closely at the different types of gambling locations. Although Las Vegas and Atlantic City are still popular destinations for casino gambling, hundreds of other options are also waiting for you. (Flip to Chapter 19 for ten cool places to gamble.)

Nevada: Viva the gambling state!

For decades, Nevada was famous for being the only U.S. state where casino gambling was legal. That limitation changed when the state of New Jersey legalized gambling in the late 1970s (although only in one town, Atlantic City). And, despite the growth of on-the-water and Indian casinos throughout the United States (primarily in the 1990s), the Silver State remains the king of casino gambling.

Las Vegas reigns supreme

Las Vegas is the jewel in the crown and far and away the biggest gambling destination in the world. Also known as *Sin City* or *Lost Wages,* Vegas is a unique agglomeration of palm trees, fountains, neon lights, and 100,000-plus hotel rooms among a wild mishmash of must-see architecture.

From its forbidden-fruit beginnings to its mobster adolescence, to its starring role in a few hit TV shows, Vegas exudes a frenetic energy that makes the city a unique place in American pop culture. And Vegas takes full advantage of its iconic position. New hotel/casino complexes continue to rise from the desert floor at an astounding pace. As of 2006, nine of the ten biggest hotels in the world were located within a few miles of each other on the Las Vegas Strip.

The city is still primarily known for its gambling — after all, where else can you expect to find slots in grocery stores and in airports? But that image is changing. At some point in the late 1990s — for the first time in its history — gambling money amounted to less than half of the total revenue brought in by the Vegas casino industry. And that change means people from around the world are seeing the city as a resort (or convention) destination first and a place to gamble second.

If you're eager to find out more about Las Vegas, check out *Las Vegas For Dummies* by Mary Herczog (Wiley).

Tahoe and Reno: Quieter cousins

Before Las Vegas rose to prominence, Reno was the epicenter of gambling in the United States, and casinos around Lake Tahoe frequently hosted celebrities, such as Frank Sinatra and his buddies. Now, their southern Nevada competitor easily eclipses both Tahoe and Reno, but these two intriguing cities remain good alternatives for visitors that don't care for the Vegas speed-of-light pace.

As "the biggest little city in the world," Reno's Wild West frontier spirit and gambling accessibility appeal to many travelers. Tahoe also boasts gambling opportunities on the Nevada side of the border while promising superb skiing in winter, a wealth of lake activities in summer, and spectacular mountain scenery year-round.

Atlantic City: Vegas of the east

In the late 1970s, New Jersey took the bold step of legalizing gambling as a way to revitalize Atlantic City. The transformation hasn't always gone smoothly, but today Atlantic City's casino industry is healthy. As one of the biggest gambling spots in the United States, it sees billions of dollars in wagers every year.

Although the Atlantic City Boardwalk can't rival the Vegas Strip, it does offer a unique blend of glitz and glamour in a carnival atmosphere and a seaside setting. More importantly, the location means convenience for people on the East Coast — they no longer have to fly cross-country just to play blackjack.

Diving into on-the-water gambling

Some people may not understand why gambling can be legal on the water but illegal on land. Nevertheless, if your state has a river running through it or you live on the coast, you're likely to find a casino within driving distance. (Of course, take your motion-sickness pills and be prepared to walk the plank.)

Riverboat casinos: A piece of the past

New laws and regulations have revived an icon from America's colorful past — riverboat casinos. Although these contemporary vessels bear little resemblance to the fabled paddleboats that plied the Mississippi, gambling fun is still rollin' on the river.

Most casino voyages are "cruises to nowhere" that last one to three hours. Some floating casinos don't even leave the dock, but they're in compliance with state gambling laws because they're on water. These casinos are typically smaller than the big boys in Vegas and aren't always open 24 hours, but they usually offer most of the same games.

Cruise ships: Sailing for international waters

What could be finer than cruising off the coast of Carolina? Okay, maybe cruise ships don't hit those waters often, but they do sail nearly everywhere in the world, including hot spots (like the Caribbean and the Panama Canal) and scenic destinations (like Alaska and Mexico).

Nearly every cruise line takes advantage of international waters (where gambling is legal) by offering casinos on board their ships (open only certain hours and only when the ship is in international waters). These casinos have most of the same games and similar odds as regular land-based casinos (with a few differences), so if you don't mind your dice rolling funny when a big wave hits, cruising may be just the ticket for you.

Indian gaming: Cashing in on less glitz

Although reservation gaming came on the scene late, it has dramatically changed the landscape of casino gambling across the country over the last two decades. The biggest and best-known Indian gaming area is in Connecticut (outside Hartford), providing an appealing alternative to Atlantic City for New York gamblers.

Today Indian gaming generates billions of dollars in revenues every year and provides significant competition for more traditional gambling destinations. In fact, the combined gaming revenue of all tribal casinos is greater than all the revenue of Atlantic City, Las Vegas, and Reno together.

Native American casinos typically offer the same machines and table games that other gambling capitals have. However, many Indian casinos don't allow alcohol consumption, and few of them can compete with the glitz of Vegas. Nevertheless, the success of tribal gaming speaks volumes about the quality of the casinos. So if you can live without exploding volcanoes or fancy fountains, you're bound to enjoy the friendly, less spectacular tribal casinos (see Chapter 19).

Beyond the borders: Gambling abroad

If you feel stuck in a gambling rut, traveling abroad for gaming may just be the adrenalin shot you need. Most foreign casinos offer the same or similar games as casinos in the United States, but the experience is often more refined and memorable, especially in high-class locations such as Monte Carlo.

But customs differ around the world, so you may be surprised at the rules across the pond. Many European casinos charge an entry fee, and many of them require more-formal attire. (Pack a coat and tie or evening dress if you plan on playing on the Continent.) Travelers should also be aware that the American traditions of megacasinos and multithousand room resorts are rare overseas.

The Caribbean is also a popular getaway for gamblers, and several islands offer casinos to complement their sun and sand attractions. The biggest casino in the tropical region is the Atlantis Casino in the Bahamas, which is truly a world-class resort.

Betting on the Internet

Gambling and cyberspace seem to be made for each other. Through the conduit of the Internet, casinos and gaming companies can invite themselves directly into the homes of gamblers. Now people can play anonymously and comfortably, without ever leaving the house.

Considered the last frontier for gaming, cyberspace has now been settled — if not fully tamed. Online gaming (check out Chapter 17) represents a multibillion-dollar industry worldwide that continues to grow exponentially every year. In spite of its convenience and fun, however, online gambling has some serious drawbacks.

✔ **The whole casino experience is missing.** You don't have any table camaraderie, shows, restaurants, or cocktail servers for variety and entertainment. The purists may not care, but many people gamble for the *experience* as much as for the game itself.

✔ **Internet gambling has serious temptations for the undisciplined player.** You can wager and play — and lose — at a breakneck pace when gambling online. And you don't have the typical safety checks, like a companion who urges you to stop throwing good money after bad.

✔ **If you lose your bankroll in cyberspace, no one can hear you scream.** That is, except for your unsuspecting (and innocent) significant other who's watching television in the next room.

Measuring Your Gambling IQ

As I stress throughout the book, individuals who find the greatest pleasure in gambling do so with

✔ Realistic intentions

✔ An understanding of the odds

✔ An informed strategy

✔ Some skill, depending on the game

To paraphrase the character Tevye in *Fiddler on the Roof,* it's no great shame to lose at gambling — but it's no great honor, either. I emphasize that gambling can be a fun experience whether you win or lose . . . but it's a lot more fun when you win.

In that spirit, I hope to arm you with the understanding and knowledge you need to maximize your enjoyment *and* success at casino gambling. Before you take a step into a casino, I suggest you answer the following ten questions to measure your grasp of gambling and the world of casinos. If you answer them all correctly, congratulations! And if not? Not to worry; after you read *Casino Gambling For Dummies,* you'll ace this test — and the many gambling experiences you encounter in the future.

The questions

1. **To come out ahead overall at sports betting, you need to win approximately**

   A. 50 percent of the time.

   B. 53 percent of the time.

   C. 20 percent of the time.

2. **You're playing Annie Duke at the final table of the World Series of Poker. She makes a big bet and then starts blinking her eyes rapidly. Is she**

    A. Flirting with you?

    B. Having contact problems?

    C. Bluffing?

3. **At which game would you lose more per hour (on average)?**

    A. Playing a 25¢ Double Diamond slot machine

    B. Playing $1 video poker

    C. Playing single-deck blackjack for $100 a hand

4. **You're at the roulette table and a black number has come up five times in a row. What are the odds that the next number will be red?**

    A. 47.3 percent

    B. 75 percent

    C. 50 percent

5. **How many states have legalized gambling?**

    A. 48

    B. 52

    C. 2

6. **Players who bet on the pass line in craps are hoping the first roll is a**

    A. 12

    B. Yahtzee

    C. 7

7. **What is the minimum number of innings required for an over/under baseball bet to be official?**

    A. 2

    B. 8½

    C. 4½

8. **Video poker is adapted from what poker game?**

   A. Texas Hold'em

   B. Strip poker

   C. Five-Card Draw

9. **Which of these games can you play while in the bathroom?**

   A. Keno

   B. Bingo

   C. Slots

10. **Where is the biggest casino in the world currently located?**

    A. Monte Carlo

    B. Connecticut

    C. Las Vegas

The answers

1. **B.** In sports betting, a gambler needs to win approximately 52.4 percent of his bets to break even because the house charges a commission (or *vigorish*) on every bet.

2. **C.** This could be a trick question because Annie Duke has bluffed and flirted on the same hand. However, rapid eye blinking is often an indicator of bluffing.

3. **C.** Surprisingly, playing high-stakes blackjack can be easier on your wallet than low-limit slot machines. Assuming you know basic strategy (see Chapter 6), your loss in a good single-deck game should be less than $14 an hour. Likewise, video poker (Jacks or Better 9/6) is a good bet and also will only set you back about $14 an hour. Neither one of those is very bad, considering that three quarters going into the slot machine every spin adds up to over $15 an hour.

4. **A.** No matter how many times one color or number comes up, the odds for the *next* spin aren't related to past spins. And the answer isn't 50 percent because there are also two green numbers (0 and 00) on the roulette wheel (in addition to the 18 red and 18 black numbers).

5. **A.** Currently 48 states offer some form of legal gambling, but just 20 years ago, there were casinos in only two states, so **C** was a reasonable answer. However, if you picked **B,** you may want to retake that high school geography class.

6. **C.** Seven is an automatic winner for pass line bettors on the come-out roll (first roll). **B** is incorrect because prowess at Yahtzee rarely translates into winning at the craps table — the pit boss is never happy when you try to throw all five dice.

7. **B.** Even though a major league baseball game is sometimes an official result after 4½ innings, an over/under bet is invalid unless the game goes at least 8½ innings.

8. **C.** Video poker has many versions, but all are based on Five-Card Draw. So you never need to worry about losing your shirt (or your socks) at this game.

9. **A.** Keno is one of the few games in which you don't have to be present to win. It's even possible to play from your room or the buffet line.

10. **B.** The Foxwoods Casino just outside Hartford, Connecticut, is the biggest casino on the planet.

Chapter 2

Taking a Quick Stroll Through the Casino

*W*hen you step into a modern megacasino, prepare to be dazzled. Blinking lights and ringing bells signal jackpots. Glittering chandeliers and rich furnishings and fabrics often mimic the sequined gowns and dapper dress of the folks at the high-roller tables. Clinking ice chills your drinks, and courteous staff appear to serve your every whim. When you see and hear these characteristics, you know you've walked into a fantasy world where every hand you play can be a winner, and every pull on the slot machine may make all your dreams come true.

Lucky gamblers make fortunes every day, but the reality is that most money ends up on the *other* side of the table. And the casino, or the *house,* is willing to pour millions of its profits into making sure you walk inside, stay inside, and — most importantly — gamble inside.

Always remember that, in addition to wanting your business, casinos provide a service to you, so you have every right to shop around for the establishment that best serves your needs. To assist you in your shopping, some casinos have Web sites where you can take a 360-degree virtual tour without ever leaving your house. I hope this chapter accomplishes a similar goal.

In this chapter I explain and prepare you for what to expect when you step foot into a casino and give you not only a glimpse of the razzle-dazzle designed to distract you but also the blueprint of the typical casino. I explain why this goes here, that goes there, and with whom you interact. Finally, I introduce you to who's watching you while you wander onward with your hand on your wallet and mind in the painted clouds on the starlit ceiling.

(Casino) Knowledge Is Power

The shrewdly packaged allure of the casino starts the minute you pull up to the glittering facade. From neon signs to valets to the smooth hum of the sliding-glass doors, the modern casino entrance is designed to attract you. Every possible consideration is given to design, color, and lighting.

The scheme doesn't end at the front steps, however. As you proceed through the casino's front door, every square inch of floor space entices you into moving forward. Like a siren call, the sounds of winning jackpots beckon you onward, as do the color schemes, floral arrangements, glittering lights, slot machines, and table games. If you aren't prepared, you may become disoriented inside a casino. The master plan behind the traffic flow is to bring you (and your wallet) into close proximity with the slot machines or table games at every opportunity. The pulsating pace of the gambling world is seductive and makes it hard for you to leave a winner.

Feeling overwhelmed — and not a little manipulated? It can be deflating to discover that the sounds, sights, and even smells are devised to lull you into a mesmerized state where you continue emptying your wallet into the casino coffers. But a casino visit doesn't have to be a Svengali-like experience.

Don't let the harsh realities of the casino world turn you off. Embrace them, because knowledge is power. And by understanding the psychology of casino design and getting to know the employees who perform their duties within the casino, you put yourself in a better position not only to enjoy the casino as an entertaining leisure activity but also to maintain the level-headedness and critical thinking required to succeed at your gambling ventures.

Your mission — if you choose to accept it — is to educate yourself *before* you enter these temples of chance. If you build your understanding of the components of a casino and the people who make it run, you're more likely to make rational decisions when it comes to the games you choose to play — and less likely to part with the contents of your pocketbook because of some subliminal pull.

Navigating the Casino Maze

From Monaco, the Las Vegas of Europe, to the *Queen Mary II,* the largest cruise ship ever to sail, most casinos of the world are laid out in a similar floor plan. Even at the smaller clubs, you recognize many of the same aesthetic and functional characteristics found at the megaresorts. This common design is no accident — casino owners have an intimate knowledge of the gambler's mind, and they design the interiors to make their guests comfortable with parting with their cash.

This section takes a stroll through a typical casino to prepare you for the sights and sounds you encounter when you walk through those neon-bathed doorways. Preparation is the key for maintaining control. You'll understand what I'm saying when you find yourself subconsciously reaching for your wallet before you finish the chapter.

Remember that gambling is the ultimate impulse buy. The casino's layout encourages this impulse. Taking away the mystique is your first step toward improving your odds and coming out a winner. I suggest that, in addition to the virtual walk-through you get by reading this chapter, you do the same in every brick-and-mortar establishment you visit before you drop your first dollar on the table or pump a coin in a slot. Prepare yourself: Stand still, take a deep breath, and look around.

Getting in is the easy part

It may surprise you how fast you can find yourself in the middle of the sensory hurricane on the casino floor. In less restrictive states, such as Nevada and New Jersey, you can walk in off the street or get dropped off by a taxi and find yourself a few feet away from the gaming areas. You're practically holding the door for your significant other with one hand and rolling the dice with the other. After all, casinos want as little as possible to stand between you and your favorite game.

But most casinos give you a chance to catch your breath and do some mental stretching prior to plunging into the action. When you walk in, you often find yourself in a lobby or foyer. Remember that most casinos are also hotels, so you may see familiar sights, such as the concierge, bell desk, and check-in counter. People bustle about and crowd together before they find the destinations suited for them. While some gamblers are anticipating the excitement just steps away, others are exiting with delirious grins on their faces — or expressions of shock and awe.

This bottleneck is no accident; it's part of the calculated marketing strategy to lure you ever closer to the games. At the threshold of the gaming floor, the sounds, colorful lights, and crowd energy all go to work on your senses, even from a distance. Just like an infant reaching for bright colorful objects, casino visitors gravitate to the sights and sounds of the casino floor.

Interior design is to a casino floor plan what aerodynamics is to automobile manufacturers; forward movement is a result of an ever-expanding array of enticements including colors that dazzle, lights that entice, and a temperature scientifically controlled for maximum comfort. You quickly find that every destination in a casino — the guest elevators, the bathrooms, or the buffet — requires that you walk through (or dangerously near) the gaming areas.

Slot machines and video poker stations are positioned just inside the casino entrance. The boys in marketing put them here so you can test the waters and feel the rush a quarter at a time — getting your feet wet right at the casino entrance. Up ahead you see the casino proper, a virtual indoor carnival buzzing with excitement. You can almost feel the energy pulsing.

Slot machines: Place them and they will come

As you enter the casino proper, you see hopeful gamblers, often two-deep, standing in line, patiently waiting their turn to reap the spitting, buzzing payoffs from the slot machines. You operate the slot machines by pushing the buttons or yanking down on the lever to the side. Larger casinos hold aisle after aisle of slots, like rows of corn.

Casinos typically place the most profitable slot machines within easy access to the main traffic aisles, such as the foyer, restaurants, and bars, and are extremely careful to place high-hit frequency slots within earshot of the thronging masses.

If you venture farther onto the casino floor, you can see this philosophy in action. Clusters of people sit at the corner slots, sometimes two-deep as the individuals standing in line patiently await their turn to enjoy the spitting, buzzing payoffs. As you venture down the aisles of slots, you may find a few open machines, but not many. As one row ends, another aisle begins. Some of the most popular machines are Double Diamond and Wheel of Fortune. (See Chapter 12 for more slot info.)

Table games: Penetrating the inner circle

Just as the sun is the center of the solar system, the table games rest in the middle of the casino system, attracting visitors ever inward and at the same time providing the main source of energy and vitality to the floor. Table games are grouped together into areas known in casino lingo as *pits*. The pits are separated from slot machines, restaurants, and other casino functions by a wide aisle, allowing nonplayers to watch the action and vicariously enjoy the thrill of turning over the winning card or nailing the winning roll.

Table games you can play include

- **Baccarat:** The classic card game is often played in a separate room to create a more civilized and secluded atmosphere; see Chapter 10.
- **Blackjack:** Determine your own fate with smart decisions and timely double downs; see Chapter 7.
- **Craps:** Roll the dice and hear the crowd roar in the most boisterous game on the floor; see Chapter 8.
- **Poker:** It's just like your neighborhood game, except you never have to shuffle; see Chapter 6.
- **Roulette:** Pick a number, place your bet, and then watch the spinning wheel go round and round; see Chapter 9.

If you're a high roller, the most exclusive gaming tables with the highest betting limits are often in adjoining rooms, separated by glass from the other tables. They feature fancy amenities, such as private cocktail servers or a bar.

But most table games are designed for moderate bettors. The loud, boisterous call of a lively crowd gathered around the craps table can seem like a siren song to players tempted to leave the boredom and repetition of the slots, and that's no accident. The intimate nature of the poker table beckons would-be strategists, while the smoky haze surrounding a blackjack game cries out to the novice with its lack of intimidation.

The bar: Quiet escape — or not?

Most casinos have a bar that's central to the main action. A large casino may offer numerous bars interspersed throughout the floor, each with a unique theme. Some feature live music, and some are simply service bars where you can take a quick pit stop away from the flow of traffic. But if you're picturing a quiet setting of soft music, hushed whispers, and clinking glasses, you're going to be disappointed. There's no escaping the games: Casino bars are in the midst of the lively pits.

Casinos profit from the fact that alcohol lubricates the ATM card. But no casino wants drunk patrons, so the line they walk is a delicate one, and the policy on pushing alcohol consumption may vary from place to place. In addition, every state has different laws governing alcohol consumption inside its casinos, so there is no single unifying rule about how alcohol is handled inside betting areas. Some tribal casinos don't serve it at all, so if sipping on a stiff one as you play is important, make sure you do you homework before you leave home. The bottom line: The drinking environment varies widely, so the smartest play is to find a scene that suits your tastes, and always strive to stay in complete control.

Sports books: Where you can cheer for a horse or a home run

In Nevada, most casinos have a *sports book,* an area devoted to betting on sporting events such as horse races or ball games. In smaller casinos, the sports book may be nothing more than a counter with a tote board hung behind it. But the larger casinos have super-sized rooms full of amenities designed for anyone willing to put his money where his mouth is. Every inch of wall space is used inside a sports book; dozens of megasized, high-definition monitors show games as they're played, and digital displays listing the current odds, scores, and available bets for the day cover the walls.

The newer places, such as the Wynn in Las Vegas, really roll out the red carpet for bettors.

Their sports book features leather sofas, couches, and chairs that are so comfortable, you could fall asleep there. Before you doze off, read Chapter 15, which tells you everything you need to know about sports betting, from deciphering the odds, to placing a bet, to (hopefully!) cashing in.

Not ready to place a bet just yet? No problem. The sports books are open to everyone. And if big ball games don't excite you, there's always horse (and dog) racing because most places simulcast horse (and sometimes dog) racing from tracks all around the country. If you don't know an exacta from a trifecta, read Chapter 16 for more about betting on horses.

 If you don't feel like leaving your table to head to the bar, most casinos have servers who take drink orders. You can pay and tip them with chips from the casino or cash. However, if you want to eat, most casinos don't allow eating at the table. You need to visit one of the many restaurants to chow down.

Cashing out: Heading to the cashier's cage

The cashier's *cage* is where you redeem your *markers* — the chips the casino uses to represent cash — for hard cash and where you buy and redeem your slot tokens. (You must buy your chips at the tables, and you must cash out at the cashier's cage.)

Every casino has cashier's cages — the larger the casino, the more cages you find. If the slot machines and gaming tables are the arteries that circulate a casino's input and output, the cashier's cage is the heart that pumps the casino's lifeblood: money. Highly trained and supremely trusted casino employees handle more cash each shift than most people see in a lifetime.

Casino cashiers: Behind bars no more

In the old days, the cashier's cage earned its moniker because it was, as the name implies, behind bars. Today's technology and construction make the modern cashier's cage much more inviting, providing maximum security without looking like Fort Knox. You can usually find casino cashiers in the core of the casino layout, as far from any exit as possible, which means the casino's money is more secure. This location also offers a beneficial side effect that casinos are happy to take advantage of. Their centrality means the cashier's cage is often in the lion's den of the most enticing betting areas, tempting many recent winners to *recycle* their bills by turning them right back into chips at a nearby table.

Cashier's cages are easy to find. Casinos typically locate them along the sides of the rooms to allow the more valuable floor space for games. Here, much like at a bank, one or more tellers deal with the public through a window.

If you're worried about leaving with your big winnings, you can request a check or get a safety deposit box in most casinos.

In addition to the cashier's cage, casinos usually offer a credit office. Depending on how big a player you are and the type of games you want to attack, you may want to ask for a line of credit. You can also cash traveler's checks, get change, receive incoming money via a wire service, and even receive bank wire transfers (with proper ID, of course!). If you're interested in a line of credit, check out Chapter 4, where I provide all the pros and cons.

Meeting the Casino's Cast of Characters

A vast and sometimes complicated hierarchy of employees with a variety of titles, responsibilities, and even different styles of dress populates a casino. These workers simultaneously cater to the needs of the guests and the casino owners. No matter who they are, the casino employees all have one goal in common: to provide you with ample opportunities to try your luck against the unevenly-stacked house odds.

Casino employees are usually pleasant, professional, and well-trained individuals (after all, if you're treated with courtesy and respect, you're more likely to stay — and spend — longer). In this section, I introduce you to the pleasant cast of characters you may encounter, and I explain their unique roles. With this knowledge, you're better equipped to take advantage of their services — to *your* advantage.

In the pits: Serving the table players

As you explore the responsibilities of the various casino personnel, it helps to split the casino into two parts:

- ✔ The area where slot machines appear in endless rows (see the section "Slot employees: The reel dealers").
- ✔ The area where you play table games, such as blackjack, craps, or roulette.

The casino arranges the tables in clusters, similar to wagon trains encircled to protect against an attack. These groups of tables are known as *pits*. Each pit is designed to be an autonomous, fully functioning business, equipped with a variety of table games and a small community of casino personnel that is always willing to usher your dollar bills into the casino coffers.

Pit bosses

Pit bosses are smartly attired, experienced professionals who are responsible for all the gaming operations in their assigned pits. As the name implies, pit bosses are just that: bosses. They supervise floorpersons (see the next section), dealers (see the section "Dealers"), and the gamers within their pit. Theirs is a very detail-oriented job, requiring not only intimate knowledge of all aspects of the games but also the ability to keep track of thousands of dollars flowing through their spheres of influence. Even though the average gambler probably doesn't have much contact with a pit boss, in the event of a serious dispute, the pit boss is the one who steps in to settle matters.

Among other tasks, pit bosses monitor *credit markers,* or the amount of credit extended to you (I explore credit markers in greater detail in Chapter 4), and they dispense *comps,* such as free meals or shows (see Chapter 21 as well as "Casino hosts" later in this chapter for the lowdown on comps), doled out according to an elaborate formula based on the number of hours you play and the amount of money you wager.

Winning or losing vast sums of money often ignites supercharged emotions. Another responsibility of the pit boss is to make sure those emotions don't explode into conflict. The pit boss is there to congratulate as well as to calm, to soothe as well as to strong-arm. The pit boss's job is part security staff, part supervisor, part gambling expert, and part public relations manager.

Floorpersons

Reporting to each pit boss (see the previous section) are several other *suits* known as *floorpersons.* The main difference from pit bosses is that floorpersons are in charge of only a couple of tables in the pit and report directly to the pit boss. They dress and act like the pit boss, and you typically can't distinguish between the two without asking. Both of them make sure that proper casino procedure is followed. These procedures include refilling dealer chip racks, monitoring markers, and handing out comps, all while remaining cool and calm.

Dealers

For most people, gambling is a social sport. Because the machine games are a more solitary venture, many players prefer the camaraderie of table gaming. *Dealers* are at the center of this emotional wheel of fun. Excellent customer-service skills are a requirement; after all, dealers stand on the front line when it comes to irate, belligerent, or inebriated gamblers. Even during high-pressure situations, dealers must promote a relaxed and pleasant atmosphere.

Dealers have their fingers on the pulse of the casino — figuratively and literally. Their hands, after all, deal the blackjacks and the full houses and take the money you lose or pay off your winners. Theirs is a high-pressure job with a demanding audience. Overseeing several players at a table, dealers must be confident in their gambling knowledge. They must know who wins, who loses, and how much to pay out on each hand. Many gamers mistakenly believe that dealers simply shuffle and deal cards, but dealers must also handle dice, chips, and money — accurately and quickly.

Dealers have a wide range of personalities. Some are polite and ebullient, others efficient and brusque. Although finding a compatible dealer doesn't change the cards or the size of your winnings, it can make your gaming experience more enjoyable and, sometimes, that's as much as you can ask for. You can spot a good dealer by his or her smile, humor, demeanor, and often the size of the crowd at the table. When you find one you like, sit down, but remember the dealer has no control over the outcome. Most dealers prefer that you win because they make their money primarily from tips.

Slot employees: The reel dealers

The average American casino makes nearly two-thirds of its profits from its various slot machines. Much is at stake along the rows and rows of cling-clanging slot machines and electronic games. Therefore, casinos are diligent when it comes to maintaining and stocking them for long-term play. Just like the pit bosses and dealers who watch over the table games (see the previous section), the staff members assigned to the slot machines — the slot attendants and the slot supervisors — keep a careful eye on their vast realm.

Slot attendants

The person you're most likely to deal with if you have a problem or question about your machine is a *slot attendant*. Slot machine attendants are on constant vigil, ever watchful for the next jackpot or flashing light requesting service. They're usually wearing a uniform and sometimes push carts with oodles of money so they can give change to bettors in need. The attendants are the perfect people to ask if you're not sure how to play a particular machine; they know every bell, cherry, and bar like the back of their hand.

If you need change, assistance with a game, or simply a bill that's just a tad crisper than the one you have, summon a slot attendant, who's usually at your beck and call. However, if a machine needs repair, the slot attendant calls a slot technician.

Slot supervisors

The slot supervisor rules the realm of the slot machines, managing employees and overseeing the maintenance and upkeep of the machines. The slot supervisor generally has several slot attendants as direct reports. For casual gamblers, slot supervisors normally play a part in your life only if you hit a jackpot that can't be paid out in coins.

Management: Running the tables

In addition to the employees who ensure the smooth-running operations on the floor, a host of other casino personnel contribute to the success of the house. As a beginning casino player, you may not come into contact with any of these people. However, if you do, management employees, such as the casino host, may become familiar (and friendly) faces.

Casino hosts

Modern casino hosts best resemble a successful hotel concierge: They're both at your service. Whether dealing with new guests, loyal customers, or high rollers, the casino host focuses on service, service, and more service.

Hitting the jackpot, baby!

For those rare but exciting payoffs when you defy the gods of gambling and win more than the machine can pay out, a slot attendant — and, in some cases, the supervisor — responds to your flashing machine. The slot attendant arrives with a big wad of cash to ceremoniously peel off the bills, one Franklin at a time, to you, the happy winner. And if the payout is $1,200 or more, you also receive an IRS form (called a W2-G) reporting your win to your favorite uncle — Uncle Sam (check out Chapter 4 for more tax-reporting issues).

A typical casino host is an affable and professional employee whose mission is to serve your every need. Hosts are hands-on people who greet VIP guests at the door and pamper them throughout their stay. Depending on the size and popularity of the casino and the thickness of your wallet, a casino host may

- ✔ Comp your rooms
- ✔ Arrange for greens fees at the golf course
- ✔ Get tickets to sold-out shows
- ✔ Give away free meals

If it's your first time in a casino, don't expect to have the keys to the *Rain Man* suite at Caesar's Palace handed to you. But even low rollers can make a relationship with the casino host profitable. Keep the following in mind:

- ✔ **Join the club:** The casino host expects you to be a casino loyalty club member before you're offered many comps. And don't forget to use your club card whenever you play (See Chapter 21 for more on club cards.)
- ✔ **Express yourself:** Don't wait for the host to find you in the penny slots area; go introduce yourself to the host.
- ✔ **Be loyal:** Find your favorite gambling locale and stick to it. Even small-scale visits can make you a valuable customer if they're repeated regularly.
- ✔ **Just ask:** The players who get comps are the ones who ask the casino host. Don't be rude or demanding, just ask politely and see what benefits you qualify for.

Player development is all about forming relationships. Casino hosts are eager to wine and dine you if they believe they can create player loyalty through these lavish perks. Although player-development departments often employ telemarketers or other representatives to reach out to gamers through databases, casino hosts achieve their goals on a one-on-one basis by working their cellphones and roaming the casino floors, seeking ways to make their clients' gaming experiences more enjoyable.

Other managers

As in other walks of life, every casino employee has to report to somebody, and those somebodies are the *shift managers*. The shift managers then report to the casino manager. As the name implies, shift managers are responsible for their areas of casino expertise (such as slots or table games) during a particular shift (day, swing, and graveyard). Most land-based casinos are 24/7 operations, so shift managers must be prepared to work weekends, holidays, and late-night shifts.

When player disputes arise, money needs to be accounted for or items need to be authorized; the shift manager takes on these duties as well. Shift managers are responsible for employee schedules, customer service, comps, credit, and a host of other duties that make for a mind-boggling job.

The only position above the shift manager is the casino manager. You rarely see this head honcho on the floor, but he's the ultimate decision-maker for most gaming operations. As a beginning casino player, you aren't too concerned about who the casino manager is. The only time you may ever interact with the manager is if you win enough money to buy the casino.

Maintaining a Safe and Secure Environment

In today's massive casinos, five-star hotels merge with gargantuan, themed buildings, encompassing entire city blocks and housing restaurants, bars, theaters, nightclubs, gaming tables, slot machines, ATMs, snack bars, gift shops, and even the occasional theme park. A casino's security division, therefore, must function much like the police department of an entire town.

This section explains who the security personnel are, lets you in on who's watching you, and details how you can be proactive to protect yourself when betting your hard-earned money.

Security personnel: The human touch

In the old days, casinos simply had hired muscle watch after the owners' millions. These days, casino security folks are considered important members of a casino's floor team. Because it's a dynamic and demanding job, casino security has become a true career; casinos offer competitive salaries and benefits so they can hire people who are mentally *and* physically fit.

Security staffs have a two-pronged task:

 ✔ Protect the casino's property
 ✔ Safeguard the casino's guests

Unfortunately, a security employee's job is made less agreeable by the fact that one task doesn't always go hand in hand with the other. For instance, some guests are also out to separate a casino from its money, either through cheating or through faking an injury in crowded conditions.

The responsibilities of security employees range from viewing the rows of surveillance cameras in high-tech rooms to patrolling the casino floors, constantly on vigil for fights, thieves, drunks, and other disturbances.

Surprisingly, security also keeps a close eye on the help — casino employees have initiated many cheating scams over the years.

You can easily spot the security staff; they're always available to help you resolve a conflict or point you in the right direction. Even though every casino is different, security staff typically wear a uniform that is quasi-military, with a shirt that says *SECURITY* or at least a nametag or badge that identifies them as such. Other identifying features include a walkie-talkie, a badge, and possibly a gun. Keep the gun in mind the next time you feel the urge to help yourself to the dealer's chips.

Bigger hotels can have several dozen security officers working at the busiest times of day and a supervisor in each major area of the casino who manages the team. Security supervisors must wear many hats, including the hat of a diplomat. Their staff is on the front lines, both protecting and ejecting guests, and when the occasional temper flares or a misunderstanding arises, the security supervisor must wade in to render an on-the-spot verdict.

Surveillance: The eye in the sky

On-site security personnel at a casino can only see so much when trying to protect the casino and its guests. To assist them in their daily rounds, security personnel rely on electronic surveillance — *the eye in the sky*.

One-way glass conceals thousands of digital cameras in any casino. Some are hidden where you least expect them. Others are prominent, large, and noticeable so that they serve as warnings. Technology is such today that sophisticated cameras can see not only a player's face but also the cards in his or her hands and even the serial numbers on dollar bills. On-site security personnel can view banks of television screens to identify cheats and save casinos millions of dollars each year.

In the most brazen scenarios, a nickel-and-dime thief reaches over from his machine to grab grandma's slot tokens. The cameras capture his attempt, and the thief is quickly arrested. In less obvious but equally common situations, security personnel carefully observe, identify, and apprehend cheats and cons.

 Although most surveillance is for the detection and prevention of cheating and swindling, the eye in the sky also protects honest gamblers from slick crooks prowling the casino for easy prey. The newer casinos have cameras outside the building, such as in the parking garages, to cast the safety net farther for you.

Taking safety into your own hands

The modern casino should be a carefree environment where you forget your troubles, spend money, and — with hope — win some money back. Although winning isn't always possible, at the very least you expect a safe environment in which to gamble. Unfortunately, where innocent, naive, and trusting people congregate in great numbers — surrounded by huge amounts of disposable income — the predators of society gather as well. Thieves are on the prowl for ways to separate you or even the casinos from hard-earned cash.

Although casinos implement the most stringent security measures and the latest in state-of-the-art surveillance technology, you, as a prudent casino guest, should assume responsibility for your own safety. The following tips can help you avoid becoming a victim of a casino predator:

- Tuck your wallet in a safe, hard-to-access spot, such as your front pocket.

- If you carry a purse, take a small one that you can wear close to your body, preferably under a jacket or wrap.

- Guard your chips or slot tokens; these work the same as money, so treat them accordingly.

- If you go to the casino solo, be cautious about the overly friendly people you meet. Maintain tight control of your personal information, get your drinks straight from the cocktail servers, and keep your big wins to yourself so you don't become a target.

Chapter 3

Probability, Odds, and a Bit of Luck: What You Need to Succeed

*W*hen I told a friend I was writing this book, he laughed and said the title was appropriate because "only dummies would ever gamble." I smiled to myself. Although it's true that most people who gamble do lose, the *real* dummies are the ones who take on the casinos without first educating themselves — especially on concepts about probability and odds, understanding the house edge, and identifying which games offer the best chance for success.

Sounds like the intro to a lecture in higher mathematics? Don't worry, this chapter is brief — just enough to prepare you to walk through those casino doors, make sound gambling choices, and get wise to certain myths and superstitions.

Defining Luck: A Temporary Fluctuation

Unfortunately, too many newbie gamblers rely on luck to guide their experiences. Casinos can be an easy place to burn through money, so your best chance for hanging on to that hard-earned cash is through a little dose of knowledge. But, you wonder, when it comes to striking it rich in the casino, isn't there such a thing as luck? Technically, the answer is *yes* — but don't count on your rabbit's foot to keep you on the path to riches over the long haul. The term *luck* can describe many situations, especially in gambling. Someone may have a lucky run at the baccarat table, or maybe your Aunt Rosemary plays a lucky slot machine that never loses.

But in order to have a realistic perspective of your chances in the casino, you need to view luck in rational and mathematical terms: *Luck* is a temporary fluctuation or deviation from the norm. In the short run, you may perceive that you got real lucky when the dealer busted eight hands in a row at blackjack. But in reality, such an event is just normal fluctuation — also known as a *random walk* — such as when the stock market drifts one direction or another.

For example, in Caribbean Stud poker, for every $100 you wager, you can expect to lose about five bucks. Yet over the short run, anything can happen. You may get lucky and finish the day ahead — or you may get unlucky and lose far more than $5.

In a purely mathematical sense, neither of these results has anything to do with luck. They are simply the normal consequences of fluctuation. For example, try flipping a coin. Half the time it should be tails and half heads. But over a short-term sampling, it can veer far away from 50 percent.

Understanding the Role of Probability

Millions of merry gamblers frequent casinos all over the world every day without a clear understanding of one important concept — probability. Mastering one of the more complex branches of mathematics isn't necessary for successful gambling. But an elementary understanding of probability is certainly helpful in making sound gambling choices.

Probability is the study of the laws of chance, the identification of how often certain events can be expected to occur. For example, to express the probability that a coin will turn up heads, you can give the result in numerous ways, such as a

- ✔ **Ratio** — 1 in 2 times
- ✔ **Fraction** — ½ or half the time
- ✔ **Percentage** — 50 percent
- ✔ **Decimal** — .50, which is the same as 50 percent
- ✔ **Odds** — 1 to 1

> *Odds* expresses the number of times something *won't* happen next to the number of times it *will* happen. So, 1-to-1 odds means the event is an even money event; it has an equal chance of occurring or not occurring.

(If you're biting at the bit to find out more in-depth info about probability, check out *Probability For Dummies* by Deborah Rumsey, PhD, [Wiley].) This section looks a bit closer at probability's role in casino gambling.

Identifying independent events

Another important term to understand here is *independent* outcomes. Being independent has nothing to do with successfully ditching your loser boyfriend in the keno lounge. In gambling, independent refers to events (such as roulette spins or dice throws) that aren't affected by any previous results. Craps and roulette are great examples. The dice and roulette table ball don't have a tiny brain inside, so each new throw or spin is independent of all previous turns. In other words, the dice or ball doesn't know what numbers are running hot or cold, so the probability of outcome for each and every spin is exactly the same.

Slot machines are also independent. Recent jackpots do *not* change the likelihood of the same combination coming up again. If your chances of lining up three cherries are 5,000 to 1 and you just hit the jackpot, the three cherries have exactly the same chances of appearing on the very next spin.

Recognizing dependent events

So you may be asking yourself, what constitutes a nonindependent or dependent event? *Dependent* events are occurrences that are *more* or *less* likely based on the previous occurrences. Imagine a bag of five black balls and five red balls. *Before* you pull a ball out, you know you have a 50 percent chance of pulling out a black ball and the *same odds* of pulling out a red ball. Then you reach in and pull out one red ball and toss it aside. Now *the odds have changed* — you no longer have a 50 percent chance of pulling either ball. Your chances of pulling out a black ball are now *greater* (56 percent).

So in some situations, the past does affect the future. Another classic example is the game of blackjack. Because cards are removed after they're played, the remaining composition of the deck changes. For example, your chances for getting a blackjack drop dramatically when a disproportionate number of aces are used up.

Almost all casino games consist of cards, dice, spinning wheels, or reels. These games almost always yield independent events. Blackjack is the rare exception, which is the main reason for its popularity.

Factoring in the odds

To be a successful gambler, you must understand the intersection of statistics, probability, and the odds. In simple terms, that means you need to understand how likely something is to happen (*statistics*), how likely that it can happen to you (*probability*), and what you're going to get out of it, if it does happen (*odds*). With a grasp of these concepts, you're ready to tackle the casino with realistic expectations, and you can understand why some games should be avoided.

The best example to start with is the coin flip. You probably know that heads and tails each have a 50-50 shot at turning up. As I say in the previous section, you can communicate the probability of the flip in terms of odds. In the case of a two-sided coin, your odds of flipping heads are 1 to 1. In other words, with two possible events (outcomes), you have one chance to fail and one chance to succeed. Clear as mud? Here's another example. Consider the roll of a six-sided die. What are the odds that you'll roll a 3? The ratio is 1 in 6, so the odds are 5 to 1.

Odds are, you'll hear the word *odds* used in other contexts. For example, the amount of money a bet pays compared to the initial bet are sometimes called *odds* too. But don't confuse *payout odds* with *true odds*. True odds refer to the actual chance that a specific occurrence will happen, which is usually different from the casino payout odds.

Examining How Casinos Operate and Make Money: House Edge

The seasoned gambler can count on true odds to dictate the chances of winning a particular game, right? Not exactly. Casinos aren't in the charity business — they exist to make money. And like all successful enterprises, they follow reliable business models. With their intimate understanding of probability and odds, casino owners guarantee themselves a healthy bottom line.

So you can't beat the odds when the house arranges them in its favor, but you can understand the odds of winning inside a casino by arming yourself with information about the *house edge*. The house edge (sometimes known as the *casino advantage* or *house advantage*) by definition is the small percentage of all wagers that the casino expects to win. Every game has a different house edge, and even certain bets within a single game have a better house edge than other bets.

To put it a different way, casinos expect to pay out slightly less money to winning bettors than they take in from losing bettors. The laws of probability tell casinos how often certain bets win relative to how often they lose. Casinos then calculate the payout odds based on the winning probabilities, or true odds. The payouts are typically smaller than the true odds, ensuring that, with enough betting action, the casino will take in a certain amount with every dollar wagered.

Table 3-1 shows the house edge for popular casino games and how much you can expect to lose for an average three-day weekend of betting for gamblers playing $10 a hand at table games. As you can see, the higher the house edge, the more you can expect to lose. For example, you cut your losses by 80 percent if you switch from roulette to baccarat!

Table 3-1	The House Edge for Popular Casino Games	
Game	*House Edge*	*Loss per $8,000 in Total Bets*
Baccarat	1.06 percent	$85
Blackjack	0.50 percent	$40
Craps	1.36 percent	$109
Caribbean Stud Poker	5.22 percent	$418
Let It Ride	3.51 percent	$281
Pai Gow Poker	2.54 percent	$203
Roulette	5.26 percent	$421
Three-Card Poker	3.37 percent	$270
Video Poker	0.46 percent	$37

This table assumes you only make the most optimal bets at games such as baccarat and craps. Also, the edge for many games, such as video poker or blackjack, varies depending on the particular type and version you find and on how skillfully you play. (Check out the specific chapters later in this book for detailed strategies.) This next section looks at the three methods that casinos utilize to assist themselves in performing profitably.

Charging a fee

With some games, casinos charge a fee, or commission. Baccarat is a perfect example. If you bet on the banker's hand and win, a 5 percent commission is deducted from your winning bet. This fee tilts the odds slightly in favor of the house and ensures that the casino makes a profit at this popular table game. Another example of fees is in sports betting. The house adds what is called *vigorish* or *vig* (a commission) to every wager (check out Chapter 15 for more on the vig).

Paying less than the true odds

Another way the casino makes money is to pay out less than the true odds (see the earlier section "Factoring in the odds"). Take roulette: With 38 numbers on the wheel, your odds of guessing the winning number are 37 to 1. So you bravely place a $100 bet on a single number and hit it. Congratulations! After you quit jumping up and down and kissing the cocktail server, dealer, and anyone else who couldn't quickly escape, you collect $3,500.

But, wait a minute. $3,500 means a payoff of 35 to 1. What happened to the true odds of 37 to 1? The fact is, even though you win, your payoff is less than the true odds. The bottom line? Casinos take $200 out of every $3,800 wagered, which leaves the house with a hefty edge of 5.26 percent.

Muddying the odds

Casinos offer three types of games — games with fixed odds, games with variable odds, and games where skill can affect the odds. They all have different styles of play and appeal to different kinds of gamblers. Although you should naturally gravitate toward the games that are the most fun for you, you need to be clear on the three classes of games. This section looks at the three types more closely

Games with fixed odds

When the odds are *fixed* (not subject to change), the bean counters in the back room can calculate exactly how much each of these games wins for every $100 gambled. That's because, no matter how much gamblers vary their play, the casino has the same edge. The house seldom has a losing day on games with fixed odds, such as

- Slots
- Craps
- Keno
- Roulette

Even though the profits fluctuate each day (due to short-term luck), casinos can easily forecast for the long run because they have hundreds of machines and tables all operating at once.

Games with variable odds

In this classification, the odds change, depending on how well gamblers play their cards or place their bets. Several of these games may yield better odds for smarter players. But the gain in these games can only go so far because over the long run, the odds still strongly favor the house. In other words, even if you play better than anyone else at the table, these games can't be beaten.

Some examples of these games include

- ✔ Pai Gow poker
- ✔ Three Card poker
- ✔ Let It Ride

Games where skills affect the odds

A few games reward skillful play and allow a tiny minority of gamblers to get an edge over the house. These games are variable-odds games, but they offer an advantage that the others don't: Gamblers actually have a chance to win money in the long run. But don't think you can walk in off the street and start pocketing Ben Franklins. Winning requires study, discipline, patience, and practice. Here are the games where skill can get you over the hump:

- ✔ Blackjack
- ✔ Video poker
- ✔ Regular poker
- ✔ Sports betting
- ✔ Horse racing

Calculating the Odds in Casino Games

If you're good at math, you often can detect when the casino payout odds are lower than true odds (see the section "Factoring in the odds" earlier in this chapter). With dice, for example, you have 36 different combinations, and the odds are 35-to-1 for each combination. But with other games, the odds can be impossible to calculate. Take slots, for example: The thousands of possible reel combinations and ever-changing progressive jackpots make it difficult for anyone to calculate the odds of winning.

One of the most confusing aspects of odds is the difference between *for* and *to*. For example, in video poker a flush pays 6 *for* 1, which means your win of six coins *includes* your original wager. So your actual profit is only five coins. However, if the bet pays 6 *to* 1, your odds are better. Your profit is six and your total return is seven (your win *plus* your original wager). This small detail may seem like a silly case of semantics, but it can make a big difference in your payout.

This section ties together the joint concepts of payout odds and true odds that will get you on the road to understanding the house *edge* (or advantage). Armed with a full understanding of that key statistic, you'll be able to discriminate between good and bad bets in a casino.

Identifying payoff odds

In almost all cases, the payoffs favor the house, and you lose in the long run. However, some unusual situations arise that give astute gamblers an edge.

Zero expectation

A *zero expectation* bet has no edge — for the house or the player. This balance means that both sides can break even in the long run. For example, if you remove the two extra green numbers (0 and 00) from the roulette wheel, the game now becomes a zero expectation game because it has 36 numbers, 18 red and 18 black. Any bet on red or black would be a zero expectation bet. In other words, when you bet on one color, your chances for winning and losing are equal, just like flipping a coin.

Negative expectation

However, casinos aren't interested in offering zero expectation games. In order to make a profit, they need to add in those two extra green numbers to change the odds in roulette. Now, when you bet red or black, your odds of winning are $18/38$ rather than $18/36$. So your even money bet moves from a zero expectation to a *negative expectation*.

Whenever you're the underdog (such as in roulette), your wager has a negative expectation, and you can expect to lose money. It may not happen right then. You may defy the bad odds for a while and win, but over time you will lose.

Most bets carry a negative expectation because the house doesn't give true odds for the payouts (as is the case for roulette). Craps provides another good example. Say you bet that the dice will total seven on the next throw. If you win, you are paid 4 to 1. However, the true odds for this occurrence happening are 5 to 1 ($6/36$).

That difference may not sound like a major change, but the house edge on that bet is a whopping 16.67 percent! And a negative expectation bet for you is a positive for the casino. (The casino makes an average of $16.67 on every $100 bet in the previous craps example.)

Positive expectation

In a *positive expectation* bet, the tables are turned on the house so that the players have the advantage. Most people can't believe casinos actually allow a positive expectation for the gambler, but surprisingly, some are out there. One example is in tournaments, where, in many situations, more money is paid out by the casino than is taken in. (I detail a few of these opportunities in Chapters 18.)

Getting an edge on the house edge

It's a fact: In most casino games, the house has the edge. But *you* can get an edge over the casino in two ways:

- ✔ **Using match play coupons to double your fun.** You can often find match play coupons in the free fun books distributed by many casinos. Rip these coupons out and tuck them underneath your bet. In most cases, they essentially double your wager without having to risk any more money.

- ✔ **Taking advantage of promotions.** Promotions can be the best way to secure a positive expectation. Here are a couple of examples: I have played at several casinos where they changed the rules for a short period of time and paid out 2 to 1 on all blackjacks. This change tipped the odds enough so that even basic-strategy players had nearly a 2 percent edge over the house.

  Another great promotion was when the Pioneer Casino in Laughlin, Nevada, offered *Double Jackpot Time* on some slot machines. Twice an hour, for a short period of time (approximately 30 seconds), they generously doubled the payout on certain jackpots. Most people shrugged off this opportunity as just another marketing gimmick, but it was very lucrative. A friend of mine made six figures a year there playing only a few minutes every hour.

  Finding out about these great deals isn't easy. However, one helpful resource for casino promotions and coupons is the *Las Vegas Advisor* (see Appendix B). Another tactic is signing up for casino mailing lists to keep abreast of upcoming special events.

Avoiding Myths, Magic, and Other Superstitions

Perhaps the biggest mistake for novice gamblers is making a betting decision based on superstitions or instincts rather than facts. I can assure you that poker superstars such as Howard Lederer and Phil Hellmuth do *not* win because they wear their lucky sweater or rely on horoscope readings.

Winners like Lederer and Hellmuth are brilliant in analyzing the complex choices each hand offers in a high-stakes tournament. This section debunks some common hocus-pocus that gamblers mistakenly turn to.

Going with your hunches

Using your intuition, going by your gut, and playing a hunch are all paths to ruin. If the odds favor the house by more than 9 percent (like they do on a hard eight bet at the craps table), then that's the rate you lose over time. Sure, you may get lucky and win in the short run, but casinos are geared to outlast you. (The only way to leave a winner on a lousy-odds game is to immediately stop playing if you're up.) They have a huge bankroll, and when they have the edge, not even the luckiest person on the planet (or even Olga, the All-Knowing Psychic) can turn the tables and beat the odds.

He took my machine!

I was in Laughlin, Nevada for a few days and decided to join my friend for some easy money during the Double Jackpot Time promotion at the Pioneer Casino. I found a machine to play, sat down, and then waited for Double Jackpot Time to begin.

Only certain machines were included in this promotion, and because I was running late, I was happy I had snagged one. Unfortunately, an older lady had been playing that same machine all day long and had just walked away for a few minutes to go to the restroom. She was furious that I had taken her machine.

I politely stood my ground because I hadn't broken any slot etiquette (she hadn't saved the chair or left anything to hold it). When I tried to appease her by saying I would only be on the machine for a minute, she calmed down slightly but still hovered over my shoulder like an impatient vulture.

When the promotion started, I feverishly pumped in dollar coins as fast as possible and hit a $1,000 jackpot just before the promotion ended. Though I was happy, the lady was infuriated. She loudly complained that the jackpot should have been hers.

I calmly recited to her the inner workings of slot machines and how the actual outcomes can be different depending on her speed and when she pulled the handle, but it didn't help. I finally quit trying to reason with her and waited for the slot attendant to show up.

After I was paid, the casino requested all slot customers to play at least one more spin to clear any jackpots from the screen (to prevent someone from trying to get paid twice for the same winner). After I put the coins in and pulled the handle, you can probably guess what happened. I miraculously hit another $1,000 jackpot! The lady, who already believed I had taken her machine, was now livid. I grabbed my winnings and said, "Okay, I guess you can have the machine now."

Instead of relying on your hunches, you're better off diverting that psychic energy to studying the laws of probability and choosing games that offer the lowest house edge. (You've made a great start by reading this book.)

Playing a lucky machine

Many people have a favorite slot machine they like to play. That's reasonable. After all, gambling at a familiar game is better than taking a chance with one you know nothing about. However, many players return to the same game because they believe they have found a lucky machine.

If you're relying on a lucky machine and think you're consistently winning, I urge you to keep records of your play. Write down how much money you start with before you sit down, and then count up what you have when you walk away from the machine. You may be surprised to see that you didn't perform quite as well as you thought, especially over the long term. Selective memory plays tricks and deceives gamblers into thinking they're ahead, which is seldom the case.

Breaking the law of probability

Many players erroneously believe certain events are *due*. For example, if the roulette ball lands on a red number five times in a row, some gamblers feel black is due to hit.

It's true that, over time, 50-50 propositions (like flipping a coin) even out and finish close to the average. But the most likely outcome for the short-term is anything but average. It's not unusual to have seven heads and three tails in ten flips of a coin. Even if you take time off work and meticulously keep track of a million flips, it's highly unlikely the results will be exactly 500,000 for each. The occurrence of heads and tails will be close to 50 percent, but there still may be thousands more heads than tails.

How does this example relate to gambling? Don't get sucked into illusory concepts such as hot dice, cold cards, or streaky machines. This fact is just the principle of random walk at work; short-term fluctuation is normal in any game. But can you predict that fluctuation or make money off it? Absolutely not!

Forecasting the trends

Some gamblers mistakenly believe that trends develop in some games — and that smart players can spot these trends and use them to predict the future.

To encourage this strategy, casinos even display previous numbers hit on the roulette wheel and give players paper and pencils to track results at the baccarat table.

Unless you're planning a future career as the scorekeeper for the Lakers, such activities are a waste of time. The previous results are only meaningful if there were a bias in the machine or wheel. But modern casinos are extremely vigilant about regulating all their games, and it's very rare for nonrandom events to creep into games of chance.

Succumbing to selective memory

All gambling superstitions and misconceptions share one common denominator — they all lose in the long run. You don't believe me? Perhaps you have a friend who always wins at slots or crushes the craps tables every trip. The truth is that people do win sometimes — otherwise no one would ever return to the casinos. But I would speculate that an average gambler finishes ahead about one out of every three trips. That's simply short-term fluctuation at work.

The problem for most people is that they don't keep records, and it is human nature to recall big wins and minimize losses. Consequently, many gamblers think that they're winners when actually they're net losers (see Chapter 4 for record-keeping tips).

Relying on betting systems

Gamblers instinctively understand that by wagering the same amount every time, they ultimately fall prey to the law of averages and will lose. They reason: "If I could somehow vary my bets, perhaps I could come out ahead. All I need to do is win my big bets and lose my smaller ones." Unfortunately, that strategy is easier said than done. But that hasn't kept numerous people from trying to find the Holy Grail of gambling — a winning progressive betting system.

Any betting system that has you change the size of your bet depending on whether you win or lose is considered a progressive system. Because most gamblers understand that the house has the edge, they vainly search for creative ways to gain the upper hand over the casino.

Betting systems generally come in two flavors: positive and negative. With positive systems, the bettor increases his bet *after a win* by some predetermined amount. The idea behind a positive system is to ride winning streaks by parlaying profits from one winning bet to the next. Negative systems are more common; they involve betting more after a loss. The idea behind a negative system is to raise your bet amount to *make up for a loss or losses* in one single bet. This section looks at two of the more common systems.

My advice: Avoid all progressive betting systems. They may look appealing, but ultimately they all fail.

The Martingale System

By far, the best known and most popular progressive gambling system is the Martingale system, which has been around for centuries. On the surface, this system seems so foolproof that thousands of hopeful gamblers think they have reinvented it, only to find out later that it's not as infallible as they thought.

The appeal of the Martingale lies in its simplicity. You start off by betting one unit — say, $5. Whenever you win, you continue with the same $5 bet, but whenever you lose, you double the next bet. If you lose the next hand, you double again ($5, $10, $20, $40, $80, $160, $320, $640, and so on).

To many gamblers, the Martingale seems perfect. However, it has a couple of fatal flaws. The first problem is that by doubling up after every loss, eventually you bump up against the maximum allowable bets in many casinos. A $5 starting unit will exceed $500 if you lose seven straight hands (which happens far more often than you may think).

But the real problem of the system is that it doesn't work. If you're playing a negative expectation game, such as roulette, you can expect to lose an amount that is close to the preset house advantage of 5.26 percent. The Martingale does give you a lot more winning sessions, but they're mostly small. Your losing trips, however, are bone rattling.

The D'Alembert System

In this scheme you increase your wager by one unit after every loss and decrease it by one unit after every win. For example, with $5 units, you bump up your bet to $10 if you lose the first bet, then drop back down to $5 if you win the second hand. However, you never go below your starting unit, no matter how many hands you win in a row.

The D'Alembert may be a good way to keep your mind occupied, but computer simulations consistently show that no progressive system improves your overall results. Again, you encounter a lot of small wins punctuated by big losses.

Quitting early

Another myth is that knowing when to quit saves you money. But quitting just postpones the inevitable results until your next trip. For example, you get off to a great start during a three-day jaunt to Tahoe and find yourself up $200 the first hour. Quitting early may have some positive psychological and emotional benefits, but it doesn't make any difference in the long run. Your gambling bankroll continues on the next trip, because your money, the dice, and the cards have no memory of what previously happened.

Playing less time *overall* in a negative expectation game can save you money, so in that sense, quitting has value. But if you plan to play 20 hours of roulette over the next year, it really doesn't matter how you split the time up per trip.

Chasing rainbows

More than half the U.S. population gambles fairly regularly. For most players, gambling is a fun diversion from the normal routine. However, you can easily cross the dangerously thin line from pleasurable pastime to deadly addiction. One of the best ways to avoid the pitfall of addiction is through education. Your chances of winning increase dramatically if you understand the odds and psychology of the games you play. That's where this book comes into play.

You can easily get caught up in the chase. Everyone enjoys winning more than losing, and no one likes to come home defeated. But you need to remember that no one wins every trip or every day or every session. Gambling is all about educating yourself about the long odds you are facing and selecting the best bets in the casino. So keep this advice in mind: Losing a small amount and walking away is far better than dumping a bundle trying desperately to get even.

Chapter 4

Managing Your Money in a Casino

· ·

· ·

*M*y accountant shares this favorite saying with clients who want to push the envelope: "Pigs get fed. Hogs get slaughtered." This adage is probably more applicable to gamblers tackling the tables than taxpayers dealing with the IRS. Greed and gambling are two words that go together like peanut butter and jelly, and they're just as likely to get you into a sticky mess.

When blinded by the possibility of winning more, you can easily end up blowing your gambling *bankroll* (money set aside just for gambling) in one evening — or faster. The prospect of striking it rich in the casino may make you forget that you have other financial obligations — paying the mortgage and feeding your children, to name a couple. I've heard and seen too many horror stories about individuals whose dream vacation to a gambling destination turned into a nightmare when they frantically began throwing good money after bad to make up for their losses early in their getaway.

In this chapter, I address nothing more than practical, pragmatic approaches to your money — the cash you come with and (hopefully) the money you win as you go along. I arm you with the same sort of no-nonsense advice your accountant or a financial counselor may offer to help you manage your budget (and keep track of your wins and losses for Uncle Sam).

Setting a Budget and Sticking to It

To enjoy your gambling experience, you must *control* your gambling experience, which means setting — and sticking to — a budget. Whether you're taking a weekend backpacking tour in a nearby state park or a once-in-a-lifetime cruise on the *Queen Mary II,* you decide what you're willing — or can afford — to spend, and then you make your plans. The same goes for a gambling getaway. First you budget for the transportation to your destination, your hotel and food expenses, entertainment tickets, and sightseeing excursions — and how much you plan to spend on gambling.

If your main priority is to retain all of your money, the best advice I can offer you is not to gamble at all. Assuming you don't want to hear that bit of wisdom, my next-best suggestion is to firmly decide, before you enter the doors of the casino, how much you're willing to spend (translation: *lose*).

Casinos are fantastic places where you can check reality at the door. Gambling should be a fun experience, a chance to get away from your daily stress and enjoy the escape that risk and winning can bring. But when the lines between reality and fantasy blur, when you buy into the dream and forget the budget, you can run into problems, and your money can quickly head south.

This section helps you predetermine exactly how much money you're willing to spend on your gambling venture. You also discover how to stick to your budget and avoid the kind of fun the casino wants to have — at your expense.

Playing within your means

For most people, gambling isn't a lifestyle. It's an escape from reality that has the same components of thrill, sizzle, and excitement as other forms of entertainment — well, maybe a little less than skydiving and a bit more than the opera.

A good starting point to determine your gambling bankroll is figuring out how much you spend on different types of entertainments and vacations, such as theme parks, ski resorts, or other sightseeing destinations. Knowing this information can help you compare your casino budget to the cost of last summer's beach vacation or that week in Paris.

Your gambling bankroll needs to reflect fiscal reality. If your other vacations cost $1,000, why should your gambling vacation cost two or three or even four times as much? Like all trips, hobbies, or flights of fancy, gambling is a form of entertainment. And, just like that Caribbean cruise, your gambling losses shouldn't affect your day-to-day lifestyle or your ability to pay bills for the rest of the month, after the vacation is over.

As you calculate the cost of your gambling trip, consider its value to you in terms of fun and entertainment. If you perceive your casino gambling adventure as a form of entertainment similar to, say, dinner at a fine restaurant and an evening at the theater, you can begin to put a price on its value. Would such an evening cost you $500 for two? Possibly. Would you pay $1,000 for it? Possibly again, although sticker shock may be setting in.

Okay, I may sound like a credit counselor, but the money for your gambling vacation should come from your entertainment budget. In other words, don't cash in a savings bond, dip into the kids' college funds, or take out a new credit card to bankroll the trip. And by all means, don't budget with money you *plan on* winning during the trip!

Determining your daily limits

After you figure out your budget for your gambling adventure (whether a five-day trip to Vegas or just a quick jaunt to a riverboat casino), you need to break down that budget into how much you can spend each day. Take your predetermined trip bankroll, and then divide that amount by the number of days you're going to be in the casino. For example, say you set aside $1,200 for gambling on your three-day getaway weekend. You have $400 to play with each day, separate from the money you budget to feed, house, and entertain yourself.

From day to day at the casino, you're either up or down. For example, on Friday, the first day of your three-day venture, you enter the casino with four crisp $100 bills in your pocket and finish the day with $600 for a $200 win. Congratulations! But how does your success affect your game plan? It doesn't. The next day, you should stick to your budget and still only gamble with $400. However, Saturday is a disaster and you lose every last penny of the $400 budgeted for that day. The carnage continues on Sunday, and once again you burn through $400. But because you stuck to your budget, you return home with $600 of your original $1,200 bankroll, which is a lot more money than less-disciplined gamblers (who never had a starting plan or failed to follow it) have at the end of their trip.

If you lose your $400 (or whatever the amount of your daily budget) early in the day, do something else. The free activities in and around casino towns can be pretty entertaining. Discover the mountain trails of Lake Tahoe, stroll the boardwalk in Atlantic City, or just hang out at the hotel and enjoy the swimming pool or workout room. A big mistake many people make is getting so engrossed in gambling that they miss out on the attractions of a beautiful resort.

Sizing up your bets

After splitting your bankroll into daily increments, the next step to budget your gambling is *bet sizing,* or breaking down your budgeted bankroll into the amount you allocate for each bet.

A general rule (for most table games) is to have a bankroll with at least 40 times the maximum bet you plan to make. So if you decide to ration your trip bankroll into daily allotments of $400, your betting units are $10 per hand. Proper proportional betting reduces your risk of *tapping out* (going home flat broke).

Keeping your bets consistent

Unless you're a professional card counter or an expert sports handicapper, you don't benefit from changing the amount of your bets. The simplest and safest strategy in most casino games is to bet the same amount each time. For slots and video poker, that may mean playing the max number of coins or credits each time, if you are playing a progressive machine (see Chapters 12 and 13).

Most players change the amount they bet on each play — typically increasing the bet size — because of two circumstances:

- They've been losing, so now they're desperately attempting to regain that money. Consequently, they *steam,* or increase the size of their bets.
- They've been riding a hot streak and are playing on *house money* (funds they've won from the casino).

Although games do run in streaks, you can't know when those streaks begin or end. After you have the money, it's yours. How you obtained it doesn't matter, but you still need to be judicious about how you spend or bet the money.

Limiting your losses

In addition to establishing a budget and portioning it out on a daily — and bet-size — basis, you can employ some simple strategies that help you stay within the framework of your budget. This section contains a few time-honored methods of limiting your losses.

Stop-loss limits: Covering your own butt

You may be familiar with *stop-loss limits* from the stock market. Stop-loss limits protect your shares from a severe downturn by instructing your broker to sell if a stock falls to a certain price.

You can apply the same rationale to gambling. An example is my earlier recommendation to decide in advance how much you're willing to risk per trip and per day (see the section "Determining your daily limits"). When you lose your preset amount, stop, head for the door, and spend the rest of the day golfing or sightseeing.

Big comebacks — erasing your gambling debt by winning big — are the stuff of legends. And that's where those stories belong. You're not gambling in the casino to make a living or pay off your bills. Treat gambling like a vacation, and leave the dreams of making a fortune in the casino for Hollywood movies. (Check out "Resisting the urge to chase losses" in this chapter for more about how this strategy can get you in trouble.)

Time limits: Knowing when you've had enough

Another good restraint is to set limits on how long you play each day. Marathon sessions at the tables usually spell disaster. The longer you play, the more likely you are to lose your focus and perspective.

Don't play for more than two hours at a time, and don't go play for more than four to six total hours a day. Casinos are tough enough to beat anyway, but when you're mentally foggy or hungry, you add an extra burden to the job.

Figure out how to take breaks because they can help you clear your head and protect your bankroll. Stopping for lunch or dinner may seem obvious, but the number of players who totally forget to eat when they're gambling is amazing. Reasons to take breaks abound. Here are just a few:

- **Visiting the bathroom:** Drink plenty of water so you have to take frequent trips to the powder room. Those short walks stretch both your legs and your bankroll.

- **Scoring in the sports book:** Place a few minimum-bet sports wagers over in the sports book (see Chapter 15 for more about this intriguing part of the casino). You'll be motivated to stand up every so often to track the progress of your teams, and these wagers provide perhaps the best entertainment value anywhere in the casino.

- **Exercising:** Even if it's just a brisk walk around the casino floor, do something to get your circulation going. Even better is a real workout at the hotel gym.

- **Calling your loved ones:** Your significant other and family appreciate a check-in call every once in a while. A check-in call can also provide additional restraints for sticking to your budget. You can easily lose touch with reality while gambling, and a quick phone call can remind you of what's important in life.

Win limits: Winning something is better than losing

Everyone wants to walk away a winner. Cashing out a winner is one of the greatest feelings in the world, and it's the ultimate goal of everyone who gambles. But remember — one of the worst feelings is dumping all your winnings back when you're up a lot and then losing for the day. So quitting when you win a predetermined amount ensures that you have some winning days during your visit.

Some people set up target goals, such as quitting when they get ahead of their daily bankroll by 50 percent or 100 percent. If you wisely add your profits back into your bankroll (rather than spending them), you have a larger buffer to withstand future negative swings.

Keep in mind that quitting early never helps you in the long term because you have absolutely no way of knowing when the cards are going to turn for the day. But you reap a tremendous psychological benefit if you stop playing when you win a certain amount.

Looking at Casino Credit and Its Risks

Most people feel safer using credit cards rather than cash on vacation because, if stolen, credit is easier to replace than cash. But you have to turn that strategy on its head on gambling vacations. If you want to play it safe when gambling, always use cash instead of credit.

The more credit you use (or perhaps *abuse*), the more you have to replace when you get home. For example, if you set a personal loss limit of $400 and blow your $400 in cash, stopping is easier because you're out of money. But with a $2,000 credit line, after you burn through the first $400, you can still tap into more funds, which can ultimately lead to serious debt trouble.

This section explains the downside of relying on casino credit. But there are also some advantages to casino credit, so I explain how to set it up and when to use that credit in a positive way.

Grasping casino credit

To understand the lure — as well as the danger — of casino credit, you first need to understand it. Casino credit is no different from store credit, something most people take advantage of every day. To make shopping easier, many department stores offer customers a little plastic card with a line of credit. Similarly, the casino offers you a line of credit based on your credit report and the size of your bank account. This line of credit allows you to borrow money from the casino in order to gamble — either because your funds have run out or because you just prefer not to carry cash.

The whole casino industry is designed to make you forget that you're playing for real money, which is why casinos use chips rather than cash at the tables. And taking the next step — playing against your line of credit — can move you one step further from the harsh reality that eventually you have to pay the piper.

Credit is convenient, yes. But, it's also a very risky venture. First, access to credit tends to make some people spend more money than they otherwise would — both in gambling and in the real world. But with casino credit, the problem is compounded. If you buy a $300 sander from the local home-improvement center on your credit card and your spouse promptly persuades you that you don't *need* that item, you can usually return it and get your $300 back. But when you borrow $300 from your favorite casino and lose it at craps, it's long gone. Even worse is when you lose that $300, followed quickly by $600 more, and return home with bigger debts than you can handle.

Definitely steer clear of casino credit if you have an impulsive nature. Can't stop eating potato chips until the bag is empty? Then casino credit may be another bag you don't want to dip into.

Crediting yourself with an account

Recognizing that borrowing from the casino can lead to gambling debt is a critical step as you consider managing your bankroll. Yet credit can benefit people who are extremely disciplined inside the surrealistic confines of the casino. And casino credit does offer the following clear advantages:

✔ Makes you a prime target for attractive comps (free meals and entertainment, for example)

✔ May lead to invitations to big casino events

✔ Allows you to cash personal checks at the casino cage instead of using the ATM or borrowing on your credit card, which can result in additional service fees

✔ Allows you to gamble without the risk of carrying large amounts of cash

High rollers: Moving up to the champagne and caviar crowd

High rollers may want to ignore my warning about the dangers of casino credit. But if you're a serious gambler (bankroll of $20,000 or higher), you may, in fact, have several good reasons to obtain a line of credit rather than play with cash.

The main advantage of credit is safety. Traveling to and from casinos with pockets full of C-notes can be a risky proposition. Also, when you gamble with markers, the casino can track your action more easily. As a result, you qualify for higher levels of comps and make the A-list for special casino events and functions.

Most casinos around the world comp high rollers to room, food, and beverage (RFB), but that's only the beginning. Other perks may include taking a free limo from the airport and skipping those long, tedious lines at check-in or at restaurants and showrooms. And frequently casinos comp airfare for their biggest bettors.

For exceptionally high rollers, comps can be truly over the top. I've been flown to big ball games, and my friend Mike Aponte (one of the most successful players on the MIT blackjack team) was whisked off to Vail for some skiing, followed by a jet to the Caribbean for sand and sun. These perks are certainly appealing and just may entice you to step up to the big leagues.

But remember, for most players, the more they gamble, the more they lose. And just because you have money to burn doesn't mean you should. Bill Gates is, without question, one of the richest men on the planet. But whenever he plays poker in Las Vegas, Billionaire Bill sticks to the $3 to $6 tables, which is probably a good life lesson for everyone else.

Establishing a line of credit is easier than you may think because the casino doesn't want to make borrowing money hard for you. You can set up a casino line of credit in one of two ways:

- ✔ At the cashier's cage upon arrival
- ✔ Over the phone prior to your visit

 Because credit approval may take a few days, call ahead and fill out an application form in advance. That way your line of credit is available to you as soon as you arrive.

Using markers against casino credit

After you establish your line of credit, don't expect to get a plastic credit card with the casino logo on the front. Instead, you use *markers* at the tables to tap into your line of credit. (A marker is basically a check or I.O.U. that you sign at the gaming table.)

Keep this fact in mind as you sign a marker for that next baccarat game: Chips and now markers serve as tools to distance you psychologically from the reality that you're spending your hard-earned money. And when you don't have to reach into your wallet when you're losing, continuing to play is a whole lot easier. If you choose to ignore my advice about sticking to cash while gambling, then be sure you're constantly aware of where you stand with the house, and never lose sight of the fact that payback will occur before the end of your casino stay.

At the end of your visit, the casino expects you to write a check to cover the cost of any losses you incurred during your visit. If you refuse to pay, the casino has the right to post the outstanding markers with your bank for collection from your account.

You use markers only after you've established a line of credit with the casino. And a line of credit is good only at the casino where you applied. In other words, you can't borrow money at the club across the street unless the same company owns both casinos.

Knowing When Enough Is Enough

Gambling, by its very definition, implies risk, something many people aren't used to dealing with. In your work life, you eliminate uncertainty by accepting a job with a fixed salary. In your daily life, you protect against disaster through a spectrum of safety precautions, from smoke detectors to seat belts.

When you walk into the casino, the house is betting that your unfamiliarity with risk will work in its favor. (Look at how easy establishing a line of credit is and how quickly the little extras, such as comps, make you amenable to spending and risking more money.)

The true cost of an ATM

Don't like the cut your bank takes when you use the ATM at home? Try using one at a casino! Not only are the odds at a casino stacked against you, but so are the ATM fees. In addition to the standard bank charges for using the ATM, the casino hits you with a stiff fee at the terminal. How can you avoid both fees? Simple: Bring a set amount of cash and spend only what you bring.

By following the advice in this chapter, you're taking the appropriate steps to reduce your risk of gambling-related problems when you enter the casino. But you're wise to continue looking for signs of trouble during, or even before, your casino visit. These problems can take many forms beyond simple financial issues; they can affect your relationships as well as your health. This section helps you identify the warning signs so you can walk away before it's too late.

Knowing the odds of failure

The best protection you can offer yourself in a casino is knowledge. Having a full understanding of the odds involved with every game allows you to set realistic limits in your play. You can know when pushing a little harder and continuing to play is okay, but you can also have a solid grasp on when it's time to tuck your tail between your legs and go home. Without a basic understanding of your chances, you won't be able to recognize when you've taken one step too far.

Because heaven knows the casino does everything in its power to help you step off the plank and into the ocean of risk, is it any wonder some people get in over their heads before they even realize they're in deep water? Chapter 3 looks more closely at odds, and each chapter on the specific games examines the odds and explains whether the game is worth playing or not.

Knowing thyself

You may have packed light for your long-weekend gambling getaway. But, trust me, you're carrying more baggage than you realize — all that other stuff that defines who you are and how you react to certain situations. So be realistic about your own personality and temperament.

If you have the tendency to get a little out of control when things go wrong, then bring along some safeguards in the event you start to lose. Have a friend hold your wallet, or simply leave access to money (beyond your bankroll) behind and carry nothing but cash. Above all else, be honest about how you've gambled in the past. Just because you haven't been a perfect angel doesn't mean you can't go, but you do have to be more careful than other gamblers.

Are you a disciplined type? Is adopting positive behaviors, such as daily exercise and saving money, easy for you? If you're cool, calm, and rational in your daily life, you're likely to be a good candidate for video poker or the blackjack tables. Or are you impulsive and undisciplined? Does a trip to the mall for a package of batteries turn into a shopping spree that sets you back a couple of paychecks? Do you struggle to stick to a diet? If you lack control in everyday activities, such as shopping and eating, then casinos can become a dangerous diversion. I'm not suggesting that you swear off casino visits if you can't stop yourself from eating just one more chocolate chip cookie. But understanding your nature and taking precautions to protect yourself from "cleaning out the cookie jar" is important.

If you choose to partake in the pleasures and excitement of a casino visit, then, in addition to strictly following the money-management advice in this chapter, you may want to take extra steps to curtail your impulsive side. For example, try traveling with someone who's more disciplined than you are and willing to serve as the designated banker.

Resisting the urge to chase losses

Even if you're a highly disciplined soul, the hypnotic sway of the casino can seduce you into uncharacteristic behavior. One typical lure that pulls gamblers off the cliff of control is *chasing your losses.* For example, say you've lost more than you intended. But, you think, if you could just win one big bet, your problem would be erased. So chasing your losses is tempting, especially in a casino where people seem to be winning all around you.

The sad fact is that most people lose when gambling. And when people lose, they tend to want to get their money back. Even though it's almost always a quick path to ruin, the urge to chase losses is a phenomenon that seems to sweep over casinos from the Mississippi River to Monte Carlo.

Don't fall victim to chasing your losses! When you seek to retrieve that lost money, you start throwing good money after bad, hoping to win it all back. To avoid losing even more of your gambling bankroll, treat a loss as just that: a loss. Say *no* to the next hand or play, and say *yes* to some other activity.

One reason some of the best professional gamblers win is because they don't chase their losses. As a matter of fact, the best pros win, not because they're lucky, but because they have a long-term perspective on their gambling. Annie Duke is one of the world's top poker players. Her philosophy is not to fixate on individual sessions or daily results. She feels that — over time — all players get dealt the same cards. The important difference is how skillfully you play those cards. Maintaining a proper emotional attitude and composure, even when you're losing, ultimately spells success.

Sipping, not sinking

Part of the casino experience is enjoying the festive atmosphere, bright lights, and free drinks. But enjoying and exceeding are two different events, and the quickest way to short-circuit your budget is to overindulge at the bar.

Overindulging is tempting, of course, with cocktail servers adeptly appearing just when the game gets tense, graciously slipping a fresh cold drink next to your elbow. As you sweat a little more, the next drink goes down more quickly. And before you know it, you've lost count of how many drinks you've had, not to mention how much money you've lost.

Monitor your drinking as closely as you manage your budget. If your game of choice requires strategy, then you play better with a clear head. And even if the game doesn't require player expertise, you're still better off without the excessive alcohol muddying your thoughts or encouraging you to go for broke when you're in the hole.

Recognizing a gambling addiction

Exceeding your established gambling budget by a few hundred dollars on a trip to Vegas or your nearby riverboat casino is one matter. Getting yourself tens of thousands of dollars in debt over the course of time is another matter entirely; this sort of trouble is a serious gambling problem. Gambling addiction is a complex problem far beyond the scope of this book, not to mention this chapter. But I'd be irresponsible *not* to address it in a chapter about managing your gambling money.

Gambling debts almost ruined Edgar Allan Poe and Thomas Jefferson and have devastated many families. Whether you're a beginning gambler, an occasional gambler, or a regular bettor, you need to know the signs of gambling addiction. A few signs include

- Trying to escape other problems in your life by gambling
- Lying to others about the frequency or amount of your gambling
- Falling behind on basic payments, such as rent or other bills, in order to feed your gambling habit
- Asking to borrow money from friends and family to cover your gambling debts

If you suspect you have a serious problem with gambling, you're not alone. Some excellent sources and support groups are available to help you fight your addiction and find ways to overcome debt and other related problems. You can start with an excellent Web site, www.gamblersanonymous.org, for answers and help. Check out Appendix B for more resources.

Understanding Taxes and the Law

After I figured out how to count cards with a friend, we tried our skills at the blackjack tables and we both won. As we left the casino, I vividly recall my friend tucking his $80 win into his jeans and saying, "The best thing about this money is that it's tax-free."

Unfortunately, that's not true. Do you remember that old saying: Only two things are certain in life — death and taxes? In casinos, two outcomes are also inevitable. First, the house always wins in the long run. Second, when gamblers somehow turn the tables and get lucky in the short run, Uncle Sam wins, too.

You may wonder how Uncle Sam actually gets his share. This section covers all the important tax-related issues of gambling and helps you keep complete records so you aren't scratching your head when tax day comes around.

Deducting your losses and taxing your wins

First problem: Classifying taxes on gambling winnings is a complex subject. Another problem: The tax code often changes from year to year. So, if you're a regular gambler, consulting with your CPA or accountant each year is critical. I'm not a tax advisor (and don't play one on TV).

One general principle is pretty much etched in stone: All American citizens who win money gambling must pay taxes on their winnings. So don't assume — like my misinformed friend — that your gambling income is exempt. In fact, currently U.S. citizens can count on forking over 28 percent of their wins to Uncle Sam. (Nonresident aliens typically pay 30 percent.) Proper tax preparation involves separating the wins from the losses. Yes, you have to consider your losses, too, but you don't automatically have a great tax return in a losing year. In fact, a recreational gambler can only deduct losses *up to* the amount of his or her winnings for the year.

Consult with your accountant or tax preparer for specific help with your tax form. Just know that losses are a little trickier than winnings. And you can only offset your wins by losses if you *itemize* rather than take the standard deduction on your tax return. So, if your losses are small, they may have no effect at all on your taxes.

For example, say you had winnings of $4,300 for the year and losses of $5,000. You may assume that the higher losses cancel out the win so you don't owe any tax. But when your total deductions (including your gambling losses of $5,000) are *less* than the standard deduction (for a married couple filing jointly, that's $10,000), you can't take any of those losses on your return because you aren't itemizing. Unfortunately, you still must pay taxes on your winnings, even though you actually lost. Confused? Welcome to the crazy world of the tax code.

Unreported winnings: Don't fool the IRS

It's a known fact that casinos typically report some activity to the IRS — but not all. In craps, for example, the house alerts the IRS with a Currency Transaction Report (CTR) when a player buys in or cashes out for $10,000 or more in one day. And in slots, the casino must complete a W-2G form, which includes the winner's name and Social Security number, for wins of $1,200 or more. Casinos file the same form for keno wins of $1,500 or more.

Don't waste your time begging casino employees not to fill out tax forms on you (either a CTR or a W-2G). U.S. laws require these forms, and trying to avoid them can land you in hot water. Casinos send the W-2G to Uncle Sam, and you get a copy at the end of the year. Make sure you include a copy when you file your return.

Hopeful gamblers may believe they only have to pay taxes on winnings that the casino reports to the IRS. Not true. *All* gambling winnings are subject to taxation, whether they come from a foreign country, the Internet, your neighbor's poker game, a church bingo night, or a casino. Many players ignore this law, however, figuring Big Brother won't find out about their small wins.

The IRS can conceivably obtain records from your favorite casino to determine your yearly win or loss, although I'm not aware of any such cases. But remember this principle: Underpaying your taxes is a crime. So even if your chance of getting caught is small, it's not worth the gamble.

Counting comps for tax purposes

Comps (the free perks that casinos give to gamblers) pose a gray area in tax reporting. Technically, casino comps are income, but the government is likely to care only when you receive substantial gifts or luxury merchandise, such as an expensive watch or a new speedboat.

Few gamblers lose enough money to have casinos ship them a luxury car for Christmas. Most comps are *soft* — meaning the casino doesn't incur a hard cost for them. Examples of soft costs are hotel accommodations or the dinner buffet. (Check out Chapter 21 for ways to score comps.)

Lowering your gambling tax

For most recreational gamblers, there aren't many ways to reduce taxes on winnings. If gambling is a hobby, which is true 99.9 percent of the time, then you can't deduct any expenses — only your losses. Professional gamblers can deduct expenses, but a rigid list of requirements prevents all but a handful of diehards from qualifying as professional gamblers.

The only tax-reducing tool for recreational players is a log of gambling activity (see the next section for what you need to record). Because you can only deduct substantiated losses, you must be able to verify your losses in order to offset your wins.

Keeping a log may seem unnecessary for people who expect to show a net loss for the year. However, one of the appeals of gambling is that the unexpected can happen. For example, you take four trips a year to Vegas and play dollar slot machines. The first three trips are losers and leave you $2,200 in the hole. However, on the last hour of the last day of your last trip, you line up three diamonds and win $2,000.

In this scenario the IRS assumes you won at least $2,000 for the year because they received notice of this $2,000 win from the casino in the W-2G form. Unless you have documentation to show your previous losses, you will have to pay tax on that win, even though you actually lost $200 for the year. But if you can substantiate the $2,200 in losses and you're itemizing on your return, you can avoid paying tax on that $2,000 win.

Keeping a gambling log

The IRS addresses the issue of proper record-keeping and documentation for gamblers. The basic requirements include

- ✔ Date and type of gambling event (poker, blackjack, and so on)
- ✔ Name and location of casino, racetrack, or gambling venue
- ✔ Table or slot machine number where gambling took place
- ✔ Who you were with when gambling
- ✔ Total dollar amount you won or lost

If you neglected to track these details, you're permitted to use airline tickets, canceled checks, bank withdrawals, credit-card cash advances, losing betting stubs, or yearly statements of your win/loss from the casino as additional collaboration. The burden of proof rests on you, the taxpayer, so the better your records, the better your chances of surviving an audit.

Sharing with Uncle Sam upfront

In some cases, Uncle Sam doesn't wait until the end of the year to collect his share. The government may immediately take out withholding on any really big jackpots in progressive slots or lotteries (the threshold is typically $5,000 or higher). As of this writing, the withholding is 28 percent for U.S. citizens and 30 percent for non-U.S. citizens. But remember, the tax code changes.

Even when the IRS takes a portion of your big win right away, you still have to include that win in your tax return. Your actual tax obligation may end up being higher or lower, depending on your other deductions and income. Also, some foreign countries don't tax gambling winnings, so non-U.S. citizens may be able to recover the money withheld.

Wagering with a group: Who pays the tax?

An old joke goes like this: Woody takes his yearly trip to Las Vegas. His friend, Dave, gives Woody $500 and tells him to bet it all on lucky number 22 at the roulette. Woody dutifully takes the money and, upon arriving in Sin City, he goes straight to the wheel and plunks $500 down on Number 22. Amazingly, Number 22 hits, and Woody wins $17,500. After raking in all the chips, Woody says, "Wow, that sure was a lucky number. Now I guess I'd better make the $500 bet on Number 22 for Dave."

If you're not as ethically challenged as Woody, you at least split the winnings with your fortunate pal. And the word from the IRS is that you can share the tax obligation as well. Form 5754 covers those situations and alerts the IRS that more than one person actually won the prize.

Chapter 5

Minding Your Gambling Manners

· ·

In This Chapter

▶ Dressing for success and indulging your vices

▶ Showing off your best table (and slot) manners

▶ Handing out tips to casino personnel

▶ Fighting off the temptation to cheat

· ·

*K*nowing how to play the games is one critical component of success in casinos. But minding your gambling manners is equally important, no matter how you cut the deck. *Manners*, you ask? You're seeking tips on how to win at cards, chips, and chance, and I'm pulling a Mr. Manners on you? What's next? Instructions on holding your cards with your pinky fingers extended? Admonishments for ladies to draw first?

I stand by my pronouncement, but in this context, I broaden the definition of *manners* to encompass your *manner* in the casino: how you conduct yourself and behave with players, dealers, and the casino staff. Manners are frequently defined not only as a way of behaving according to polite standards but also as the prevailing way of acting in a specific culture or class of people. And, indeed, a casino exudes its own unique culture, with a social (not to mention legal) code of conduct. In order for you to fit in and maximize your casino experience, you need to know the code.

Most gambling etiquette harkens to two issues: respecting other players and discouraging cheating. In this chapter, I reveal the keys to the casino code of conduct, which encompasses those issues (you've seen enough Westerns and gangster movies to know that this info is serious stuff). But it's not just about following rules. You also need to know how to fit in, so I also offer advice for tipping dealers and casino personnel and for communicating to others in the middle of a hand. And I promise I won't tell you to extend your pinkies.

Dressing (And Acting) the Part

James Bond sported a tuxedo. The Rat Pack wore ties and fedoras as they roamed the Vegas Strip. And a woman wouldn't be seen at the roulette table without her flashiest sequin-and-gem outfit.

True, the traditional dress code for casinos is more akin to a night at the opera than a day at the track (and I'm not talking about the Kentucky Derby, where you see plenty of high fashion). Traditional players tend to dress to the nines, pulling out their formal evening wear. Today's modern dress code, however, means that you're more likely to see T-shirts, tank tops, and flip-flops. Although overseas casinos may make more sartorial demands on gamblers, most Vegas casinos, riverboats, cruise ships, and Indian reservation casinos are far more casual and tolerant of the clientele's new fashion informality.

Dress codes, unwritten or enforced, still exist in some casinos, however, so check out this section before you head to the casino to make sure you don't make a fashion faux pas.

Getting comfortable

For table play, restaurant dining, or touring the casino, most people go for comfort, especially during the day. Most establishments tolerate even the most casual of casual attire — tank tops, cut-offs, flip-flops, and other casual beachwear — but don't dress down too much. Dressing too casually may make you feel out of place and uncomfortable. And if you hope to get the very best service or even comps, dress like you deserve them. A good rule to remember: Dress as you would if you were taking a short airplane flight (or a long elevator ride); go for what's comfortable to you, but also keep in mind that you'll be sharing close quarters with other people.

In most cases, men should feel comfortable wearing short-sleeved or long-sleeved shirts — collared or collarless — jeans, casual pants, or moderate-length shorts, and sneakers or sandals. Women are safe to consider capris, pants, jeans, skirts, moderate-length shorts, and blouses from long-sleeved to sleeveless.

Casinos strive to regulate the temperature in the gaming areas, but there's no guarantee that it's just right for you. Some casinos crank up the air conditioning, so taking a sweater is always a wise precaution. But if you're walking between casinos in the summertime (especially in Vegas), you don't want to bundle up. So dress in layers that are easy to add and subtract as needed without requiring a full change of clothes

Dressing up for evenings

The casino landscape often changes at night, especially on the weekends in the bigger resorts and on cruise ships. In the evening, you're bound to see more formal wear as people are moving to and from night clubs, shows, and the gaming tables themselves. Add to that the array of high-end restaurants available in Vegas, Atlantic City, and other destinations, and you'll likely come across some sharply dressed ladies and gentlemen.

Nothing prevents you from wearing at night what you wear during the day. But looking snappy is part of the fun of casino gaming. When preparing for an evening out, just consider the same outfits you'd wear for attending a nice party or a night at the symphony. For men, a jacket of some kind is always a winner. Slacks and good dress shoes go well. But what goes in between is up to you. The more adventurous player may go without a button-down collared shirt; the more formal may opt for a necktie. For women, the range includes dresses, skirts or slacks, fancy tops, and heeled sandals or dressy shoes. Remember, it's not a funeral, and it's not work, so have some fun with your threads!

If you're off to a night on the town and are unsure about the proper attire, a hotel concierge is an excellent resource for help. He knows the dress code for every place in town and can help you avoid any potential embarrassment. Most hotels have a concierge on speed dial from the room phones, and if not, their desk is usually adjacent to the front desk. If you're in a casino without a hotel, you can ask the casino host about attire, although he may be less knowledgeable about requirements for other establishments.

Smoking permitted (sometimes)

In contrast to almost every public venue, most casinos allow smoking throughout their many public areas and offer only token nonsmoking arenas. For many gamblers, their entire casino experience depends on the ability to puff while playing. If you're in that camp, you'll find yourself among friends virtually everywhere you go in a casino. However, you should always check first before you light up, just in case you stumble across a nonsmoking table game or find yourself in a smoke-free section of the casino. You can also show good manners by asking other players at the table if they mind your firing up a cig or stogie.

As more casinos restrict smoking, do your research and make sure you're visiting a place that allows smoking before you find out the hard way. In addition, casino restaurants and bars may also have nonsmoking policies or sections, so look for the signs, or ask a casino employee about the smoking policies.

Butting out

City and state governments across the country have been steadily reducing the opportunities to light up in public places. These new regulations have affected virtually all non-open air space, such as businesses, bars, restaurants, and, yes, casinos. Smoke-free gaming is currently available in many places, but for some states, such as Connecticut and New Jersey, the statewide smoking ban has a casino-specific exception.

If you're not a smoker, don't automatically assume the advanced filtration systems will remove all secondhand smoke from the casino air. If you're playing in an older casino that has low ceilings and allows smoking, you're essentially playing in smog. For the occasional visitor, a few days won't bother you. But if you have any medical conditions (such as asthma) that bad air may aggravate, don't expect a smoke-free table in a smoke-filled casino to do you much good.

Like just about everything else in a casino, smoking has its own set of unspoken rules for nicotine fiends to be mindful of, including the following:

- Casinos that allow cigarette smoking may have a prohibition on cigars, so double-check before you fire up that stogie.

- Cocktail servers are often able to buy packs of cigarettes for you; just be prepared to pay higher prices and make sure you tip generously for going the extra mile.

- Dealers for some games ask you to take extra care with a lit cigarette. For example, if you're playing craps, never hold your cigarette over the rim where ashes could drop on the table.

Drinking encouraged

Drinking and gambling seem to go hand in hand, so you shouldn't be surprised to find out that drinking at the tables, slots, restaurants, clubs, and shows isn't only permitted but also — many would argue — encouraged. After all, how many places aside from casinos offer free drinks on the house with cocktail servers coming to your table to take and deliver your orders? Drinking doesn't get any easier: however, in some casinos, drinking isn't free or allowed, especially on Indian reservations.

Keep in mind that, from the casino's perspective, alcohol is a lubricant that helps loosen your inhibitions — translation: purse-strings or wallet clips. If you've had a drink or two, you're more likely to take risks with your money. So, yes, many casinos encourage alcohol consumption — as long as you're of legal age, that is. Don't be surprised if you have to provide proof of age before you can place your drink order. Keeping your identification with you is a wise idea.

And because I focus on etiquette in this chapter, you'd be smart to control the amount you drink while gambling. A sober head not only helps you play better but also keeps rein on your emotions and your mouth. Loss of either may lead to trouble with the dealer, other players, and casino security.

Playing Well with Others: Minding Your Table Manners

Most of your interaction with other players comes within the context of the games themselves. So whether you're playing poker, blackjack, baccarat, or roulette, you want to know how to play the game, and you want to have an understanding of the house rules that dictate your conduct before, during, and after the game. House rules help ensure respect and sensitivity to all players participating, and they protect against cheating.

Knowing your limits

Before you cash in your money and make any bets at a table game or slot machine, be sure you know the rules and parameters of the game you're about to play. Even popular standards, such as blackjack and video poker, may have weird variations or unusual rules. Avoid disrupting other players — and save yourself some embarrassment — by confirming that you're playing the game you *think* you are before you join in. Just ask the dealer (while she's shuffling is the best time) to give you a quick overview of the game. But most specialty or unusual games have their rules printed at the table, so you can typically read them before you play.

Always check the *table limits* — the betting minimums and maximums — before you sit down. Casinos usually print the limits on a small, colored placard on the table to keep you from inadvertently joining a high-limit game where you can't afford even the minimum bet. Making a $5 bet only to have the dealer point out that you're sitting at a $100-minimum table can be humiliating.

Joining a game

Sitting down at any table or slot machine that has an empty chair is acceptable, but remember these caveats when joining a game:

- ✔ Ask at a crowded table if a position is open. (For example, someone may have merely run to the restroom.) Craps doesn't have chairs or stools, so sometimes you can't obviously determine whether the table has room for you. If in doubt, ask the dealer closest to you or the stickman if the table has room for one more. Some blackjack tables have a sign saying *No midshoe entry*. At these tables, you need to wait until the shuffle before you can play.

  As you discover in Chapters 7 and 8 (on blackjack and craps, respectively), some games are played in natural cycles. If the table you want to join has any big bettors, you should politely ask before jumping in mid-shoe or in the midst of a hot roll. Many players are superstitious, and if they have great runs going, they often prefer you wait. In blackjack, you hold off until the shuffle so you don't break up the *sacred order* of cards. In craps, you wait until the next come-out roll.

- ✔ When you do sit down, you need to *buy in* (convert money to chips), unless you bring chips with you from another table. To do so, place your money on the table (but outside any betting areas) for the dealer to exchange into chips.

Thou shall not touch. . .and other table commandments

In many games, what you can do with your hands (the ones on the end of your arms, not the ones made of playing cards) is strictly defined, and the reason is simple: The casino wants to minimize your opportunity to disrupt the game or, worse, cheat. You can discover the protocol of specific games in the respective chapters of this book, but for now, be aware that casinos are very sensitive about how you handle all gaming material, such as chips, cards, or dice.

- ✔ In craps, don't touch the dice unless you're the *shooter*.
- ✔ In table games, if the cards are dealt face-up, don't touch them after they hit the felt.
- ✔ After you place a bet and play has begun, you aren't allowed to touch your bet again, even to tidy up a toppled stack of chips. (There are a few exceptions to this rule in craps.)

- ✔ Use only one hand to touch your cards. This is primarily because cheaters use two hands to switch cards.

- ✔ Understand and use all hand signals or gestures that are part of the game. (Although the dealer or the other players may help you, you need to know the rules before you sit down to play.)

- ✔ Don't do anything to mark or damage the cards in any way, such as bending, warping, or scraping with your fingernail.

- ✔ Don't give unsolicited advice to other players. Even if you're offering good strategy, players aren't likely to accept it in the generous spirit in which you gave it. And if they do take your advice and lose, guess who they'll blame?

- ✔ If you bring a friend to cheer you on, remember that the chairs are only for players. However, if the casino isn't crowded, nonplayers usually can sit in a chair as long as they're prepared to vacate when the table begins to fill up.

- ✔ At the end of the hand, place your cards in front of you; don't hand them to the dealer.

- ✔ Some slots and video poker fanatics play more than one machine at a time. Before you sit down at a machine, make sure someone isn't playing the machine; arm pullers can be very territorial.

- ✔ Casinos are sensitive to any kind of electronic devices around the gaming areas. In some places, you aren't allowed to snap pictures, talk on a cell phone, or tap away at a two-way pager.

Giving Gratuities to Dealers and Others

Tipping is a difficult subject for gamblers to stomach and for gambling authors to write about. For years, blackjack was my business, and every dollar I tipped eroded the slim edge I held as a card counter. Too many tips and I could easily turn my winning profession into a losing venture.

Most people, however, don't view the casino as their office or gambling as their livelihood. Most people view gaming as a form of entertainment. And just as you tip a restaurant server, valet, coat-check assistant, or cashier at your favorite coffee shop, offering gratuities to the service staff you encounter in the casino is customary.

Most of the casino employees, like other workers in the service sector, rely heavily on the generosity of the people they serve in order to supplement their wages. Hard-working dealers, cocktail servers, bellhops, and the like depend on your support, so offering tips — or *tokes,* as they're known in gambling lingo — is a customary practice in the casino.

Although some people feel that casino staff have become jaded — eagerly expecting (if not outright demanding) a tip whether or not their service justifies it — most staffers genuinely strive to serve and make your casino experience a pleasant one. So be prepared to tip your service providers; maybe you'll increase your odds of generating positive casino karma!

Tipping your dealer

Servers, valets, bartenders, housekeepers — you're already familiar with tipping many of the service personnel you encounter on a daily basis. But dealers are unique to the casino world, so tipping can pose a dilemma to the gambling novice. When do you tip? How much do you give? How exactly does the money change hands? This section helps pare down when tipping your dealer is appropriate and how to tip correctly.

Spreading the wealth

Dealers make most of their income from tips. But casinos don't work the way a restaurant works. When your food comes on time and your server remembers to put the horseradish on the side, the extra buck you toss him goes directly into his pocket. However, casino tips are almost always pooled, and with good reason.

- ✔ Pooling eliminates any direct incentive for a dealer to cheat on behalf of a player.

- ✔ Pooling provides equality for dealers, some of whom deal at low-end tables while others get the high-rollers who toss black $100 chips around like they were nickels.

Tips are usually pooled based on shifts, which allows for a simple daily calculation for everyone who worked at the same time.

If you think you can get by without tipping your dealer, you may be surprised to feel the overt pressure to tip at the table. Some dealers are out-and-out rude if a winner fails to share his good fortune with them.

So the first question is, under what circumstances is a tip to the dealer customary? The standard practice is to tip when you're winning, but winning or losing has nothing to do with the dealers. Tipping is a way of showing appreciation, but it doesn't change the odds, help you in the future, or give you better cards. Tipping only changes the way dealers, players, and pit bosses treat you while you're sitting at the table. So if you want to be loved, tip generously whether you win or lose.

How to tip the dealer

The most common method of passing a tip to your dealer is placing an extra bet in front of your regular bet. You also can place any amount on top of your bet for the dealer. Adding to your bet basically makes your dealer a *partner* with you on that hand. Dealers usually enjoy being able to participate in the game.

Giving the dealer a chip or two when you leave the table after collecting your winnings is also common. Dealers often have you *color up* (exchange your many smaller denomination chips for chips of higher value) before you leave a table, so make sure you set aside some small chips for the dealer before this process.

How much to tip (or not)

Casinos have no universal tipping standards such as those recognized for valets or bellmen. Most dealer tips are based on how much you're betting or how much you're winning. Unfortunately, most gamblers tip far more than they realize — and win far less than they think.

For example, suppose you bet $10 every hand at a full blackjack table (typically six players). You decide to tip only when you get a blackjack (an ace and a face card, or 10). Because a blackjack pays you an extra $5 (at 3-to-2 odds), you share that bounty with the dealer by placing a $5 bet for her on the next hand. That action translates into approximately $15 worth of tips for the dealer every hour (or one tip every 20 minutes).

Your expected loss during that same time period is $6.70 (assuming that you master the condensed basic strategy for blackjack in Chapter 7). So your modest tipping actually gives the dealer more than twice as much money as you lose to the casino. If everyone at your table follows this same tipping practice, the dealer averages close to $100 an hour in tips!

Now that I've told you how *not to* tip, you may still be wondering how *to* tip. Keep these few guidelines in mind when tipping:

- **Think of tips like dog treats.** The quantity of cheddar cheese is less important to Fido than the frequency. He'll roll over just as enthusiastically for a sliver as he will for a chunk. So spread out your tips and make them in small amounts.

- **Start off on the right foot.** Making a small bet for the dealer when you first join a table is always appreciated.

- **Make amends.** If you're getting bad service or you're playing with a rude or indifferent dealer, a tip is a good way to end the cold war and get the dealer back in your corner. But if that's not your style, or if you simply don't think he deserves it, by all means don't hand over a gratuity.

- **Keep track of your tips.** Most important of all, keep a very rough estimate in your head of how much you've tipped. The number may surprise you.

Tipping doesn't have any hard-and-fast rules. A casino or dealer will never kick you out or ban you for refusing to tip. Remember that these guidelines are simply that — guidelines. Observe how more-experienced players at your table give gratuities and make note of the rapport they build with the dealers. Before long, you can develop a feel for what's appropriate and what isn't. Just as important, you get a feel for what kind of tipping pattern fits your personality and budget.

Tipping other casino employees

From the valet who parks your car to the cocktail server who delivers your complimentary drinks to the hotel housekeeper who turns down your bed, you encounter plenty of casino employees who anticipate a gratuity of some sort. Some services — waitresses and concierges — are universal, and others — slot attendants — are unique to casinos.

This section provides a quick rundown of tip situations you can expect to encounter on your casino adventure. Table 5-1 breaks down the customary tip amounts for all the different service workers who may serve your needs.

Table 5-1	Tips for Proper Tipping	
Occupation	*Standard Tip*	*High-Roller Tip*
Bartenders	$1 per round	$5 per round
Casino cocktail servers	$1 per round	$5 per round
Dealers	$2 to $10	$25 to $100
Hotel bellhops	$1 to $2 per bag — more for heavier bags	$3 to $5 per bag — more for heavier bags
Limo drivers	Minimum of $5	Minimum of $10
Maids	$1 per night	$5 per night
Room service personnel	15 percent of check	20 percent of check
Servers in restaurant	15 percent of check	20 percent of check
Slot attendants, Keno runners, change personnel	$1 to $5	$10 to $25
Taxi drivers	Minimum of $2	Minimum of $5
Valets	$1 to $2	$5 to $20

Pay attention to the following tips for tipping the different casino personnel and hotel, restaurant, and bar staff in a casino hotel:

✔ **Cocktail servers.** Many casinos provide free drinks while you're playing any game in the house. Like most other casino employees, cocktail servers receive low wages and count on your tips. Depending on your first few tips, cocktail servers can leave you either high and dry or refreshed and relaxed. A standard tip is $1 for every one or two drinks, and you can always use chips for tips.

Servers record what you order based on where you sit in the casino. They work by sections, and each server stays in her area. Therefore, if you move, don't expect your server to find you and deliver your drink.

✔ **Slot attendants.** You can tip your slot attendants at any time, but normally they expect tips only when you hit the bigger jackpots, which are paid out by hand. A customary tip is 1 to 3 percent of the win to the employee who pays you. The amount is solely at your discretion, however, as the attendants do the same amount of work when paying out $2,000 or $20,000.

✔ **Security personnel.** Casinos require security officers to attend to all money transactions (hand pays) on the slot machines, and the officer who attends your transaction is allowed to accept tips for this service. A modest tip (1 percent of the jackpot) for security at the same time you tip the slot attendant is usually good form — particularly because they stand right next to each other, and one of them has a gun.

✔ **Other hotel workers.** Just as in any resort hotel, the service personnel at a casino hotel expect a commensurate gratuity, more or less, depending on the level of luxury and hoopla provided by the house. Therefore, even though you only pay $1 to park your 1988 olive-green Chevy at your hometown country club, consider upping that amount to at least $5 if you've rented a Ferrari and pull into the driveway of Caesars Palace. The same goes for your other service providers.

Be prepared to tip the cast of characters by having plenty of one-dollar and five-dollar bills handy before you arrive. You can snap them off as smoothly as James Bond when the occasion merits or as audaciously as Jim Carrey in *Dumb and Dumber.* Up to you!

The richest valets in the world

Tipping is a voluntary practice, so don't ever feel obligated to tip if the service is bad. Alternatively, if the casino employee you encounter is incomparably entertaining or incredibly pleasant, tipping liberally is certainly appropriate.

Just don't tip out of compulsion or guilt. At high-end casinos like the Wynn, dealers take home more than $300 a day in tips, cocktail servers make around $125,000 a year, and valet parkers bring in $150,000 annually.

Avoiding the Appearance of Cheating

Cheating in casinos is a subject worthy of its own book because it has a long and not-so-distinguished history. But as a novice casino visitor, you need to understand some basic facts about the subject and how it affects you.

With so much money flowing, casinos are an inevitable target for cheats. But put your mind at ease because the casino virtually can't cheat you. Gaming commissions and competition ensure fair games these days, and besides that, casinos don't *have* to cheat. Probability theory guarantees them long-term profits on the games. Nevertheless, some cheating still goes on — from both sides of the table — just not in the way you may think. Casinos catch dealers cheating from time to time, but the dealers' targets are rarely the gamblers at their tables. The few dishonest dealers try to swindle the casino by palming chips, overpaying an accomplice, or some similar technique.

Of course, the era of the Wild West, when a cheater could end up with a bullet through the heart — or hanging from the gallows —.is over. And, despite their gangster heritage, modern casinos don't make it a practice to provide their dishonest guests with cement overshoes.

Even though you may not end up sleeping with the fish, make no mistake about it: Cheating when gambling is an extremely serious offense. If a casino catches you cheating, jail time is in your cards!

You may not be able to imagine yourself cheating in any shape or form to win. But if you devote any good amount of time to gambling, chances are you'll be confronted by temptation. A dealer may overpay you, or your slot machine may malfunction and spit out extra coins.

You may also experience casino protocols that, on the surface, seem irrelevant but are actually in place to avoid situations that can be interpreted as attempts to cheat. One example is the marking of cards. Of course, you didn't mean anything by getting your chili-cheese-fry fingerprints on the ♥Q in the last hand. But you find that casino personnel are very unsympathetic to your tragic lack of a napkin.

Following are some efforts made by casinos to eliminate cheating among players. Some examples appear elsewhere in this chapter, but they bear repeating.

> ✔ Casinos typically have the legal right to ask anyone to leave their premises at any time for any reason. If casino employees suspect a customer of cheating, they can detain the person and possibly arrest him or her.

✔ Even though casino personnel do their very best to be polite about it, touching taboos are taken very seriously. Casinos expect neophytes to accidentally violate these rules from time to time, but repeat offenders are eventually asked to leave.

✔ Theft is a problem that casinos take seriously even though they aren't directly in harm's way. Gamblers are caught snagging chips from stacks of other players every day. You're especially vulnerable at craps and roulette tables because attention is so often focused away from your stack.

✔ Casinos are also sensitive to violating interstate gaming laws, so they're wary of cell phone use in certain areas. For example, don't make or take calls while you're in the race and sports book. (For more details, turn to Chapter 15.)

✔ Casinos invest millions of dollars in security technology to protect themselves against cheaters. You can use this technology to your advantage as well. For example, if you believe a dealer made a mistake, the tape can be rolled back to see what really happened. And the lens doesn't lie.

Losing like a champ

Being a magnanimous winner is easy. Being a gracious loser is much more difficult. Although you have limited control over your luck, you can control how you behave. An upbeat temperament is not only helpful in making more friends at the tables but also a key ingredient in your long-term gambling success. After all, your emotions are one of the few factors you can control when you're gambling, so why let the house have the edge by giving in to self-indulgent behavior?

Don't get me wrong. I'm not espousing some mind-over-matter mantra that magically changes your cards into winners. But how well you deal with adversity ultimately affects your prosperity.

Russ Hamilton won the World Series of Poker main-event championship in 1994 and is widely believed to be one of the world's best all-around gamblers. He asserts that keeping a proper attitude is fundamental to his success in poker. Russ suggests you ask yourself the following questions:

✔ Do you complain when you take a bad beat?

✔ Do you say, "I'm never lucky"?

✔ Do you ridicule other players when they beat you?

✔ Are you a jerk at the table?

If you answer *yes* to any of these questions, you're not maximizing your potential. A negative attitude never helps you win and possibly costs you money.

Part II
Conquering the Table Games

The 5th Wave · By Rich Tennant

"I'm sure he's just kidding. Still, why don't you just <u>ask</u> for another card."

In this part . . .

In this part, I put it all out on the table! From poker to blackjack to craps to roulette to the more exotic games (such as Caribbean Stud poker, Let It Ride, and Pai Gow poker), I explore the spectrum of casino table games and offer a thorough mini-course on each. In addition to a general overview of each game, I provide insider strategies to improve your win record — or slow down your spending — and share some secrets from the pros.

Chapter 6

Will Bluff for Food: Poker

*P*oker is currently exploding in popularity. But what makes poker so fascinating and alluring? Poker has an element of emotion and energy that enthusiasts find lacking in other casino games. When you sit down at a poker table, your opponents are the other players at the table rather than the house. They're betting *their* money so that they can take *your* money. When you beat your opponents in poker, raw emotions and bitter disappointments flare up into full display. Poker players have diverse personalities and individual styles of play — all of which makes poker a highly intriguing and exhilarating game.

So you may as well jump on the wagon and ante up! But before you take the plunge, read this chapter. It can help you master the basics of poker so that you don't throw away your hard-earned money. It also shows you some key tactics and the best ways to act when playing. Finally, it covers the most popular types of poker in more detail — Seven-Card Stud, Texas Hold'em, and Omaha poker — and provides some basic strategies for each game. (If you're itching to master poker and take your game to the next level, check out *Poker For Dummies,* by Richard D. Harroch and Lou Krieger [Wiley].)

Uncovering the ABCs of Casino Poker

In this chapter, I walk you through two of the most popular casino poker games: Seven-Card Stud and Texas Hold'em. I also introduce you to a few other versions. But in this first section, I explore the aspects that are universal to all games of poker — as well as factors that make playing poker in a casino different from playing poker at your kitchen table. The following are a few poker basics that you need to remember:

- ✔ The goal in poker is to win the pot of money by having the highest hand (or, in some versions of the game, the lowest hand) or persuading the other players into believing you do.

- ✔ Betting is a critical part of the game.

- ✔ Players don't play with cash on the table in a casino — they bet with chips.

- ✔ A professional dealer sits in on all games.

- ✔ The dealer passes out the cards, clockwise to the left, using a standard 52-card deck.

- ✔ In casinos, you play poker at an oval table seating seven to ten players, depending on the version of poker.

- ✔ To join a poker game in a casino, you must speak to a floor supervisor or poker-room host, also known as a *brush,* who finds an available game for you or puts you on a waiting list for a game.

Poker's popularity reigns

For years, poker was relegated to smoky back rooms. However, today the game is booming, and massive poker rooms now take center stage in the nation's biggest casinos. When you look at all the different casino card games, poker is clearly the hottest game in town. Television has elevated poker champions Phil Hellmuth Jr., Annie Duke, and Doyle Brunson into cult figures as admired as rock stars. And not just in the United States. Their fame is so far reaching that some foreign fans are virtually ready to bestow royalty status on poker celebs.

The poker bug bites nearly everyone, from *Spiderman* (actor Tobey Maguire) to Baptist ministers, who practice their skills with the shades drawn. Flip through your cable channels on any given night, and you're apt to run across more than one televised poker tournament airing simultaneously — from the World Series of Poker to celebrity tournaments featuring Hollywood stars to the dazzling glitz of the World Poker Tour. And to punctuate just how popular the game has become, poker chips are now a favorite Christmas gift for men (and even women).

Paying homage to hand hierarchy

Before you can play poker, you need to understand the basic order of the cards. You play most poker games with a standard 52-card deck consisting of four suits:

- Clubs ♣
- Diamonds ♦
- Hearts ♥
- Spades ♠

Each 52-card deck has 13 cards of every suit (A-K-Q-J-10-9-8-7-6-5-4-3-2), and all suits are equal in value. A 52-card deck has more than 2 million possible five-card combinations. How likely you are to hold a particular hand determines a poker hand's value.

The ace is the key card because it ranks highest, although you may also use it as the lowest card for a *wheel straight* (5-4-3-2-A). Consequently, the ace is far too valuable a card to not use.

Don't sit down at any poker table until you understand what the *nuts* are. *Nuts* is a poker term for the best possible hand. To determine your chances of winning, you need to know the ranking of poker hands. Check out Figure 6-1 for a complete listing of poker hands, from highest to lowest. These hand rankings are fairly consistent throughout all variations of poker.

Figure 6-1:
Poker hands in descending value, with a royal flush being the best hand.

- ✔ **Royal flush:** The best possible hand, a royal flush is an ace-king-queen-jack-10 of the same suit. The royal flush beats all other hands. When two players have royal flushes, the hands tie. An example of a royal flush is A♥-K♥-Q♥-J♥-10♥, all of the same suit. No suit (spades, hearts, diamonds, or clubs) has any higher rank than another.

- ✔ **Straight flush:** A straight flush is five cards in numeric order of the same suit. A straight flush can be 6♣-5♣-4♣-3♣-2♣ or any other succession of ordered cards up to K♣-Q♣-J♣-10♣-9♣. If the straight flush runs all the way to ace high, it's no longer just a straight flush but a *royal flush* (see the previous listing, and then consult your financial planner for ways to open up your Swiss bank account).

- ✔ **Four-of-a-kind:** Four-of-a kind, or *quads,* is four cards of the same rank — for example, four kings or four 3s or four 8s. The higher the ranked cards, the better the hand. Four queens beats four jacks, for example.

- ✔ **Full house:** A full house is three cards of the same rank, combined with a pair of other ranked cards — for example, three jacks and two 8s. The set of three ranked cards determines the value of a full house, not the paired cards. For instance, a full house of 5♥-5♣-5♠-3♥-3♦ beats 4♦-4♣-4♠-A♦-A♥. Even though the aces are the highest-ranking cards in the deck, the three 5s are higher than the three 4s.

- ✔ **Flush:** A flush is any five cards — not in numeric order — of the same suit. If two or more players are both holding a flush, the flush containing the single highest card wins. If the high cards are tied, the next card, then the next, and so on determines the better hand.

- ✔ **Straight:** A straight is five cards in numeric order, not all of the same suit. If two or more players hold a straight, the straight with the highest card wins. For example, a queen-high straight of Q♦-J♣-10♥-9♦-8♠ beats a 9-high straight of 9♠-8♦-7♠-6♥-5♣.

- ✔ **Three-of-a-kind:** Three-of-a-kind is three cards of the same rank with two other cards that aren't paired. If two or more players hold a three-of-a-kind, the highest-ranking set of three cards wins, regardless of the two other cards. For instance, K♦-K♥-K♠-4♠-2♦ beats 9♦-9♥-9♣-8♠-7♠.

- ✔ **Two pair:** Two pair consists of a pair of one rank, a pair of a different rank, and an unmatched fifth card. When two or more players have a two pair, the best hand is the one with the highest single pair. For example, K♦-K♥-2♠-2♥-7♦ beats Q♥-Q♦-J♠-J♥-10♠ because the kings are higher than the queens. The second pair matters only if two players each have the same top pair; for instance, 9♥-9♠-6♥-6♦-A♠ beats 9♦-9♣-4♦-4♣-7♦. In the case of two players' hands each containing the same two pair, then the fifth card determines the best hand. For example, J♥-J♣-7♠-7♦-9♥ beats J♠-J♦-7♥-7♣-5♥.

✔ **One pair:** One pair is two cards of the same rank along with three cards of different ranks. The highest-ranked pair wins. If two players have the same pair, the next highest card each player holds determines the best hand.

✔ **High card:** A high-card hand, the lowest-ranking hand, contains none of the previous hands, just five unmatched cards not of the same suit. If players face each other with just high-card hands, the hand with the highest-ranked card is the winner.

Knowing the dealer

Unlike at your weekly home game, a dealer is part of the package in casino poker games. The dealer has no financial interest in the game (he is paid by the casino and through tips, known as *tokes*). The dealer's job is to see that all the players abide by the rules and that the house takes its share of the pot, or *rake*. (The rake is the house's portion of each pot — a predetermined amount that is usually capped at 10 percent of the pot but is often much less.)

Even though the casino provides the dealer, the position of dealer moves from player to player around the table. The rotation of the dealer position is critical to ensuring the fairness of the game because one of the most important aspects in playing poker successfully is being *in position*, or being one of the last players to act. A disc or puck called the *button* designates the dealer position. As the dealer deals each successive hand, the button moves from player to player so that everyone starts from the position of dealer once each round and has the advantage of playing after everyone else.

Following basic poker etiquette

Before you sit down at the casino table, always be sure you understand the rules and limits of any game you choose to play. Knowing proper poker etiquette is also critical. Otherwise, the dealer may reprimand you for making novice mistakes, and other more experienced players at the table may criticize you. Keep the following tips in mind so you can stay out of trouble when you first start playing:

✔ **Keep your cards hidden from other players by shielding them, but don't take them off the table.** Even though modern casinos are far removed from the seedy Wild West days, cheating is still a valid fear for many players, and consequently everyone is expected to keep all their cards on the table at all times.

✔ **Never fold or bet or out of turn.** Doing so is considered rude and can also give an unfair advantage to other players. For example, knowing you're either going to fold or *raise* (increase the bet) your hand behind them makes their decision making easier.

✔ **Never turn your cards face-up for others to see when you fold.** Simply slide your cards toward the center of the table and into the *muck* — the area on the table where you and other players place all the dead cards, including hands that have folded.

✔ **Protect your cards when you have a good hand.** If you watch any poker on TV, you probably notice players putting a chip or a lucky memento over the top of their cards. For example, 2005 World Series of Poker champion Greg Raymer uses a fossil to protect his cards. This safeguard helps prevent your good cards from getting mixed into the muck. If that happens, your hand is dead. When you place an item over your cards, you show the dealer that your hand is still active.

✔ **Raise either by saying "I'm raising five dollars" or by silently pushing out five dollars in chips — or do both.** When raising, however, you aren't allowed to make a *string-raise,* where you make a bet and then go back to your stack to add more chips. Perform all raises with one hand motion, unless you verbally announce your bet. Then count out the chips.

✔ **Never *splash* the pot, or toss your chips into the center of the table, and mingle them with other chips.** The correct technique is to place your chips (when you call or raise) slightly in front of you and let the dealer pull them into the pot when all the betting action is complete.

✔ **Never add chips or money to the amount in front of you during the play of a hand.** The reason for this piece of advice is that most casino poker games are based on *table stakes* (amount you have on the table at the start of a hand). If you run out of chips in the middle of a hand, you can stay in, but only for that portion of the pot that your bets cover. You normally buy your chips when you first sit down, but you can also purchase more chips later — but only *between* hands.

✔ **Don't talk about hands in progress — even when you're no longer in the hand.** Your discussion about possible holdings or what you held may influence the remaining active players.

Betting the Farm (Or Other Parcels of Real Estate)

Betting is what elevates poker from an amusing card game into the next stratosphere. Without that element in the equation, poker would have as much chance of being on ESPN as high school cribbage championships.

Betting is the single most important aspect of poker. Over time, everyone is dealt his or her fair share of great hands and weak hands. Though streaky, these cards even out in the long run. So what separates successful poker pros from everyone else at the table is their skill at betting. The only player left standing with any chips when the sun goes down (or comes up, for some games) is the one who outplays his opponents with skillful bets, *bluffs* (misrepresenting the strength of a hand), or *judicious folds* (laying down a good hand when you're most likely beat).

Grasping the betting basics

Strategies on betting vary from one poker game to the next, but you need to keep a few key principles in mind. Most poker games start with an *ante,* an upfront wager that buys you the right to play. This amount is typically a percentage of the game's minimum bet and goes in the *pot,* or pile of chips in the center of the table. You make the ante before the cards are dealt.

Most poker games consist of several betting rounds — the exact number of rounds varies from game to game. After the cards are dealt and you review your cards, you can take one of four actions:

- Determine that your hand is a no-hope loser and *fold* (throw the hand away).
- *Check* — opt not to bet, but stay in the game.
- *Call* — bet the same amount as the original bet (in the case of the first player, the bet typically is the established minimum bet for the table).
- *Raise* the amount wagered, increasing the original bet.

The betting round continues until all players take a turn. If only one player remains in the hand, that player automatically takes the pot. If two or more players remain, subsequent rounds of betting take place. After the final round, if two or more players are left, then the hands are turned over for a *showdown* to determine who wins the pot and who is left crying for his mommy.

Following betting limits

Poker junkies addicted to TV tournaments are no doubt familiar with *no-limit* poker — where players can bet any amount of chips at any time. But most poker tables have *fixed-limit* games. In fixed-limit games, you can't bet or raise more than the fixed limit of that table, although the limit may change from round to round. For example, if you sit down at a two- to four-dollar Texas Hold'em table, the maximum bet is $2 through the first round; then it doubles to $4 for subsequent rounds.

Less common versions of limit poker are *spread-limit* games. At these tables, you can bet any amount within the assigned limits at any time. For example, at a one- to five-dollar spread-limit game, you can fire away any size bet from $1 to $5, provided it's at least equal to any previous bets made on that round. Meanwhile, *pot limit* is a cross between limit and no-limit poker. In pot limit, only the amount of money in the pot restricts the bets or raises.

Knowing when to check or fold

Your opportunities to use the *check option* (opting not to bet but staying in the game) are limited. After you make a bet in the round, no other player may check. For instance, if you as the first player bet, then the rest of the players may call, raise, or fold — but not check. If you fold, then the second player has the option to check because you didn't make the initial bet.

If you check, you still retain the right to call or raise any bet made by players who follow. A *checkraise* occurs when you first check but raise a bet made by an opponent later in the same betting round. A checkraise is a common trapping technique you can use when you've made a monster hand.

When you fold, you say *adios* to any chips you previously put into the pot. But don't stay in just because you have money invested in the pot. Always call or raise depending on the current strength of your hand, not on how many bets you already have put into the pot.

Upping your knowledge of raising

When you raise the bet, you convey to the other players that you're confident of your chances of winning. This action forces the other players to bet this amount as well (they have to at least match your bet or fold). Those who suspect their hand won't stand up to yours are more likely to fold, improving your odds of taking the pot.

In most poker games, you can have only three or four raises per betting round. That means other players can reraise an opponent who has already raised. As soon as the game reaches the maximum number of raises, the betting is considered *capped* — you can make no more raises until the next round.

Bluffing: When deception pays

Some casino games demand skill and experience; others are based on sheer luck. Poker is unique in that it's a blend of skill, luck, and one other critical component, the art of the *bluff*. It's a great feeling when you win not because you *have* the best hand, but because you make everyone else *believe* you have the best hand.

Familiar with the term "poker face"? Poker is a game where the flicker of an eyelid or the twitch of a lip may give away a full house — or a losing hand. Because your poker hand isn't entirely revealed to the table — and you and the rest of the players have the opportunity to withdraw, or fold— even a poor hand has a chance of winning a big pot. Observing your opponents — trying to pick up on their unique mannerisms and weaknesses — can help you win. If you employ skill and timely bluffs, you leverage luck to create a strategy that improves your chances of walking away a winner.

Betting when you're low on chips

What happens when you find yourself running out of chips in the middle of a poker game? No, you can't bet your watch or shake your pockets out into the pot. Unlike your kitchen-table game, casino poker adheres to a bit of decorum, and you make wagers with chips that you bring with you to the table. If you find the game heating up and your chip supply dwindling, you may be forced to declare that you're *all-in*. In other words, you come to a round where you must place the last of your chips in the pot.

Are you out of the game? No. You may continue playing, but a *side pot* is created. Those players who aren't all-in can continue to make bets into the side pot. If you win the hand, you get the contents of the original pot, but not the side pot.

Eating (and drinking) at the table: A poker tradition

At most casinos, you can order and eat right at the tables without even missing a hand, which is not only convenient but highly fitting to the grand history of food. About 300 years ago, a British nobleman named John Montagne instructed a servant to put his roast beef between two slices of bread so that he could eat with one hand and play cards with the other.

His "invention" lives on today and bears his name, as John Montagne's titled position was the "Earl of Sandwich."

You can also drink at the table. However, don't bring your own six-pack. The casino has a cocktail server who comes to your table to take your order.

A long winter's Stud game

Seven-Card Stud is the game my baby-boomer generation grew up playing. I still have vivid memories of a marathon poker game of Stud my dad played with some friends back in the winter of 1964. A blizzard pounded our small town and kept any of the players from leaving for several days, so they just kept dealing the cards. Finally, the bravest member of the crew offered to snowshoe into town for supplies (the roads were impassable). He returned a few hours later. But the only supplies he brought back — much to the consternation of my mother — were beer and cigarettes.

Checking Out the Most Popular Versions

Poker boasts a spectrum of variations — more than 120 different games — and each version has its own unique rule twists. In some games, you're dealt five cards, in others, seven. In some versions, the cards are dealt face-down, in others face-up — and in some, face-up *and* face-down. In some games, you draw for additional cards (Five-Card Draw, for example); in others, you play the hand that's dealt you (Seven-Card Stud).

The biggest casinos typically offer a variety of games and limits in their poker rooms. This section examines three of the most common games: Seven-Card Stud, Texas Hold'em, and Omaha/8, and a few related versions.

Playing Seven-Card Stud

Seven-Card Stud used to be the favorite game for many players. Today, you can still find it in most poker rooms, but it has taken a severe back seat to Texas Hold'em in popularity. However, Seven-Card Stud is easy for even novice players to get a handle on, making it a great entry-level game.

In Seven-Card Stud, you receive a total of seven cards — two dealt face-down, followed by four face-up, and then a seventh card face-down. You and every other player play your seven cards to make the best five-card hand possible.

If you want to win, you first have to survive all the way to *seventh street* (each round is called a street, culminating with the seventh and final card) without folding. And then you need to have the best hand (according to the rankings in Figure 6-1), or have everyone else fold. You should fold weaker hands and stay to the end with only your better holdings.

Playing the game like a stud: An overview

Before you sit down for a game of Seven-Card Stud, read through the following steps to understand the game:

1. **You and the other players put an ante into the pot.**

2. **The dealer deals each player two cards face-down and a third card face-up.**

   The downcards are called the _hole cards_ (because no one else can see them — as if they're hidden in a hole).

3. **The deal pauses for a round of betting.**

4. **The player with the highest face-upcard _opens,_ or has the first opportunity to bet.**

   If you tie with another player for the highest face-upcard, the player nearest the dealer's left is first to bet.

5. **The first player checks, calls, raises, or folds.**

   However, some versions require the lowest upcard to go first (rather than the highest upcard) and to make a forced bet, called the _bring-in._

6. **You and each other player (in clockwise order from the first person to act) take a turn to call, raise, or fold.**

7. **Assuming active players are still in the game after the round, you and each other player are dealt a fourth card face-up.**

8. **Another round of betting occurs.**

9. **The player with the highest-ranking poker hand showing makes the first bet.**

   For example, one player may have an A♦-K♥ showing, but you have 2♠-2♣. You (with the pair of deuces) bet first, because a pair ranks higher than no pair.

10. **The dealer deals you and each other player a fifth card face-up.**

11. **Another round of betting occurs.**

12. **The dealer deals a sixth card face-up.**

13. **Another round of betting occurs.**

   You can fold at any time. Don't be afraid to give up on a bad hand that doesn't improve. Or you may also want to fold if you see that one of your opponents appears to have a stronger hand than yours based on his visible face-upcards.

14. **The dealer deals the seventh card face-down — the last of the three hole cards.**

15. **Another round of betting occurs.**

16. **You and all remaining players reveal your hole cards to determine the best five-card hand.**

17. **The winner takes the pot.**

Implementing Stud's basic strategies

Seven-Card Stud is lively because it features five rounds of betting. The decision you make in the first round is the most important one. The strength of your starting hand — your two hole cards combined with your upcard — determine whether you should stay in or fold when someone makes a bet before you.

The best possible starting hand is a three-of-a-kind, especially three aces. Other good starting hands include three-suited connectors, such as J♥-10♥-9♥; three cards suited J♣-9♣-5♣; three cards connected, such as 10♦-9♠-8♣; a high pair; or even a hand with just a couple high cards, like A♦-K♣-5♣.

If you have a good starting hand and are first to play, you usually want to bet. When you're in a later position with a strong hand and someone ahead of you has already bet, you should call, raise, or reraise. As long as you think you have the best hand, continue to bet.

Exploring variations of Seven-Card Stud

Seven-Card Stud has some close cousins: Razz, Seven-Card Stud/High-Low Split, and Seven-Card Stud/8. In these games, the seven cards are dealt in exactly the same way as in regular Seven-Card Stud: two down, four up, and one down. And the betting rounds also are the same. The only difference is what constitutes a winning hand.

Turning it upside down with Razz

You can describe Razz as Seven-Card Stud turned upside down. Instead of the best poker hand winning the pot, in Razz the worst hand wins — or in other words, the best *low* hand wins.

What's a low hand? The lowest-ranked hand is simply a lousy hand with no pairs or better (check out Figure 6-1). *In Razz, you ignore straights and flushes, and the ace is always low.* Thus, the best low hand is A-2-3-4-5. To win at Razz, you want a junk hand (no three of a kind, full houses, quads, and so on). The five-card hand with the lowest high card wins.

Even though ace through 5 makes a straight, this hand is still the lowest possible hand in Razz. Likewise, if the five low cards make a flush, you still have a low hand because straights and flushes don't count in Razz. If two players have hands that are six-high, a 6-4-3-2-A beats a hand of 6-5-4-2-1. Because the 6 is tied for low, you go to the next card, then the next, and so on to determine the winner.

A good starting hand in Razz is three low cards of different ranks. Betting is the same as in regular Seven-Card Stud, but keep in mind the low hand wins (just turn Figure 6-1 upside down).

Mixing it up with Seven-Card Stud/High-Low Split

This game (you can call it *High-Low* for short) combines Seven-Card Stud with Razz. The best high hand (as in Seven-Card Stud) wins half the pot, while the best low hand (as in Razz) wins the other half (hence, the *split*). The main difference between High-Low and the other two games is that you can use all seven of your cards in different combinations of five-card hands. Consequently, you can sometimes win both the high hand and the low hand, which creates some interesting twists and some crazy betting.

For example, if your seven cards are A♠-J♠-8♥-5♣-4♠-3♠-2♠, your high hand is an ace-high flush A♠-J♠-4♠-3♠-2♠, and your low hand is a cool-looking 5♣-4♠-3♠-2♠-A♠. Each of these hands should be a winner against your opponents.

You don't have to win both high and low to collect any chips. High-Low is a split-pot game — half the pot goes to the high hand, and half goes to the low hand. Winning *both* in a single hand is called *scooping* the pot.

Betting is the same as in Seven-Card Stud, with five action-packed rounds. This game can yield monster-sized pots because some people are betting their low hand, while others are betting on a high hand.

As always, your starting cards are very important — particularly your hidden hole cards. Getting aces in this game is particularly valuable because you can play them both high and low.

Another variation: Seven-Card Stud/8

A popular variation of the game is Seven-Card Stud Eight-or-Better High–Low Split (that's a mouthful, so it's often called Seven Card Stud/8). What distinguishes this game is that the low hand must be *8 or better* — meaning the highest card in any low hand must be 8 or less. If at the end of the hand, neither you nor any other player has a qualifying low hand of 8 or less, the winner of the high hand takes the entire pot — no split.

Holding your own at Texas Hold'em

Texas Hold'em is clearly king today. No other poker game gets as much television exposure. The reason for this exposure is because Texas Hold'em has nearly perfect ingredients for the TV screen. The *community cards* (five cards shared by everyone) make visually tracking what's going on easy for the viewing audience.

In fact, the most successful Hold'em players have become famous celebrities. The catchy Full Tilt Poker commercials give pros such as Chris "Jesus" Ferguson the kind of exposure that promises more than a mere 15 minutes of fame.

Even if you don't seek any TV celebrity fame, you can still play Texas Hold'em and have tons of fun. Who knows? You may even get lucky. And if you do decide to enter tournaments after you master the game, you may be the next budding star. The game has made instant millionaires of tournament winners and turned them into household names to the dedicated fans who religiously follow every episode of the World Poker Tour. (Check out Chapter 18 for more info on tournament play.)

Flops, turns, and the river: How Hold'em differs from Stud

Although Texas Hold'em shares some characteristics with Seven-Card Stud, it's quite a different game. (To grasp how to play Seven-Card Stud, check out "Playing Seven-Card Stud," earlier in this chapter.) In Texas Hold'em, you and each other player start with two cards face-down just as in Stud, but then the action quickly diverges.

Hold it! I see a Texas Hold'em star

Texas Hold'em is all the rage in television poker tournaments with big names and big personalities. I've even got sucked up into crazed hero worship of poker icons. After returning from a trip to Las Vegas, where I competed against some well-known poker personalities in the inaugural Ultimate Blackjack Tour, I found myself beginning conversations with complete strangers on the airplane with "I rode in the same car with Phil Hellmuth" or "I shook hands with Annie Duke." Most of my fellow flyers were impressed that I'd actually met Hellmuth, although a few passengers' eyes glazed over or frantically scanned the plane for emergency exit doors.

The remaining five cards are dealt face-up as community cards, which you share with all the other players to complete your best five-card hand. This places far more importance on the two hole cards (also called your two *pocket cards*) because they're the only cards that separate your hand from your opponent's hand. (Check out Figure 6-2 for an example of a Texas Hold'em hand.)

Figure 6-2:
A Texas Hold'em hand.

Player's hand   Flop   Turn   River

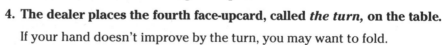
Community cards in center of the table

Betting in Texas Hold'em is different from Stud, too. In Stud, the first round of betting occurs after the third card — when you have two hole cards and one upcard. Texas Hold'em has four rounds of betting (Seven-Card Stud has five), which unfold as follows:

1. **The first round of betting occurs after you and each other player have your two hole cards, called *preflop* play.**

2. **The dealer places three cards face-up on the table (see Figure 6-2), called *the flop.***

3. **The second round of betting takes place.**

4. **The dealer places the fourth face-upcard, called *the turn*, on the table.**

   If your hand doesn't improve by the turn, you may want to fold.

5. **The third round of betting occurs.**

6. **The dealer places the fifth card face-up on the table (see Figure 6-2).**

   This final card is called *the river.* If you've been holding out for that miracle card to help you complete a flush or a straight and your ship doesn't come in, you may drown here.

7. **The fourth and final round of betting takes place.**

8. **If you remain in the hand, you show your cards to see who wins (after all the betting, baiting, and trash-talking is over).**

   The best five-card poker hand — using any of your own hole cards and the community cards — is the winner.

Each time before the flop, the turn, and the river, the dealer *burns* one card, placing it face-down. No one sees the burn cards, and they serve no useful purpose (sort of like the vice president).

Substituting blinds for antes

Another critical difference exists between the two most popular casino poker games. In Texas Hold'em, you use *blinds* (forced bets before any cards are dealt) rather than antes to create the starting pot. Where does the name *blind* come from? The first two players to the left of the dealer have to make these blind bets *before* looking at their cards — they're betting blind.

The first player posts the *small blind,* and the second player posts the *big blind.* The table stakes at each game determine the amount of the blinds. The big blind is normally twice the amount of the small blind ($10 and $5, respectively, for example). A dealer button keeps track of which player is in the dealer position, and the small blind is to the immediate left of the dealer, followed by the big blind. This button moves one player to the left after each hand, ensuring that all players take their turns in posting the small and big blinds.

Lassoing basic Hold'em strategies

As Mike Sexton likes to say on the World Poker Tour, "Texas Hold'em takes a minute to learn and a lifetime to master." The fact that it does look deceptively simple to play on TV causes many to fail to understand the deeper nuances of the game. The biggest misconception comes from believing that poker is all about *bluffing* and that the best players are the ones who move all-in with any two cards. Although bold aggression may work for some pros, it's a bad strategy for normal players, especially at lower-limit tables.

Knowing when to fold 'em

Probably your most important decision in Hold'em comes before the flop, your first round of betting. This is where you may make a lot of errors that can prove very costly later. Are your first two cards good enough to play? Because you have only two cards of your own (the remainder are community cards), the entire outcome of the game hinges on the strength of those two precious cards.

Make sure you always evaluate your style of play in order to identify and plug any potential leaks (weaknesses that drain money from your pocket). Many different styles of play exist, but the one I recommend for most people is to *play tight.* In other words, be extremely selective about which hands you're willing to risk your money on. That style may not always be optimal, but it does keep you out of trouble and should put you on the path to becoming a consistent winner. (Check out "Avoiding Poker Pitfalls" later in this chapter for other mistakes to avoid when playing poker.)

Getting into position: When last is best

One of the most important considerations in Texas Hold'em is your position. At a full table (nine to ten players), the first two or three players (after the small and big blinds) are in *early position* — they take their turns first. Next to act are the fourth, fifth, and sixth players. They're in *middle position.* Middle position is slightly better than early position because some players have already acted before you.

The last two players, in *late position,* are called the *cutoff* and the *button,* respectively. These players are in the *catbird's spot;* they play after they see what everyone else does. Their advantage continues, because they always go last on the flop, turn, and river. (Check out "Flops, turns, and the river: How Hold'em differs from Stud," earlier in this section, to understand the differences between flops, turns, and the river.)

The type of hands you play varies greatly by position. For example, you may often throw K♣-J♣ away *under the gun* (first to act in early position). But you may raise with it from the button. If you're playing in late position, the more people ahead of you who only *limp in* (just call the big blind rather than raise) or fold, the stronger your hand can become.

Flirting with Omaha/8

If you compare Texas Hold'em to Omaha/8 poker, the resemblance is remarkable. They each have the same betting rounds and the cadre of flop, turn, and the river. But the difference lies in the start of the game: In Omaha/8, each player is dealt four rather than two down, or hole, cards.

Players originally played Omaha poker for only the best high hand, commonly called Omaha High. But the most prevalent variation today is Omaha 8-or-Better High–Low Split Poker — called *Omaha/8* for short, and that is what I will discuss in this section. Like Seven-Card Stud/8, which I discuss earlier in this chapter, in "Another variation: Seven-Card Stud/8," in Omaha/8 the pot is split for the best high hand and the best low hand.

The game's splitting of the pot has fueled the game's popularity because it gives you two possible chances to win. And with people betting for both a high hand and a low hand, the pots build quickly.

Playing your hole cards: Take two

When making your five-card hand in Omaha/8, you can use only two of your four downcards in combination with three of the five community cards. Even if you have four aces as the four hole cards, you may use only two of those aces when making your best five-card hand. Conversely, if among your four hole cards you have an ace as your only spade, you can't use four spades on the board to complete a flush — you must play two of your hole cards and three from the community cards.

More cards, better odds

If you've been playing a lot of seven-card games, such as Texas Hold'em or Seven-Card Stud, get ready to see many better-ranking hands in Omaha/8. Because you have nine cards to build a hand from, the chance to make straights, flushes, full houses, or better hands increases accordingly.

With five community cards, as in Texas Hold'em, the strength of your hand is again in your hole cards. Good starting hands are as important as ever before you enter into a pot. And because you have four hole cards in Omaha/8, you have six possible combinations for using any two of those cards. This creates far more opportunity to combine them with the community cards to make winning hands.

Sizing up the strongest hands

Strong starting hands in Omaha/8 are *double-suited* — which means that two of your four hole cards are of one suit, coupled with two other cards of another suit. Because you can play only two of your hole cards, no advantage exists to having all four hole cards in the same suit. But being double-suited gives you opportunities to make a flush in two different suits. And because Omaha/8 is a split game, the best starting hands include those with a combination of both high cards and low cards. Consequently, aces are powerful because they play either way.

The worst-possible starting hand is 2-2-2-2. Because you must play exactly two of your hole cards, you have no chance of making three of a kind — and the hand is neither *suited* nor *connected* to easily make a flush or straight.

Play Omaha/8 similar to how you play Texas Hold'em. Don't get into a pot unless you have a good starting hand. But in Omaha/8, you have two opportunities to strike *pay dirt* — either the best high hand or the best low hand.

Avoiding Poker Pitfalls

To call poker a complex game is a massive understatement. Even the masters who have successfully plied their trade at the tables for decades still uncover new tricks nearly every day. Hence, *tilt* is a word you frequently hear at the poker tables. It describes players who lose their rudder and play poorly, normally after a bad beat. Top pros aren't immune to this affliction; the pressure of big tournaments causes some to implode before a national television audience. But the best players understand that becoming a poker champion is a never-ending process, so keep looking for new hidden layers of enlightenment.

Delving into advanced strategies for poker is far beyond the scope of this book. For more advanced theory, I recommend *Poker For Dummies,* by Richard D. Harroch and Lou Krieger (Wiley).

Although I don't go into advanced poker strategy, this section provides you with some basic advice that can elevate your game. The key to winning at casino poker is to play aggressively (raising your good hands relentlessly like a schoolyard bully). Simply checking and calling through the flop, turn, and river and overlooking the strength of your opponent's hand is a sure recipe for disaster.

The following are some common mistakes that people make in poker. Poker may be a social game, but to be a success in the casino, you have to care more about winning than making friends at the table. If you steer clear of these pitfalls, you're already a leg up on your competition.

✔ **Playing too many hands.** Without question, the biggest strategic mistake most beginning poker players make is playing as if any two cards can win. Although this is true in theory, going to war with weak starting cards is a suicidal battle tactic. Sometimes you may hit your long shots and rake in big pots, but over the long run this approach burns through money faster than a wildfire.

Instead of worrying about multiple hands, focus on playing fewer hands than you do in your home game. Then with the hands you do play, be as aggressive as you can be. Doing so creates a tough table image, which is critical to your success. Being feared is far more profitable than being loved.

Keep this saying in mind: Any two cards can lose. (What — you wanted something catchier?) In Texas Hold'em, the first step toward becoming a winning poker player is to be extremely selective about *what* two cards you play. Admittedly, throwing away hand after hand is no fun, but playing *tight* yields far more profit than playing like a maniac.

✔ **Playing like you're at your kitchen table.** Even if you regularly play poker every Saturday night, you'll experience a bit of culture shock the first time you play in a casino. The pace is much quicker, the game is more formal, and far fewer people play each pot. On your first hand, a tough player to your right may checkraise you — despite the fact that you consider checkraising poor manners in your home game. However, if you're able to adapt, the game can actually be more stimulating than the slow, constantly interrupted weekly version you play with your buddies.

✔ **Overreaching your bankroll.** Stay within your financial comfort zone. A big loss is the primary factor that commonly drives people over the edge and puts them on tilt. Proper money management can help you sleep better at night. If you stay within prearranged limits, you should never lose more than a small portion of your overall bankroll on any given day. (Check out Chapter 4 for tips on helping you manage your money in a casino.)

If you do find yourself in a losing streak, *don't* jump to a higher-limit game in a desperate attempt to win back your losses. You may, instead, spiral into greater loss. Better to stick to the same limits until you consistently win. Then if your $1,000 bankroll grows to $1,500, you can move up to $3- to $6-limit games. But never make such a move out of panic or desperation.

✔ **Checking and chasing.** Staying in the hand all the way to the river even when your hands don't improve isn't smart poker. The player who stubbornly calls bets all the way to the end while hoping for a miracle card is as foolish as the driver who's lost and refuses to ask for directions (you know who you are). Many players charge ahead to the bitter end with bad cards when pulling off the road and getting out of the hand would be far better.

✔ **Losing sight from tunnel vision.** Tunnel vision plagues many new players. The natural tendency when they see the flop is to only evaluate how it improves their hand. Although this evaluation is important, reading the table and determining how the flop may improve your opponents' hands is critical.

Poker isn't a solo sport. To be a successful poker player, you must constantly keep your eye on the big picture — not just how your hand is playing out. Especially in games where community cards are part of the package, you have the opportunity to read how others may fare from the deal.

✔ **Overvaluing the top pair.** In Texas Hold'em or Omaha/8, whenever someone flops top pair (pairing the top card on the flop with one of your hole cards), his first thought often is *"Cool, I have the best hand."* That *may* be the case — but two pair or better are usually needed to win. So be careful about going gangbusters with only one pair, even if it is *top* pair.

Almost everyone knows that the weakest starting hand in poker is a 2 and 7. But few people know that the absolute worst finishing hand in poker is when you have a good hand but it's only second best. This kind of hand sucks you in for several bets before you find out the bad news that you have a loser. You encounter few worse feelings in the poker realm than getting oh so close to the pot of gold, only to watch someone else snatch it away.

✔ **Getting married.** Many poker players heartily agree that casinos and the open road should be your only mistress in life, but the mistake I'm talking about has nothing to do with your domestic status. I'm warning you about the danger of falling in love with and committing to a particular hand. The result of such an unfortunate attachment is that you're unable to release that hand later when the fact that you're beaten should be obvious. Even if you start with a great hand — a pair of kings or queens, for example — you're likely to find yourself in a situation where you must get a divorce and throw the hand away after the flop.

✔ **Not giving any respect.** Too many players are oblivious to bets that indicate unusual strength. When a player makes a raise from early position, he usually has a premium hand. Or if a player checkraises you on the turn, alarms should go off in your head screaming that you're beaten.

Poker rewards aggression. But sometimes your best strategy is to quietly retreat. Being able to fold a good hand is an important skill that every top player has in his arsenal. Carefully watch the other players at your table and if someone rarely raises, or only plays the very best hands, then you need a strong hand yourself to play against them when they bet big.

✔ **Being too predictable.** Poker is a game that is best played by keeping your opponents off balance. If you always check when you have a weak hand or bet when you have a strong hand, your opponents can read you like a cheap paperback with a formula ending. Mix up your game with the occasional bluff or unexpected checkraise. If you normally bet when you have a flush draw, check it next time. Anytime you feel your opponents think they know your tendencies, surprise them.

✔ **Getting emotionally involved.** Never lose your edge by focusing on just one person at the table. Some obnoxious player may be pushing all of your buttons and making you hot under the collar. If this jerk recently beat you out of a big pot and then gloated, you'd like nothing better than to bust him out and inflict some revenge.

Don't let another player get under your skin. Take a deep breath, ignore that obnoxious player, and concentrate on the entire table to play optimally. If these tips don't work, look for a new table or at least take a break for a while to cool down.

✔ **Telegraphing your hand.** I was fortunate enough to play college basketball. Because I was too short to dunk, the move I enjoyed most was making a key steal. I often succeeded because I was adept at reading the eyes of my opponents and discerning where they were going to pass the ball. Likewise, at the poker table many mannerisms, or *tells,* give away the value of someone's hand. What is a tell? A player may stop talking or breathing when she has a big hand. Another tell may be the presence of perspiration on a player's forehead or shaking hands. If someone plans on betting or raising, he may take a quick glance at his chips. If a player wants you to call her hand, she may lean back in her chair; if she prefers that you fold, she may lean forward as an attempt to intimidate you.

Always observe your opponents for any clues to their hands. But more importantly, study *yourself* to make sure you're not giving away valuable information to your opponent.

Knowing when to quit: The 30-bet rule

Normally I'm not an advocate of any artificial stop-loss controls in gambling. However, the emotional and psychological aspects of poker make these artificial barriers valuable because they can keep you from going on tilt.

Annie Duke's brother, Howard Lederer, taught her a great rule. When she first started playing, he told her to quit if she ever lost more than 30 top bets in any game. This 30-bet rule kept her from steaming and playing poorly during bad sessions. It also helped protect her bankroll from taking a big hit (more than 30 bets) in games where she may have been overmatched, and prevented her from being the sucker at the table without even realizing it.

Chapter 7

The Easiest Game to Beat: Blackjack

*B*lackjack is the most popular table game in casinos because it offers the best chance for beating the house. Rather than relying on the cold, mechanical whim of slot machines, you make decisions at blackjack that help determine your fate. Each hand of cards at the blackjack table offers several options, and the choices you make with your cards may ultimately affect whether you return home a winner or a loser.

You may have avoided blackjack in the past — because you felt as out of place as a Playboy bunny at a Billy Graham crusade. But blackjack is a fairly simple game to understand, and with just a few lessons and strategies, you can feel comfortable and confident at the tables. This chapter lays out the basics and gives you the tools you need for your first venture into the world of blackjack.

Dealing Out Blackjack Basics

Blackjack, or *21* as it's also called, is a card game with a very clear-cut objective: You try to beat the dealer. Not your neighbor to the left. Not everyone else at the table. Just the dealer. And you have three — count 'em, three — ways to win:

- ✔ The dealer deals you a *blackjack,* any starting hand consisting of an ace and a 10 (10s and all face cards — jacks, queens, and kings), equaling 21 points. However, this is only a tie if the dealer also has a blackjack.

- ✔ The dealer's hand *busts* — or exceeds 21 points — and your hand doesn't.

- ✔ Your hand — which doesn't exceed 21 — is higher than the dealer's hand. For example, you have 19, and the dealer has 18.

The news gets even better — the dealer must stick to some restrictive rules that favor the players. (I explain these rules in "Drawing the dealer's curtain" later in this chapter.) And following a number of simple strategies helps you to improve your odds of beating the house.

In this section, I set the stage for your game of blackjack. I explain the arena in which you play and the cards' values. I also provide a brief *script* on how to play the game.

Setting the scene

Even if you've never set foot in a casino, you're probably familiar with blackjack from the movies. For example, who can possibly forget Raymond Babbitt, the savant in *Rainman,* crushing the tables at Caesars Palace?

Whether on the silver screen or in the real world, you play blackjack on a semicircular, felt table that seats up to seven players on the half-moon side of the table, while the dealer stands opposite (see Figure 7-1). These blackjack tables are clustered together into *pits,* which you usually find in the middle of a casino. The only other accoutrements to the game are the cards — the game uses anywhere from one to eight decks (more about that in "Dealing what's in the cards" later in this chapter) — and the chips, which you use to make your bets. In addition, small placards indicate the table limits and minimum and maximum bets allowed. (Check out "Eyeing table bet levels" later in this chapter for more information about bets.)

Blackjack

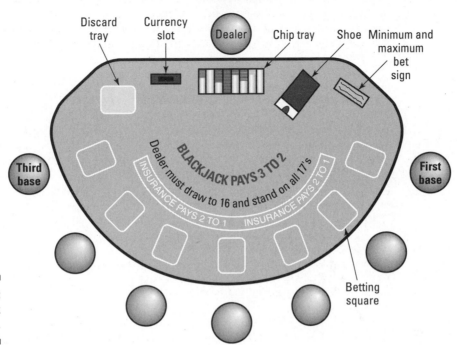

Discard tray   Currency slot   Dealer   Chip tray   Shoe   Minimum and maximum bet sign

Third base   First base

BLACKJACK PAYS 3 TO 2

Dealer must draw to 16 and stand on all 17's

INSURANCE PAYS 2 TO 1   INSURANCE PAYS 2 TO 1

Betting square

Figure 7-1:
A blackjack
table.

Valuing your cards

In blackjack, the cards are normally worth their face value, or their *pip number*. A 4 counts as four points, an 8 is equal to eight points, and so on. The only exceptions are that 10s and face cards all are worth 10 points, and an ace can count as either 1 or 11 points, depending on how you want to use it. The ace is also the most important card in the deck — the combination of an ace and any ten-point card (10, jack, queen, or king) on your original two cards results in a *natural,* or a blackjack.

Unlike games like poker, individual suits — clubs, hearts, spades, or diamonds — make no difference whatsoever in blackjack.

Preparing to Play

Yes, understanding the basics of blackjack is relatively easy. But, before you can walk away a winner, you need a deeper understanding of the nuances of the game and casino protocol. In the previous section, I briefly discuss how you play blackjack. In this section, I delve a little deeper and plumb the many facets that, when mastered, lead to blackjack success. I begin with the warm-up acts — getting seated, purchasing chips, and placing bets — all of which are important steps before you actually begin playing the game.

Finding a table: Strategic seating

Blackjack begins by selecting a seat at the table. Typically, a blackjack table allows for five to seven players. Whenever you see an empty seat at a blackjack table, you may assume it's for your taking (unless chips or a coat are holding the spot for a player who just stepped away for a moment or unless some player is playing two hands). In most cases, joining a game in progress is okay, although some tables have a *No-Midshoe Entry* policy (usually marked by a sign at the table), which means you have to wait until the shuffle before playing.

For your first trip to the tables, you're better off finding a nearly full table. Although the number of players at the table hardly affects the odds on your hands, the game is much quicker with fewer players. A fuller table gives you more time to think about each hand without being rushed or pressured.

The following sections provide a few more pointers to keep in mind when looking for a seat. Ideally, you want to search for a table with fewer decks and favorable rules.

Seeking single-deck tables

Without getting into a lot of math, here's a good rule to follow: The fewer decks the casino uses, the better for you. Your chances for success increase if you can find a single-deck game. Most casinos worldwide have gone to six or more decks in an attempt to thwart *card counters* (skilled players who keep track of cards). But some places still deal blackjack the old-fashioned way — with one deck of 52 cards. Most of the casinos in northern Nevada (Reno, Lake Tahoe, and Wendover) still use one deck of cards at many of their black-jack tables. If you aren't sure how many decks the casino is using, just ask.

Abracadabra: Can a certain seat give you an edge?

Unfortunately, nothing is magical about seat selection. Despite some popular myths, no spot at the tables gives you more of an edge over other seats. Some players like to sit in the last spot (commonly called *third base*), thinking that they can somehow control the cards right before the dealer acts. But, unless they're psychic, this position won't improve their chances of winning.

Staying original

Blackjack has undergone many revisions and changes over the years. Some of these variations have stuck, and others have disappeared. My advice: Steer clear of the hybrids and stick to plain, old, basic blackjack. One of the more popular hybrid games is called *6-5 blackjack*. It may look like a normal game, but, because it pays only 6 to 5 on blackjacks ($12 for every $10 bet), this variation doesn't provide the return that a traditional game offers. Stay clear of it.

Other more-common new breeds of blackjack are *Spanish 21, Super Fun 21,* and *Double Exposure.* If you're ever unsure of the rules at your favorite casino, just ask, because games and rules often change.

Spotting tables with favorable rules

When searching for your table, you also want to know which rules favor you. Some rule changes are beneficial and help players — dealer standing on *soft 17* and *surrender* are good examples (look at "Homing in on house rules" later in this chapter for specifics on these rules). Sometimes these rule variations are spelled out at the table, but if you're unsure, just ask the dealer what the specific rules are.

Eyeing table bet levels

Before you actually sit down, look for the table's minimum and maximum betting limits. Every table has these fixed limits, which the casino usually posts on a small sign located on the table to the right of the dealer.

For example, you may sit down at a table where the placard says $5–$500, which means you have to bet at least $5 on every hand and can never bet more than $500 on any one spot. Typically, the higher the minimum starting bet, the higher the maximum bet for that table. (Check out "Eyeing table bet levels" later in this chapter for more about bets.)

When you're starting out, find the lowest minimum table in the casino and begin there. Making smaller bets keeps you out of trouble until you understand the game better — and you're less likely to end up sitting next to a high roller (who may not appreciate a novice at his table).

Purchasing chips

After you select your seat, you need to buy chips from the dealer. Select the amount of money you want to start with and lay your cash on the felt in front of you. The dealer changes your cash into chips and slides them across the felt to you.

Don't hand your money directly to the dealer; doing so is a breach of etiquette and brands you as a greenhorn.

After you receive your chips, leave them on the table in front of you. Chips come in several denominations and are color-coded. Although every casino uses distinctive chips, most colors are standard. (Check out Chapter 1 for a list of the different color chips and their values.)

Start off with a small amount of chips. A good approach is to cash in no more than 25 percent of your daily bankroll for chips. For example, if you budget $400 for the day, buy in for no more than $100 to start. This way, when you're losing, you minimize the temptation to bet more than you planned. You can always buy more chips later if necessary.

Homing in on house rules

Blackjack rules are fairly similar worldwide — with a few variations. Sometimes a small placard sitting on the table indicates where the casino stands in regard to certain scenarios. If you don't see a placard, you may ask the dealer what the house rules are, even when you're in the middle of a hand.

Does the dealer hit on a soft 17?

A *soft hand* is any hand that counts an ace as 11 rather than 1. The hand is soft because it can't bust on the next card. For example, if you hit (take another card) a soft 18 (an ace and a 7) with a 6, the ace automatically reverts to 1 (rather than 11), and the hand total is now 14 (rather than 24, which would be a bust).

Whether a dealer hits or stands on a soft 17 is usually spelled out in bold white letters right on the felt.

Cuts and burns: Ensuring shuffling safety

Cutting the cards is a time-honored tradition in gambling that helps protect the honesty of the game. In blackjack, the dealer places the shuffled deck or decks in front of one of the players to cut the cards. (This job rotates, and you can decline.) You cut the cards by placing a plastic cut card into the middle of the deck or decks.

The dealer then takes the bottom section of cards and places it on top of the other half.

To further ensure the integrity of the game, the dealer takes the top card, known as the *burn card,* and removes it from play.

Is doubling down restricted to certain card combinations?

In Las Vegas, casinos typically allow *doubling down,* an option that allows you to double your bet, on any two cards, but other places may restrict this move to just totals of 10 or 11. The placard probably won't list restrictions to doubling down. If you aren't sure whether restrictions are in place, don't be afraid to ask the dealer, even if you're in the middle of a hand.

Can you surrender?

A playing option known as *surrender* is an extremely profitable option for you as a player, but not many casinos offer it. When you surrender, you lose half of your initial bet and give up your hand. For example, if you bet $10 and are dealt a 16, you can surrender and only lose $5 (half your bet) rather than risk the entire $10 on a bad hand. Once again, the placard may not readily advertise this rule variation, so always ask if surrender is available.

Dealing what's in the cards

All right, you're situated at the table, you've made your bet in the betting box, and your heart is pumping like a jackhammer. The dealer flashes you a warm smile, wishes you good luck, shuffles the deck, and asks you to cut the cards. (Check out the sidebar "Cuts and burns: Ensuring shuffling safety" for what you need to know about cutting the deck.)

If you're playing a one- or two-deck game, the dealer holds the cards in his hands and deals you two cards face-down. You can pick up these cards, but make sure you only hold them in one hand.

However, the majority of blackjack games today use six or eight decks. In these cases, the dealer deals your two cards face-up from a *shoe* (a boxlike device that houses the cards).

Whether your cards are dealt face-up or face-down really doesn't matter — dealers follow strict rules, and seeing the values of your cards doesn't influence them. Dealers' hands always start off with one card exposed and one card hidden, regardless of the number of decks.

Betting Your Bottom Dollar

On the felt in front of you is a *betting circle* or *betting box.* Place your chips in this spot to indicate how much you want to bet on the upcoming hand. You must make all bets before any cards are dealt.

After you make your bet, you aren't allowed to add, take from, or touch the wager again. After the hand is *resolved* (the dealer has paid out the winners and collected chips from the losers), you may change the amount you wager for the next hand.

Ah, but of course, exceptions apply to every rule. And in blackjack you *may* alter your bet in two ways:

- **Doubling down:** You double your original bet.
- **Splitting:** You break your original hand into two separate hands.

For more information about these two lucrative options as well as other playing options, check out the next section, "Playing Your Hand."

Playing Your Hand

After dealing, the dealer addresses the players from left to right, asking them to take action. At last — the moment of truth. Now your skill and understanding can improve your chances of beating the dealer.

Unlike many of the casino's games, blackjack isn't based entirely on luck. Skill and strategy play a significant role in who wins at the blackjack tables — and part of the fun and challenge is weighing the various options you can use in a hand.

Exercising your options

Depending on your hand and the dealer's *upcard* (the one you can see), you have a number of options to consider. The great appeal of blackjack lies in the many decisions available to you, and each hand presents a wide range of choices. The two most common ones are the following:

- **Hitting:** Taking another card to improve your hand.
- **Standing:** Passing up the opportunity for another card if you're satisfied with the total you already have.

The following sections explore your other options. (You can also check out "Identifying Common Mistakes" later in this chapter for help with some specific blackjack circumstances.)

Act natural: Holding 21

If your first two cards total 21(an ace and a 10 or a face card), you're the proud owner of a natural, also referred to as a *blackjack*. A natural is as good as it gets — you no longer have any agonizing decisions over whether to hit or stand. (Check out "Drawing the dealer's curtain," later in this chapter to find more information about whether you win.)

Stand and deliver: Staying put when your total is high

If you don't have 21, but your total is still pretty high — 17 or more — your best strategy normally is to stand.

Communicate that you're standing by waving your hand over the top of your cards in face-up games or by tucking your cards gently under your bet in face-down games.

Hit me, baby: Asking for another card

If you don't get a natural, and your hand total is very low — say a 5 and a 4 for a total of 9, you should hit. Even if you get a 10, you won't bust, so you're safe to request another card. Signal you're hitting either by motioning with your finger in face-up games or by scratching your cards on the felt behind your bet in face-down games.

Anytime your hand totals 12 or higher, there is a risk in adding another card. If your hit card is a face card, your hand now exceeds 21 and you lose, regardless of what happens to the dealer's hand. (I provide correct basic strategy for all hands in "Strategizing in the computer age.")

Get two for one: Splitting pairs

If you hold two cards of equal value — such as two 8s — you have the option of *splitting,* or making two separate hands from the pair. With this tactic, you must match your original bet. In other words, if you bet $10, you increase your bet by $10 more for the new hand. You then play two separate hands, each starting with one of the original 8s. You play these two hands out, one at a time, with the normal options of hitting, standing, splitting, or doubling down. Splitting is one of the rare opportunities you have to alter your bet in the middle of a hand.

Double the fun: Increasing your bet

Doubling down is an option that allows you to double your original bet. The tradeoff is that you receive only one more card, which the dealer traditionally deals face-down. Most casinos permit doubling down on any first two cards.

Going beyond Lady Luck

Most new players have two primary goals for their first session of blackjack: win money and avoid looking like a rookie at the table. But to become a successful blackjack player, you need to master the principles of basic strategy.

And relying on Lady Luck or a rabbit's foot isn't a basic strategy that works in blackjack.

In this section, I simplify and condense basic strategy down to six bite-sized blocks — tactics that help you reduce the house edge to approximately 1 percent. If you want even better odds, then I suggest you skip this simplified version and learn regular basic strategy (see the section "Strategizing in the computer age").

Basic strategy for hard hands

A *hard hand* doesn't have an ace or, if it does, the ace counts as 1 rather than 11. Use the following strategies for hard hands:

- On 17 or more, always stand.
- On 12 through 16, hit if the dealer shows a 7 through an ace as his upcard; otherwise stand. If the dealer's card is lower, stand.
- On 11 or less, always hit. (However, if your total is 10 or 11 on your first two cards, the double down options (see "Basic strategy for double downs") take precedence over hitting.)

Basic strategy for soft hands

A soft hand is a hand in which an ace counts as 11 rather than 1. Remember these two basic strategies for soft hands:

- On 18 or more, always stand.
- On 17 or less, always hit.

Basic strategy for double downs

Doubling down permits you to double your original bet but restricts you to receiving just one more card. The following are the best times to use this strategy:

- On 11, double if the dealer's upcard is a 2 through 10; otherwise hit.
- On 10, double if the dealer's upcard is a 2 through 9, otherwise hit.

A starting total of 10 or 11 is the best time to double down because you have approximately a 30 percent chance of receiving a 10 or a face card.

Basic strategy for pair splits

When you hold two cards of equal value, you can split your cards and make two separate hands from the pair by matching your original bet. You play the hands out one at a time.

Keep the following strategies in mind for pair splits:

- **Always split aces and 8s.** Aces are great to split because of the chance to make 21; you split 8s more for defensive reasons (16 is a poor starting hand).

- **Never split 5s or 10s.** Never split 5s and 10s because their totals (10 and 20, respectively) are great starting hands.

Basic strategy for stiff hands

Stiff hands are any hard totals between 12 and 16. Stiff hands are obviously your worst nightmare because any 10 busts your hand. Follow these strategies for stiff hands:

- Stand when the dealer is weakest (upcard of 2 through 6).

- Hit whenever the dealer is strong (upcard of 7 through ace).

Basic strategy for pat hands

Pat hands are any hard hands of 17 to 21. Because of their high starting total, pat hands deliver most of your winnings. Whenever you have a hard hand of 17 or more, stand.

The founding father of card counting

Once upon a time, craps was king of all casino games, and blackjack lagged far behind in popularity. That pecking order changed dramatically when Dr. Ed Thorp, a professor from MIT, developed a system for counting cards in 1961. His work showed that blackjack is a game of skill; how you play the cards and vary your bets can dramatically affect the outcome. Thorp's powerful pen set off a stampede of players eager to make their fortune at the blackjack tables. Unfortunately, very few got rich. The reason they failed was simple: Most of them couldn't master Thorp's complicated strategy.

This history lesson should provide one clear insight — players can beat the game of blackjack, but the complex math often proves more than players can comprehend. Far too many gamblers still don't know how to correctly play their hands. Therefore, the first step for any budding blackjack pro is to study *basic strategy*, a computer-simulated model, for the optimal way to play each and every hand of blackjack.

There's only one way to consistently win at blackjack — by learning to count cards. Anyone with average aptitude can become a card counter — but this skill takes discipline and drive, and most players don't want to get that serious about their hobby. Counting cards is a strategy a bit advanced for this book. However, if you want to try moving up to the next level, I explain several different counting systems in my book *Play Blackjack Like the Pros* (HarperCollins).

Strategizing in the computer age

After you have a little experience under your belt at the blackjack tables, I recommend studying the complete version of basic strategy in this section. Mastering basic strategy definitely takes a little work, but the additional gain is very worthwhile. Following basic strategy (rather than the simplified strategy offered earlier) cuts the casino edge against you in half — to a half percentage point or less — by far the best odds of any table game played against the house.

If you aren't able to memorize Tables 7-1, 7-2, and 7-3 right away, you can always buy a basic strategy card at most casino gift shops and use it right at the tables. Strategy varies, depending on rules and decks, so if you want to know exactly how to play at your favorite casino, go to www.blackjackinfo. com. There you can input any variables for blackjack and come up with the optimal strategy.

Table 7-1	Strategies for Hard Hands
Hard Hand	*Playing Strategy*
8 or less	Always hit.
9	Double versus 3-6. O/W (otherwise) hit.
10	Double versus 2-9. O/W hit.
11	Double versus 2-10. O/W hit.
12	Stand versus 4-6. O/W hit.
13	Stand versus 2-6. O/W hit.
14	Stand versus 2-6. O/W hit.
15	Stand versus 2-6. O/W hit.
16	Stand versus 2-6. O/W hit.
17 through 21	Always stand.

Table 7-2	Strategies for Pair Splits
Pair Split	*Playing Strategy*
A-A	Always split.
2-2	Split versus 2-7. O/W hit.
3-3	Split versus 2-7. O/W hit.

Pair Split	Playing Strategy
4-4	Split versus 5-6. O/W hit.
5-5	Never split.
6-6	Split versus 2-6. O/W hit.
7-7	Split versus 2-7. O/W hit.
8-8	Always split.
9-9	Split versus 2-6, 8-9. Stand versus 7, 10, A.
10-10	Always stand.

Table 7-3	Strategies for Soft Hands
Soft Hand	Playing Strategy
A-2	Double versus 5- 6. O/W hit.
A-3	Double versus 5-6. O/W hit.
A-4	Double versus 4-6. O/W hit.
A-5	Double versus 4-6. O/W hit.
A-6	Double versus 3-6. O/W hit.
A-7	Double versus 3-6. Stand versus 2, 7, 8. Hit versus 9, 10, A.
A-8 or A-9	Always stand.
A-10	Always stand.

Making a side bet

Occasionally you may sit down at a blackjack table that offers *side bets*. You can make these bets in addition to your basic wager (typically before the hand is dealt) in a separate, distinct betting box. The appeal of side bets is their huge payoffs for certain card combinations (up to 1,000 to 1 in *Lucky Ladies,* for example).

Although several popular blackjack side bets exist (you may have heard of some, such as *Super Sevens* and *Royal Match*), only one — *insurance* — is generally available at all blackjack tables. Insurance is a hedge bet you can take whenever the dealer's upcard is an ace. You wager up to half of your original bet that the dealer's hole card is a ten (that the dealer has blackjack). If the dealer does have blackjack, your side bet pays back 2 to 1.

Side bets are almost always bad, and you should avoid them. Unless the bean counters in the backroom make an error on their slide rules, every side bet in a casino favors the house with odds far worse (for you) than regular blackjack. The insurance bet is a good example; it's just another tactic to separate gullible gamblers from the contents of their wallets.

Drawing the dealer's curtain

Now the dealer. . .drum roll, please. . .reveals that mysterious face-down hole card that can make or break your successful outcome (see Figure 17-2).

Figure 7-2: The dealer's hand is revealed.

© Lynn Goldsmith/Corbis

The following possible scenarios can result:

- ✔ If the dealer has a natural (21), the game is over — you lose (unless you also have a natural; then you tie).

- ✔ If the dealer's total is 16 or less, the dealer has to hit.

- ✔ If the dealer busts (exceeds a total of 21), the game is over — you win if you haven't also busted.

- ✔ If the dealer's hole card reveals a total of 17 or more, the dealer must stand. Your hand must beat the dealer's hand to win.

The dealer is bound by these rigid rules. For example, if the dealer has 15, she can't choose to stand, even if doing so is beneficial, because she must always hit until reaching 17 or higher. And the dealer doesn't have the options that are available to players, such as doubling down or splitting.

Looking at payouts

After the dealer has completed her hand, you know whether you win, lose, or tie. The following are some of the payout possibilities:

- ✔ **You're dealt a natural** (your first two cards equal 21). The house pays you 3 to 2 — at least in most casinos — which means that a $10 bet wins $15 ($25 total, for a profit of $15).

- ✔ **You bust, exceeding 21.** You lose, no matter what happens with the dealer's hand, and the casino wins your $10 bet (a loss of $10).

- ✔ **Your hand is higher than the dealer's hand.** For example, your hand totals 20, and the dealer has 18. You win even money on your wager — $10 for every $10 bet ($20 total, for a profit of $10).

- ✔ **Your hand is lower than the dealer's hand.** For example, you have 17, and the dealer has 19. You lose, and the dealer keeps your chips (a loss of $10).

- ✔ **You and the dealer tie, or have a *push*.** Nobody wins, and no money changes hands.

Mathematically speaking, the casino game of blackjack is the best table game to play because of its favorable odds. The small house edge comes from the simple fact that the dealer goes last and that many players bust out and lose their money before the dealer even acts on his hand.

Blackjack protocol: How to avoid trouble

When playing blackjack, you want to ensure that you don't make any faux pas. Just like in other casino games, etiquette is important when playing blackjack (check out Chapter 5 for general casino etiquette). Blackjack is a fairly social game, and talking openly about your hand with other players is common. But make no mistake, blackjack — along with poker — boasts a long history of innovative or desperate players who cheat in order to get an edge. And modern casinos are vigilant about stopping any suspicious activities that suggest card-marking or other nefarious techniques. Consequently, you want to be careful, especially as a rookie, how you handle yourself — not to mention your cards and chips. For example, you can easily bend cards without realizing you're doing anything wrong.

Here are some tips to help you be a good citizen of the blackjack table:

- ✔ If you're uncertain as to what behaviors draw suspicion, explain to the dealer that you're new to the game and ask him to inform you if you're making any mistakes.

- ✔ Follow the game protocol by turning over your cards when you bust or have a natural (in a face-down game).

- ✔ Remember that you aren't competing against other players at the table, so don't feel like you have to hide your cards like you do in poker.

- ✔ Lastly, don't give any advice. Although you have good intentions, other players rarely welcome your help, which can backfire if they follow it and lose. Telling other people how to play or how to spend their money is also poor etiquette.

Identifying Common Mistakes

In order to help you play your cards correctly and understand basic strategy principles, Table 7-4 includes six examples of common mistakes and the rationale for how to avoid them.

Table 7-4   Common Blackjack Mistakes — and How to Avoid 'Em

Common Mistake	Scenario	Strategy	Explanation
Hitting with a stiff hand when the dealer's card is low	You have a 12 (a 5 and 7), and the dealer's upcard is a 4.	Stand	A general rule for these troublesome stiff hands is to stand against a dealer's upcard of 2 to 6 and hit against a dealer's upcard of 7 or higher.
Standing with a soft hand, ace and 6 or less	You have an ace and a 4.	Hit	Always hit or double down on soft 17 or less (when you hold an ace and 2 through 6).

Common Mistake	Scenario	Strategy	Explanation
Not splitting when you have two 8s	You have two 8s. and the dealer's upcard is a jack.	Split	Splitting the 8s considerably reduces the house edge on this difficult hand. If you chicken out and don't split, the dealer has an advantage higher than 50 percent against you.
Splitting two face cards	You have a queen and king.	Stand	Close to 70 percent of your gain in blackjack comes from being dealt either 20 or 21, so don't be too quick to part with your gift horse.
Not doubling down on 11 when the dealer has a 10 up	You hold a 5 and a 6 and the dealer's upcard is a 10 or face card.	Double down	The odds favor the brave in this scenario, and you'll make more money over the long run by taking the extra risk and doubling down.
Not taking advantage of a weak dealer upcard	You hold a 5 and a 5, and the dealer's upcard is 2.	Double down	When the dealer has a small upcard (2–6), you typically want to go gangbusters and double down or split whenever you can. Against the bigger upcards (7 through ace), you tend to split and double down less often.

If you can avoid these six common mistakes, you're ahead of 95 percent of the players in the casino. Very few gamblers understand that a correct way exists to play each and every hand of blackjack. After you acquire that knowledge, you can whittle the odds against you down to nothing at a good single-deck blackjack game.

Chapter 8

Rolling the Dice: Craps

. . . .

In This Chapter

▶ Understanding craps basics

▶ Playing the game

▶ Placing the best bets

▶ Steering clear of *bad* bets

. . . .

Step into any casino and follow the noise — and you no doubt end up at the craps table. Craps is loud. Craps is fast. And craps is definitely where the action is. While the baccarat room exudes a genteel hush and the poker tables emit a restrained energy, the mood of the craps corner is one of exuberance — irrational and otherwise. Above the jabbering of slot machines, whirring of roulette wheels, and *ca-ching*-ing of payouts, you can hear the craps crowd cheering and moaning as luck shifts with each roll of the dice, the heart of the game.

Despite all its heart-pounding intensity, craps can be one of the best games in the house. Depending on which bets you make, the house edge can be less than 1 percent. And even though craps may seem incredibly complex, it's easy to play. After all, in essence, you're betting on the outcome of two rolled dice.

This chapter gives you the lowdown on craps, including how you play and what your best (and worst) bets are. So let your ears lead the way. Listen for the roar of the crowd and get ready to rock — and *roll*.

Setting the Craps Stage

Craps is like no other casino game. The sheer variety of bets means that you and other players at the same table may all be playing different games. A single dice roll may mean a win to you, a loss to another player, and absolutely nothing to a third.

Before you can start making your bets, you need to know how to play craps. This section looks at the game's objective and its important props and characters. I also have a short section on how to properly behave at a craps table.

Casting the dice

The dice are the heart and soul of the craps game. No doubt, you know a die (the singular form of dice) when you see it: that six-sided cube, one to six dots (or *pips*) marking each face.

In the game of craps, the objective is to bet on the outcome of the roll. So you can help yourself by understanding the various combinations of dice throws. Take a look at Figure 8-1. A pair of dice has 36 possible ways to land on a given throw, which means that you have a 1-in-36 chance of rolling any single combination. But for the most part, the dice *total* is what matters in craps. A 7 is still a 7, whether the dice come up 5 and 2, 6 and 1, or 3 and 4. Because some totals have multiple combinations, certain rolls are more likely than others.

Number Rolled		True Odds		
2		35	to	1
3		17	to	1
4		11	to	1
5		8	to	1
6		6.2	to	1
7		5	to	1
8		6.2	to	1
9		8	to	1
10		11	to	1
11		17	to	1
12		35	to	1

Figure 8-1: The possible dice combinations.

In craps, you have the following possibilities of outcomes:

- ✔ Six ways to roll a 7, or 16.7 percent
- ✔ Five ways to roll a 6 or an 8, or 13.9 percent for each
- ✔ Four ways to roll a 5 or a 9, or 11.1 percent for each

- ✔ Three ways to roll a 4 or a 10, or 8.3 percent for each
- ✔ Two ways to roll a 3 or an 11, or 5.6 percent for each
- ✔ One way to roll a 2 or a 12, or 2.8 percent for each

Don't think of craps as a game of just dice rolls but as a game of dice-roll *sequences*. Craps is more than a toss of the dice; it's a series of tosses. Most bets win or lose based on numbers thrown in a certain order. Knowing the terminology can help you keep it straight: A *throw* is a single toss of the dice, and a *roll* is the series of throws that result in a win or loss for the main craps bets. Sometimes you even hear the word *hand,* which refers to every *roll* (as in sequence of throws) a single *shooter* (see "Shooting for the whole table," later in this section) has before relinquishing the dice to the next player.

Surveying the lay of the table

Before you can start to play craps, you need to know the landscape. You play craps on a long, narrow, felt-covered table (see Figure 8-2) that has a foot-high ridge running all the way around, making it the perfect mini-arena for tossing dice — or racing hamsters. The standard craps table is large in order to accommodate up to 14 players at a time. Craps is a *stand-up* game — no chairs for you or the other players. At the top of the ridge is the *rail* with two grooves (the *rail rack*) perfectly sized to hold casino chips. But make sure you keep your drinks, purse, cigarettes, and everything else off the rail. A built-in shelf at your knees keeps your personal items safely out of the way of the game.

Going on a dice dig

Dice have been around since the dawn of recorded history. Many Roman emperors were hooked on dice games. Caligula was a notorious cheater — but who was going to argue with a sadistic despot who forced his enemies to commit suicide?

Archaeologists have unearthed loaded dice in Pompeii and ancient India, as well as limestone dice dating from 600 B.C. in Egypt. Another early version of dice was carved from the box-shaped knuckle bones of pigs, which explains why people sometimes refer to both dice and dominoes as *bones*. As popular as they were for gambling games, dice were also used as tools in rituals to predict the future.

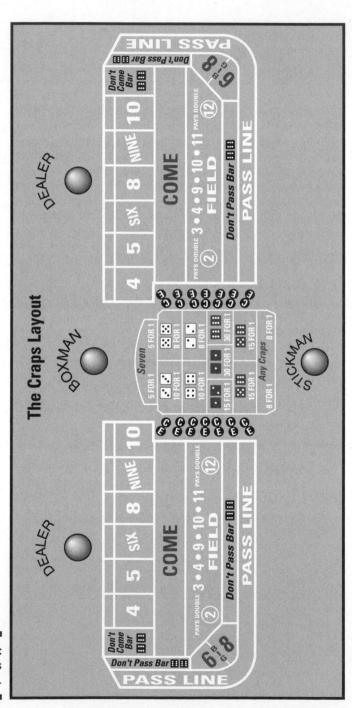

Looking at superstitions: Craps rites and rituals

Beliefs and superstitions closely intertwine with the customs and habits of craps. And because craps brings out obscure beliefs and quirky superstitions more than any other game in the casino, I suppose that intertwining is only fitting. Even the most rational people develop strange habits, like rubbing the dice three times on the felt, refusing to look another player in the eye, or blowing on their dice for luck.

You take turns rolling the dice with other players, but the outcome of everyone's good fortune rides on the shooter, who can be the hero or the *goat* with a flick of the wrist. The bettors loudly cheer a hot shooter if he can hit a series of point numbers, but they shun him like a leper if his dice turn cold.

Depending on how you choose to bet, you place your bets in the designated area of the *layout* (the playing surface). Figure 8-2 shows the jigsaw puzzle of betting boxes. (I explain these boxes in "Relying on Strategy to Place the Best Bets," later in this chapter.) The layout consists of two parts:

- The center section is for long-shot bets (see "Avoiding 'Sucker' Bets" for more on high-risk bets).
- The left and right wings are for the main bets.

The left and right halves of the table are identical to each other, so you can pick either one. Some space-constrained casinos have smaller craps tables consisting of a center section and a single wing. But other than the truncated table (and reduced dice trajectories), game play at those tables is identical to play at full tables.

Getting to know the craps crew

Before you start to play, you need to understand who's who at a craps table. The following four people man a standard craps table. (You can also check out Figure 8-2 to see where these people stand during play.) They're listed according to how much you interact with them during a session at the craps table.

- **Two dealers:** Each dealer covers one wing of the table. The dealer's job is to change your currency into chips, help place your bets, and pay off winners.
- **Stickman:** The stickman, who stands at the middle of the table and opposite from the dealers, is in charge of the dice. His job is to retrieve and deliver the dice to the felt in front of the shooter by using a long,

straight, putter-shaped stick. The stickman also makes the *call* (announcing the results of the roll to the entire table), oversees the central betting area (placing all bets in that area for players), and instructs the dealers to pay out winners.

✔ **Boxman:** Sitting across from the stickman at the center of the table, the boxman is also the *bossman,* overseeing the entire game, releasing stacks of chips to the dealers, and collecting cash for the house. He watches the bets and keeps a wary eye on the dice, the other dealers, and you and the other players to make sure everything's on the up and up.

Shooting for the whole table

The *shooter* is a key character in craps because she's the player who's rolling the dice. In craps, *shooting,* or dice rolling, is a rotating affair. Each player gets a turn to roll for the entire table, and the honor moves clockwise around the table. When your turn comes around, the stickman pushes five dice toward you, and you select two. The only requirement to shoot is that you have a bet riding.

If you're a craps newbie, you can refuse your turn to roll the dice. But I recommend you give it a try. Shooting is part of the experience of craps. Even if your first roll goes completely off the table or lands in someone's drink, pocket, sleeve, mouth, or cleavage, the game continues, and nobody gets too upset. The stickman (when he's done laughing at you) calls, "No roll." Then the boxman inspects the errant die and gives you another shot at getting it right.

Minding Mr. Manners at a craps table

When you're playing craps, most of the etiquette-related manners focus on the dice, so pay attention to where the dice are at all times. When the stickman yells, "Dice are out!" the shooter has permission to roll the dice. This is your signal to get your hands up and out of the way (assuming you're not the shooter).

The following are some of the simple do's and don'ts of craps etiquette:

✔ **Keep drinks away from the rail.** And definitely don't hold your drink *over* the rail. Craps is a fist-pumping, back-slapping, wild game, so you're bound to get jostled and splash your whiskey on the felt.

✔ **Don't touch the numbers.** Craps dealers keep a lockdown on parts of the layout. Players are only allowed to place chips on the bets right in front of them: the pass-line and don't-pass bets, plus the come, don't-come, field, and Big 6/8. The unspoken demarcation line is the come box; any bet in the numbered squares requires a dealer's assistance. The same is true for all bets in the middle area; the stickman places those bets for all players. (Check out "Avoiding 'Sucker' Bets," later in this chapter, for more info about these bets.)

✓ **Handle the dice with one hand only.** When your turn comes, never use two hands — and keep the dice where the crew can see them. Casinos are justifiably obsessed with cheaters who might sneak crooked dice into the game, so these rules limit those chances of cheating.

✓ **Do your best to toss a valid throw.** Toss the dice so they hit the far wall of the table and bounce off. This move ensures a random outcome and is considered a valid throw. Also, don't toss the dice too high or too soft, and keep the arc lower than the tallest player at the table.

✓ **Leave the fancy pitches to baseball.** Don't fling the dice like a hotshot grounder to third — you're likely to leave piles of rubble in your wake and generate a dirty look from the boxman. As a dealer once said of dice, "They're small, light, and not made of dynamite."

Walking through Craps, Step by Step

Craps is definitely a luck-based game, but estimating the odds successfully does require some homework so you understand the chances of rolling certain number combinations. The good news is that your odds of coming out ahead of the house are some of the best in the casino if you stick to the basic bets (despite the numerous fancy bets available).

Before you decide to join the game, make sure you've read the previous section, "Setting the Craps Stage," for the lowdown on a craps table layout and the important members of the cast and crew.

Buying in

The game cycle starts as you place chips — or have the dealer place them — onto the marked betting boxes on the table. Minimum craps bets typically begin at $5. (The table minimum and maximum appear on the standard casino betting-terms placards on the inside wall of the table in front of each dealer.)

After you elbow your way in and claim a spot at the rail, you need to get some chips to play with. Wait until after the dealers pay out the winning bets and the dice are sitting idle at the center of the table in front of the boxman. Then ask the dealer for chips by saying "Change please."

Dealers can't take money directly from your hand, so drop the bills on the table. If the dealer is busy doing something else, just wait a few seconds. The crew has its own ways to keep track of all the players. After the dealer notices your bills, she takes them and slides a stack of chips back to you. Pick them up and put them in your *rail rack* — the two grooves on the rim of the table that act as trays for your casino chips.

Coming out (no, not of the closet): The first roll in craps

Before the game starts, most players at the table place *line bets,* which means they put money on the pass line or the don't pass (see "Relying on Strategy to Place the Best Bets," later in this section, to understand what these actual bets mean). The action begins when the stickman pushes five dice to the shooter, who selects two for the throw. The shooter tosses the dice to the opposite end of the craps table for the *come-out roll,* the first step in the game sequence. Although this throw looks like any other, certain rules apply for come-out rolls that are different from subsequent rolls.

If the come-out roll is 7 or 11 (a *natural*), all bets on the pass line win even money. If the roll is a 2, 3, or 12 *(craps),* then all pass-line bets lose. For example, a player sets a $25 chip on the pass line and the shooter throws a 3 and 4 on the dice (to make a 7 for a natural). That player's bet wins, and he is paid immediately; the dealer on his side of the table places a $25 chip next to his original bet. Had the shooter rolled a 1 and 1 for a total of 2 (craps), the pass-line bet would lose and the player's $25 chip would be removed by the dealer.

Making a point

If the come-out roll is a 4, 5, 6, 8, 9, or 10, that number becomes *the point.* The line bets are neither paid nor raked if a point number is rolled on the come-out; the fate of those bets now depends on the next roll.

As soon as the point is established (assume it's the number 9), the shooter is no longer coming out. Instead, he now makes point rolls: throwing the dice until he either hits the number 9 again *(makes the point)* or throws a 7. If he makes the point by rolling a 9, the sequence starts over — the table reverts to a new come-out roll with the same shooter. However, if he throws a 7 before a 9, then the roll is a loser, the shooter's turn is over, and the dice move to the next shooter.

If you make your way to the edge of the action in the middle of a game, you can quickly tell what type of roll it is by looking for the *marker puck,* a small plastic disc. If the roll is a point roll, the puck sits white-side-up in the square above the point number on the felt. During the come-out roll, the puck sits black-side-up in the *don't-come area* (see Figure 8-2)*,* and the dealer moves it as soon as the point is rolled. For example, if you see the white puck over the 4, you know that the table is currently in the point roll, and the shooter continues to roll until she hits a 4 *(makes the point)* or throws a 7 *(sevens out).*

Relying on Strategy to Place the Best Bets

Craps offers more than 100 different kinds of bets. The table layout (Figure 8-2) gives a mere hint of all the betting options to consider, from bets that depend on a series of rolls to one-roll bets that hinge on only the next throw. But with a variety of bets comes a variety of odds. Many of the bets in craps tilt too heavily toward the house to be worth considering.

Before you toss down your cash and buy in at a table, make sure the table betting minimum is within your budget so you don't make a quick exit. Minimum bets are as low as $5, sometimes even $3, but during busy times or at ritzier clubs, the minimums rise accordingly, with many tables sporting $25 or $100 minimums.

You may have a good understanding of how to play craps if you've read the previous sections in this chapter. (If you haven't, I suggest you check them out to get a good foundation of how to play craps.) If you do understand the very basics of craps, then this section is for you. Here I focus on betting and how you can utilize strategy to make the best bets.

You don't need to understand every single bet on the table to become a good player. In fact, some bets have such poor odds that you're better off avoiding them altogether. With so many options, you want to concentrate on the most advantageous bets. If you're fairly new (or even an old pro) at playing craps, I suggest you focus on the following bets.

The pass-line bet

The main wager in craps is the *pass-line bet,* also called the *front-line bet.* The pass-line bet is popular because it offers eight ways to win and only four ways to lose, yielding a low house edge of only 1.41 percent (the casino wins an average of $14 out of every $1,000 bet). The pass-line bet works as follows:

- ✔ On the come-out roll, a 7 or 11 wins.
- ✔ A come-out roll of 2, 3, or 12, known as a *craps,* loses.
- ✔ If the come-out roll is a 4, 5, 6, 8, 9, or 10, that number becomes the point, and the next sequence of rolls is point rolls.
- ✔ A 7 is a loser after the point is established.

During point rolls, all pass-line bets can still win if the point is rolled before a 7, which can happen on the very next roll. However, the shooter may have to throw the dice dozens of times before the bet is resolved by either a 7 or the point number coming up on the dice. If the shooter *sevens out* — rolls a 7 before the point — all the pass-line bets lose. For example, if the come-out roll is a 10, the dealer moves the puck white-side-up into the 10 square. For the next roll or sequence of rolls, your pass-line bet wins if the roll is a 10 but loses if it's a 7. All other numbers rolled will be meaningless (at least for the pass-line bet).

You aren't allowed to *take down* (remove your pass-line bet) after the point is established, but you may increase it with an *odds bet,* which I discuss later in "The odds bet" section.

Most casinos allow you to make a pass-line bet (called a *put bet*) after the point is established. Some gamblers place these bets if they walk up to a table in the middle of point rolls. This move lets them play immediately instead of waiting for the next come-out roll. But put bets aren't smart moves, even if they look attractive when the point is 6 or 8. The better play is to make a come bet. (See the next section for more on the come bet.)

The come bet

After the point is established on a come-out roll, only the point and the 7 can affect bets on the pass line. Because it can take a dozen or more rolls to hit one of those two numbers, the *come bet* offers extra playing excitement to bettors. With a come bet, *every* point roll can be an independent come-out roll.

You can place come bets only after a point has been established for the pass-line bettors. To place a come bet, slide a chip to the large area on the layout marked *Come*. Make sure you slide the chip directly in front of you so the dealers know it's yours. Now you're betting on the next throw of the dice. Just like a pass-line bet,

- 7 or 11 win outright.

- 2, 3, or 12 loses.

- If a 4, 5, 6, 8, 9, or 10 is thrown, that number becomes your point number. You win if that point number is thrown again before a 7, but you lose if a 7 is rolled before the point number.

So, for example, you have a pass-line bet on the board and the established point is a 6. That bet is only resolved if a 6 (win) or 7 (loss) is thrown. Before the next throw, you place a new bet in the come area, subject to the same minimum betting rules as the pass-line bet. Now the shooter throws a 2. Your original pass-line bet is unaffected, but you lose your new come bet. You put another chip on the come area, and this time the shooter throws an 8. The dealer moves that come bet to the 8 square. Now you're rooting for two different numbers, the 6 and the 8. If either number appears, one of your bets will pay off. Of course if a 7 appears, you lose both the original pass-line bet and the come bet on the 8.

When you hear about players going on great craps rolls, some time period is usually associated with it . . . 30 minutes, 45 minutes, an hour. You lose your turn only when you *seven out,* or throw a 7 after the come-out roll. Only on seven outs does the whole table lose all its pass-line and come bets. So for a hot shooter to roll the dice over and over, she must be hitting point after point after point.

The don't-pass line bet

The *don't-pass line bet,* or *back-line bet,* plays the opposite of the pass-line bet. If you make this bet, you're called a *wrong-way* bettor. But don't worry, it's not immoral or against the rules to bet this way. The word *wrong* just means you're betting opposite the dice, or opposite the way most people bet. How you win your bets is also opposite. If the come-out roll is a 2 or 3 (craps), the *don't-pass bet* wins even money. But if the shooter throws a 7 or 11, the bet loses. The don't-pass line bet is fairly safe, yielding a house edge of 1.36 percent, which is slightly better than the pass-line bet.

You can only place chips on a don't-pass bet before a come-out roll. As soon as a point has been established and the shooter is throwing point rolls, the don't-pass bet is off-limits.

As a don't-pass bettor, you want the opposite of what pass-line bettors want. You don't want to see a 7 or 11 on the come-out roll (automatic loser). Instead you're rooting for a 2 or 3 (automatic winner) and are indifferent to a 12. If a point is established, you're hoping a 7 appears before the point number is rolled again. If that happens, your don't-pass bet wins.

People who play the don't pass are typically in the minority at a craps table. Playing against the dice goes against one of the major appeals of the game: its community spirit. You cheer as the others are shaking their heads and cursing. But because the odds are slightly better, playing the wrong way is absolutely fine. Some people prefer the dark side approach, and over time the don't-pass bets keep more money in your wallet than the pass-line bets.

In a pass-line bet, the 12 (along with the 2 and 3) means craps. But, even though the 2 and 3 win even money in a don't-pass line bet, wrong-way bettors *tie* (no money is won or lost) if 12 is rolled. (The don't-pass rules can't be completely opposite the pass-line rules or the wrong-way player would have the same slight statistical advantage that the casino enjoys with the pass-line. So one number, usually the 12, becomes the odd man out.) Two dice of 6s *(box cars)* appear on the table in the don't-pass space to indicate that the don't-pass line *bars* the 12, preserving the advantage for the casino. Even with this negative feature, the don't-pass line is still a good bet.

Betting against the dice

Craps players come in two basic flavors: right-way bettors and wrong-way bettors. Most players bet on the pass line and follow up with come bets. In other words, they bet *with* the dice. On the opposite side are the wrong-way bettors. They bet on the don't-pass bets and follow with don't-come bets — betting *against* the dice.

In addition to their polar-opposite strategies, right-way and wrong-way bettors hold another important difference: The right-way bettor must stick with the bet, while the wrong-way bettor can take down the bet at any time. Because wrong-way betting has the advantage of the bet after the point is established, the wrong-way bettor has no reason to ever take down the don't-pass bet.

Wrong-way bettors enjoy the thrill of bucking the crowd and betting the "don't." But you're definitely not going to win friends around the table when you win and everyone else loses.

The don't-come bet

You make a *don't-come bet* after a point has been established for the pass-line bet. But like don't-pass bets, these bets are wrong-way, too. The don't-come bets are at risk on the first throw — they lose if a 7 or 11 is thrown, but they win outright on a 2 or 3. The 12 is a *push* or tie — the same as the don't-pass bar. After the don't-come bet gets safely on base, it wins if 7 is rolled before the come-point is repeated, and it loses if the come-point is thrown before the 7.

The don't-come bet is to the wrong-way bettor what the come bet is to the regular craps bettor. The bet allows him to have more numbers *working* instead of having to wait for a new come-out roll.

The odds bet

One of the best bets in the entire casino is the *odds bet,* offered on pass-line and come bets. The odds bet is also advantageous for wrong-way bettors playing the don't-pass and don't-come bets, although the payout is less. Because taking odds is such a good deal, casinos sometimes don't advertise this option. But if you look carefully, you can see the odds limit posted on the end zone under the rim where the dice bounce. If your bankroll can afford it, you should almost always take the odds bets.

You have no designated spot or box to place your odds bets, but the standard practice is to tuck them in right behind your pass-line bet. (See Figure 8-3.)

Figure 8-3:
The pass-line bet with odds placed behind it.

Original Pass-Line Bet

Odds Bet

PASS LINE

Odds Bet: Pass Line

Taking odds on pass-line and come bets

After a point is established for the pass bet, you can take the next step and *take odds.* All you need to do is place your odds bet directly behind your pass-line bet (this is done between dice rolls). As long as your pass-line bet is still alive (whether it's right after the point was established or ten rolls later), you're free to take odds or *back your bet*. The amount allowed on this bet varies from casino to casino and can range from 1 to 3 times the norm — or up to 100 times the odds in rare instances.

For example, three times the odds means you're allowed (but aren't obligated) to bet up to three times your original pass-line bet or come bets with an odds bet. Some casinos vary the amount of odds you can take from number to number, allowing several times more on the 6 and 8 than they do on other points. If in doubt, just ask your dealer about maximum odds allowed.

Odds bets are called *free odds* because the house has no advantage over the player — the bet is a break-even proposition. By taking odds, you can reduce the house edge to less than 1 percent, so the bet is definitely worth making. If the point is rolled before a 7, you win both your pass-line bet and your odds bet. But if the 7 comes first, you lose both bets.

Say you put $5 on the pass line before a come-out roll in a casino that allows 3× odds. The shooter then throws a 4, a tough point number to hit because the shooter is twice as likely to throw a 7 before he throws a 4 (refer to Figure 8-1 earlier in this chapter for outcome possibilities). Not only is the house more likely to win the bet, but even if a 4 *is* thrown, your pass-line bet only pays even money, putting you at a serious disadvantage.

During the 10 to 20 seconds between dice throws, while other bettors place additional bets, you reach down and place $10 in chips behind your $5 pass-line bet. (You could have placed $15 because the casino allows 3× odds, but it's fine to place any multiple of your pass-line bet.)

As the game continues, the shooter tosses the dice and, sure enough, it's Little Joe! (That's craps lingo for a 4.) The casino pays your pass-line bet even money ($5 for $5) and puts $20 next to your odds bet. Payout odds on a 4 are 2 to 1, a reward level that exactly matches the bet's risk. Your odds bet did nothing to improve the likelihood of the shooter throwing a 4 before a 7, but you should take advantage of the odds bets because they vastly improve the amount you're compensated for hitting your point.

Although the pass-line and come bets pay even money, the payouts for taking odds are as follows:

- ✔ When the point is 4 or 10, the odds bet pays 2 to 1.
- ✔ When the point is 5 or 9, the odds bet pays 3 to 2.
- ✔ When the point is 6 or 8, the odds bet pays 6 to 5.

Always make sure you place odds bets in increments the casino can easily pay off. At $5 tables, the odds cause minor problems when players take single odds on pass-line and come bets. For example, if the point is 5 or 9, your odds bet should be an even number (such as $6 or $10, rather than $5), so the dealer can quickly pay out the 3 to 2 on winners.

Laying odds on don't-pass and don't-come bets

The wrong-way bettor can *lay odds* on don't bets just like the right-way bettor takes odds on the pass-line and come bets. However, the *don't* bettor (a wrong-way player who bets on don't pass and don't come) gets only a fraction of his odds bet when he wins. For example, he has to risk $40 to win $20 with odds on the 4 or 10. Even though the numbers may not look like it, these are actually true odds; laying odds reduces the house advantage to less than 1 percent over the player, which makes laying odds a good option for players. (Check Figure 8-4 to see what this bet spot looks like on the layout.)

Original
Don't Pass Bet   Odds Bet

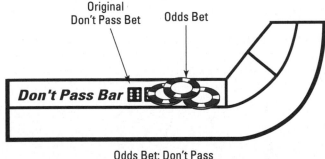

Figure 8-4:
The don't-pass bet with an odds bet.

Odds Bet: Don't Pass

Unlike the come-bet odds, which are temporarily suspended during come-out rolls, the odds bets on don't-pass and don't-come bets are always *working* or *on*.

The payouts for laying odds are as follows:

- ✔ When the point is 4 or 10, the odds bet pays 1 to 2.
- ✔ When the point is 5 or 9, the odds bet pays 2 to 3.
- ✔ When the point is 6 or 8, the odds bet pays 5 to 6.

The odds calculation is slightly different for wrong-way betting. Use the example of placing a don't-pass bet of $5 and the point number 10. When you lay odds (place odds behind a don't-pass or don't-come bet), you calculate based on what you would win. At a double odds table, the most you could win is twice your $5 bet, or $10. To win that $10, you'd place $20 behind your bet because the odds pay 1 to 2 when the point is 10.

Taking the maximum odds

After the point is established, you usually want to take the maximum odds that you can safely afford on your bets. Most casinos offer single or double odds, but you can occasionally find a table that offers up to 10 times — sometimes even up to 100 times — the odds for games with low table minimums. If the table limit sign indicates "3× – 4× – 5× odds," the maximum allowed bet is three times the odds on the 4 or 10, four times on the 5 or 9, and five times on the 6 or 8. The house edge decreases as the odds increase, making the odds bet one of the best plays in the casino.

Avoiding "Sucker" Bets

Like any casino game, craps has bets that have better odds for you as well as bets that have a higher edge for the house. In craps, bets of the one-roll variety aren't player friendly — you win or lose depending on the next roll of the dice, and the odds are poor on these bets.

Most of the *bad* bets are in the center box in front of the stickman, but — be warned — danger is everywhere, and some of the riskiest (translation: "sucker") bets are oh so close to you. In this section, I tell you about some of the not-so-good bets and show why they're not the best way to make money at a craps table.

Resisting the lure of Big 6 and Big 8

A bet on the *Big 6* or *8* (found in the corner of the layout, temptingly close to you and next to the pass-line bet box) is a wager that the shooter rolls a 6 or 8 before a 7. This bet pays only even money and has a whopping house edge of 9.1 percent. (In other words, it's a horrendous bet to make because the casino wins an average of $91 out of every $1,000 bet.)

If you want to play something with a 6 or 8 in it, just mere inches away from the Big 6 and Big 8 is the more advantageous *six or eight place bet,* which pays 7 to 6 and has a house edge of only 1.52 percent!

Swearing off the place bets

A *place bet* on one of the point numbers (4, 5, 6, 8, 9, or 10) is a wager that the shooter will roll that number before a 7. For example, you can place this bet at any time by saying to the dealer "I want to place number 5" and dropping your chips in the come area. The dealer then moves your chips to the appropriate number box. Place bets are identical to established come bets in how they win or lose. But their payout odds are different, and you have the option of taking them down and getting your chips back, should the whim hit you. Place bets are *off* on the come-out roll unless you ask for them to be *on*.

The house pays place bets at slightly less than correct odds, giving the house an edge of 4 percent on a 5 or 9 and a 6.67 percent edge on a 4 or 10.

The following are the payouts for a place bet:

- ✔ A winning place bet on a 4 or 10 pays 9 to 5 (bet $5 and get paid $9).
- ✔ A winning place bet on a 5 or 9 pays 7 to 5 (bet $5 and get paid $7).
- ✔ A winning place bet on a 6 or 8 pays 7 to 6 (bet $6 and get paid $7).

Steering clear of buy bets

Buy bets resemble place bets but with one difference — they pay out at true odds in exchange for a 5 percent commission. Remember, the house normally reduces payout odds slightly, so the player isn't compensated in proportion to the risk level of his bet. (*True odds* means the house pays in exact proportion to the actual risk of the bet.) Buy bets are *off* by default on the come-out roll, meaning they're in suspended animation: They can neither win nor lose, no matter what's rolled. Bettors are also free to bet or remove buy bets at any time. For example, the 4 or 10 buy bet is slightly more advantageous to the player than the 4 or 10 place bet because the buy bet has a 4.76 percent house edge versus the place bet's 6.67 percent house edge.

Be sure to factor the 5 percent commission into your bets ($1 on a $20 bet, for example). The 4 or 10 buy bet is the only buy bet worth making; for the 5, 6, 8, and 9 numbers, you're better off making a place bet. Nevertheless, players often use buy bets as a way to simplify their betting; they pay the commission and then enjoy correct odds on all their bets. Of course, the money all comes from the same place, but, as they say, "Different strokes . . . ."

Laying off lay bets

A bet on one of the point numbers (4, 5, 6, 8, 9, or 10) is to lay odds that the 7 rolls before the point number — the opposite of a buy bet (check out the previous section for more info on buy bets). But like the buy bet, you can place or remove a *lay bet* at any time, and it's always *working* — which means the bet is active and can win or lose even on the come-out roll. Because the 7 is more likely to appear before the point number, lay bets have a better-than-even chance to win and, therefore, pay less-than-even money: A 4 or 10 lay bet pays 1 to 2; a 5 or 9 lay bet pays 2 to 3; and a 6 or 10 lay bet pays 5 to 6.

The casino takes a 5 percent commission on a win (not on the bet). So if you bet $60 on a 9, your net win is $38 ($40 minus $2 — or 5 percent of the $40 you win, not of your $60 original bet). To place these bets correctly, you need to lay $41 to win $20 on the 4 or 10 (your best bet), lay $31 to win $20 on the 5 or 9, and lay $25 to win $20 on the 6 or 8.

Passing up field bets

You can find *field bets* in the middle of the layout. These one-roll bets consist of the numbers 2, 3, 4, 9, 10, 11, and 12. They pay even money, except for 2 and 12, which pay 2 to and sometimes 3 to 1. The house edge on field bets is 5.56 percent and is popular with inexperienced players because it's a one-time roll that's simple to understand. But you rarely see craps experts placing field bets because of the ugly house advantage.

Saying no to proposition bets

Proposition bets (also known as *center bets*) are one-roll bets you place on a 2, 3, 7, 11, or 12, and they're bets you can make on any roll of the dice. You can see the *prop* bets in the center of the table layout (check out Figure 8-2 earlier in this chapter). The stickman places these bets for you.

Some proposition bets indicate the bet pays 30 *to* 1, while another table layout may state the payoff odds as 30 *for* 1. Be careful because these two types of bets are different. A bet that is 30 *to* 1 is paying 30 times the bet — but a bet offering 30 *for* 1 pays 29 times the bet. Although *for* seems like an innocent little word, don't let semantics fool you into thinking a bet pays more than it really does!

The smartest and simplest strategy is to ignore all bets in the center of the table (see Figure 8-5). If you feel an urge to play these bets, go for it. Just remember that I'm offering you my expert advice because I want to help you keep your losses at a minimum. The following proposition bets can suck your wallet dry:

> ✔ **Any 7:** A one-roll bet that pays if the next roll is a 7 and loses if any other number appears. Although the probability of rolling a 7 is 5 to 1, this bet pays only 4 to 1 (or 5 *for* 1, which is the same thing). The casino's edge is 16.7 percent. Can you say ATM?

✔ **Craps-eleven:** A one-roll bet on any craps (2, 3, or 12) or the 11, represented by all those circled *C* and *E* initials on both sides of the center box. The payout is the same as for the bets for any craps (8 for 1) or the 11 (16 for 1). House edge is more than 10 percent.

✔ **Horn bets:** A one-roll bet that pays out if the next roll is 2, 3, 11, or 12 and loses if any other number appears. Horn bets may not even appear on all center-box layouts, but it's the same as craps-eleven. You make a wager with four chips as if you're making four individual bets; you're paid 16 for 1 (for the 3 or 11) or 31 for 1 (for the 2 or the 12) — but you also lose the other three wagers. House edge is 12.5 percent.

✔ **The 2, 3, 11, or 12:** One-roll bets in the center box offering typical payouts of 16 for 1 on numbers 3 and 11 and 31 for 1 on numbers 2 and 12. (Some casinos may offer 30 for 1.) The house edge on these bets ranges from 11 to 14 percent.

✔ **Any craps:** A one-roll bet that pays if the next roll is a 2, 3, or 12 and loses otherwise. A box is available for this bet at the bottom of the center-bet layout. A win on any craps pays 8 for 1, and the house edge is a stiff 11 percent.

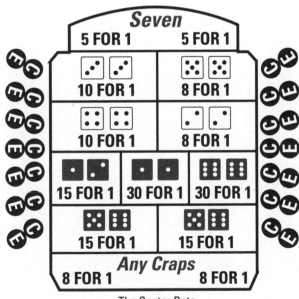

Figure 8-5:
The center bets.

The Center Bets

Finding out the hard way

Four different *hard-way* bets are available to players on the following numbers: 4, 6, 8, and 10. A bet placed on a hard way wins if that number is thrown as a pair (for example, a dice roll of two 4s is a *hard 8*) and loses if that number comes *easy* (for example, a 6 and a 2 is an *easy 8*). You also lose the bet if any 7 is rolled.

The bets are placed in the center of the table, but, unlike the proposition bets, they aren't single-roll wagers; they remain on the board until resolved one way or the other. Hard-way bets are some of the worst bets on the table with the house edge a hefty 9 to 11 percent.

Chapter 9

Spinning Wheel Goes Round n' Round: Roulette

In This Chapter

▶ Getting the roulette lowdown

▶ Understanding bets inside and out

▶ Reviewing roulette etiquette

▶ Exploring strategies to improve your odds

▶ Recognizing strategies that don't work

*T*he roulette wheel is a readily recognizable casino icon, conjuring up images of tradition and nobility, creating an ambience of luxury and elegance. In fact, roulette is the oldest of all the casino games and is still around for two good reasons: It's fun, and it's very easy to play. Roulette is probably the best place for you as a novice to start your gambling experience (although not always the smartest because of the odds).

The centerpiece of this age-old game is the beautifully crafted wheel in which a small, white ball spins around a groove and drops down into one compartment, or *pocket,* on the wheel. Over the centuries, a number of scientists and mathematicians have tried to figure out how to beat the wheel, but such systems and theories always end in failure.

The fact is that where the roulette wheel stops is a matter of chance. And chance rarely favors the players because the stiff house odds virtually ensure a profit for the casino. So playing roulette isn't what I call the likeliest route to becoming independently wealthy.

The game still has a seductive appeal, and if you catch on to some time-tested betting strategies, you can manage your gambling bankroll and stretch it into an enjoyable casino pastime. In this chapter, I explain the game's basics, some important betting tips, and some helpful strategies.

Getting the Spin on Roulette Basics

You probably have a good sense of the basics of roulette — after all, you've seen enough movies to know that you place piles of colored chips on a long, rectangular table. After all the bets are made, the *croupier* (dealer) spins a large, bowl-shaped wheel with corresponding slots marked by colors and numbers in a counterclockwise direction, and then she releases a small, white ball in a clockwise direction. Anticipation builds as the ball and wheel spin, whirr, and slow. You wait for the ball to drop into one of the numbered pockets (hopefully in one of the spots you bet on!).

The goal of roulette is basically to guess where the ball will land when the wheel finishes spinning. But, of course, you need to know a little more than that. This section takes a look at the wheel and the table betting area, walks you through a step-by-step roulette play, and explains the role of the croupier.

Starting with the wheel

The first step toward understanding the game of roulette is to decipher the roulette wheel — the most recognizable casino gambling symbol in the world. Beautiful and flawless, the wheel is a finely crafted device weighing in at 100 pounds (45 kilograms) and costing thousands of dollars. A roulette wheel has the following distinguishing characteristics:

✔ The outside rim of the wheel is divided into numbers in alternating pockets of black and red.

✔ The outside rim also has one or two pockets in green (0 and 00).

✔ The numbers on the wheel are mixed up — they don't run consecutively or in any discernible pattern, such as alternating odd and even.

And how many number segments are on the wheel? The answer depends on where you're playing roulette.

✔ **United States:** If you're playing in Las Vegas, Atlantic City, or anywhere else in the United States (including cruise ships and Indian reservations), the roulette wheels you encounter most likely have a total of 38 numbered slots, or pockets, containing numbers 1 through 36, and two green compartments, one with a single zero and the other with a double zero. (This wheel is often referred to as the *American wheel.*)

✔ **Europe and South America:** If you're gaming in Monte Carlo or another location in Europe or South America, your roulette wheel (often referred to as the *European* or *French wheel*) has one pocket less than its American counterpart (it doesn't include the double-zero pocket).

Check out Figure 9-1, which shows the major differences between the American wheel and the European wheel.

The European Wheel   The American Wheel

Figure 9-1:
The European wheel with a single zero (left) and the American wheel with zero and double zero (on the right).

Roulette is more popular in Europe than in the United States mainly because the European wheel offers better odds with one less possibility to bet on (no double zero). But don't buy that plane ticket to Paris quite yet. Although most of the wheels in the United States have 38 pockets (two green numbers), you can find European wheels in some upscale American casinos.

Taking in the table layout

The other key component to a roulette game is the *betting table* where the players place their chips for wagering. The betting table is situated adjacent to the wheel and is inlaid with a variety of squares and bars. Take a look at Figure 9-2 as I dissect the roulette table to make some sense of it.

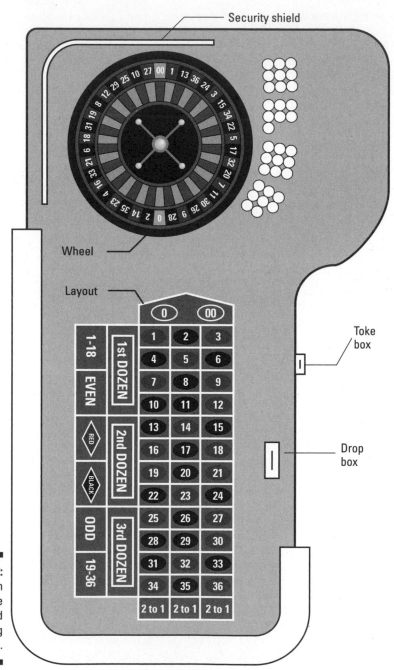

Security shield

Wheel

Layout

Toke box

Drop box

Figure 9-2: American roulette wheel and betting layouts.

Two sections make up the roulette table:

- ✓ **Squares showing numbers and colors corresponding to the number and color pockets on the roulette wheel.** These squares take up the most space on the layout. Unlike the wheel, the numbers on the table run in sequential order in rows of three. For example, in the third row from the top in Figure 9-2, you find the number 8 in black between 7 and 9. This betting spot corresponds to the black 8 pocket on the wheel, and it's where you place your chips if you want to bet on the 8.

- ✓ **Bars wrapping around the outside of the rows of sequential numbers.** For example, you can see in Figure 9-2 bars containing the words *odd*, *even* and diamonds containing the words *red*, and *black*. As you may guess, you place chips in these areas to bet on other aspects of the wheel outcome. For example, placing chips on *odd* is a bet that the ball lands on an odd number — *any* odd number.

I explain more about these various betting areas in the section "Betting: The Inside (and Outside) Scoop." *Inside bets* are bets you place on any of the columns of numbers; *outside bets* are — no surprise — bets you place in the outside areas.

The table normally accommodates up to six players, but some double table layouts can handle a dozen or more players. Try to get a seat right in the middle so you can place a bet in any area on the table. If you're stuck sitting at the end of the table or standing, you must slide chips toward the croupier and ask her to place bets on any area that you're not able to reach.

Betting with chips of a different color

You make bets by placing chips on the squares that correspond to the numbers or colors on the roulette wheel. Roulette doesn't use normal casino chips, however. Instead, it features special color-coded chips unique to each player at the table and the particular roulette table you're playing at. You can't play the chips you use at one roulette table at a different game because the chips have no value marked on them.

Each player gets a different color of chip, allowing the croupier to distinguish one player's bet from another's. For example, your orange chips may be worth $5 each, while another player's blue chips may be worth $1 each. The distinctive chip color allows all players to have bets on the table without fear of mixing the bets up. In other words, if the player next to you places a stack of blue chips on your favorite number, go right ahead and stack your yellow chips on top of his.

Roulette's roots: Philosophic origins and creepy coincidences

Many of you probably played spin the bottle (don't deny it) when you were kids (and maybe you still play it at your company's holiday party), so the idea of playing a game of chance by spinning an object isn't foreign. And if spin the bottle isn't gambling, I don't know what is — especially if you were one of the unlucky girls stuck in my circle.

The exact origins of roulette are unknown, but you can trace the modern components of the game (the flywheel and red/black slots) back to the famous 17th-century mathematician and philosopher Blaise Pascal. He'd been tinkering

with perpetual-motion devices and gave the name *roulette* to the wheel he was working on.

In 1842, a couple of French brothers named Francois and Louis Blanc invented single-zero roulette to attract more players. The idea was a hit, and Charles III, the Prince of Monaco, invited Francois to establish a casino in Monte Carlo. Legend claims that Francois sold his soul to the devil in exchange for the secrets of roulette. And if you want to enter the realm of the sort of creepy (cue the *Twilight Zone* music), add up the numbers 1 through 36 — the sum equals 666.

When you join the game, or *buy in,* you generally ask for a *stack,* which consists of 20 chips. Let the croupier know what value you want assigned to the chips. The croupier keeps track of the value by placing a marker called a *lammer* on your color in the chip stacks. (Although at smaller casinos or when everyone is playing the same-value chips, lammers may not be used.) When you leave the table, the croupier exchanges your roulette chips with casino chips, which you take to the cashier's window and cash out.

Dealing with the croupier

In the game of roulette, the dealer is called the *croupier* (pronounced croop-ee-*ay*) and performs a variety of tasks to facilitate the play. When you're playing roulette, just remember that the croupier does all of the following:

✔ Converts your cash or casino chips to the colored chips unique to roulette.

✔ Places your chips on the table if you're unable to reach the spot on the table where you wish to bet them.

- ✔ Spins the wheel counterclockwise and releases the ball clockwise, even as you continue to put down bets. Players may place bets until the croupier announces, "No more bets" and waves a hand over the table.

- ✔ Announces the winning number and color as soon as the roulette gods determine the ball's fate. Then the croupier places a marker (it looks like a chess piece) on the corresponding winning number on the table.

- ✔ Rakes in losing bets and pays off winning bets (starting with those players farthest away). Don't grab your chips or place any new bets until the croupier completes paying off everyone. And be sure to pick up your winning chips if you don't plan on betting them again on the next spin.

Betting: The Inside (and Outside) Scoop

As I discuss in the previous section, the roulette table layout breaks betting down into two sections: the inside bets and the outside bets. Inside bets involve betting specific numbers on the wheel; a winning bet on a single number pays 35 to 1. The outside bets are outside of the numbers on the table layout. They pay either *even money* (1 to 1) on red/black, high/low, or odd/even, or 2 to 1 on *columns* and *dozens*. (Check out "Making outside bets: Better odds but lower payouts" later in this section for more on columns and decks.)

Although you know what the bets mean, that information doesn't help much if you don't know how to make them. This section gives you the lowdown on identifying the table limits and placing your bets.

Knowing your (table) limits

Most games establish a minimum wager of, say, $1. In addition, inside bets may require a minimum *spread* — $5, for example. You can achieve a spread by making five different $1 bets (betting numbers 2, 13, 21, 28, and 33 for example), or by making one $5 bet (on just a single number). Basically a spread is the total of all your bets.

The roulette table usually has a sign displaying a table minimum and a chip minimum, but you can't mix and match inside and outside bets. For example, at a $5 table with a $1 chip minimum, you must place a minimum bet of $5 on the outside bets, or you can place five $1 number bets on the inside bets. You aren't allowed to bet $2 on the outside and $3 on the inside.

Making inside bets: Long shots and big payouts

Inside bets (betting on single numbers or a combination of numbers) have just the right elements for drama, nail biting, and impressing others. After all, when you set your chips down on a single number on the inside of the table, you're basically betting that, of all the 38 (or 37 on the European wheel) slots on the roulette wheel, the ball will land in that particular number. But players typically bet on more than one number at a time to increase their chances of hitting a winner.

Although most croupiers review the layout and point out any ambiguous bets before dropping the ball in the track, make sure that the croupier properly places your bets, and watch that other players don't accidentally knock your bet onto a different spot. You don't want the croupier to have to eyeball an imprecisely placed wager and tell you that your winning three-number street bet (paying 11 to 1) is so far out of place that it looks like a six-number line bet (paying 5 to 1).

Take a look at the circles on Figure 9-3. The following are examples of bets that players can make on the inside:

- ✔ **Straight up:** This bet is on an individual number, such as 21. If the ball drops on this number, the bet pays 35 to 1. For example, if you bet $1, you receive 35 times your bet, plus your original bet, for a total of $36. (See Circle A in Figure 9-3.)

- ✔ **Split:** This bet is on a line between two adjacent numbers, such as 29 and 32. If the ball lands on either number, the bet pays 17 to 1. (See Circle B in Figure 9-3.)

- ✔ **Street:** This bet is on the outside line of a row of three numbers, such as 13, 14, and 15. If the ball lands on any one of these numbers, the bet pays 11 to 1. (See Circle C in Figure 9-3.)

- ✔ **Corner:** This bet (also called a *quarter* or *box bet*) is on the corner of a group of four adjacent numbers, such as 7, 8, 10, and 11. If the ball lands on any one of these numbers, the bet pays 8 to 1. (See Circle D in Figure 9-3.)

- ✔ **Line:** This bet is on the end, on the intersecting lines of a group of six numbers, such as 25, 26, 27, 28, 29, and 30. If the ball lands on any one of the six numbers, the bet pays 5 to 1. (See Circle E in Figure 9-3.)

- ✔ **Five-number bet:** This bet is on the end of the line of the zero, double zero, one, two, and three boxes. If the ball lands on any one of the five numbers, the bet pays 6 to 1. (See Circle F in Figure 9-3.)

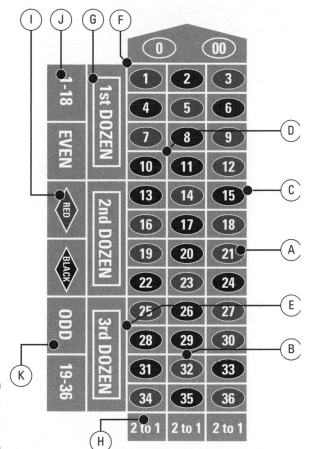

Figure 9-3:
Zooming in
on the table.

Just say *No* to five-number bets! They have the distinction of being the worst bet on the table. The problem lies in the improper payout of 6 to 1 — less than the *true* odds (actual odds of bet hitting) — leaving the house with a hefty edge of 7.89 percent and making this bet extremely hazardous to your bankroll.

Making outside bets: Better odds but lower payouts

The outside bets involve the designated spots on the table that are *not* numbers — the ones on the rim of the table layout, nearest you and the other players. These bets are more likely to come up than the inside bets, but the payoffs are much less (either even-money or 2 to 1). However, if the ball lands on a green number (0 or 00), all of the following outside bets lose.

All or nothing on red

In 2004, Ashley Revell of London became the stuff of legends when he sold everything he owned and bet his life savings on one spin of the roulette wheel in Las Vegas. All along, he'd planned to make a bet on black but changed his mind at the last minute and put $135,300 on red. If he won, the house would pay him even money; and if he lost, he wouldn't have a penny to his name. The croupier launched the ivory ball as the cameras rolled and...and...and...it landed on red seven! Revell doubled his money and walked away with $270,600.

The corresponding circles (G through K) in Figure 9-3 indicate outside bets:

- **Red/Black:** This bet says the winning number will come up either red or black. A win is paid at even money, or 1 to 1. For example, if you have a $10 bet on red and the ball lands on red 21, you win $10, plus the return of your original bet, for a total of $20. (See Circle I in Figure 9-3.)

- **High/Low:** This bet says the winning number will be in the low half (1 to 18) or the high half (19 to 36), excluding 0 and 00. The house pays a win at even money. (See Circle J in Figure 9-3.)

- **Odd/Even:** This bet says the winning number will be odd or even, excluding the 0 and 00. The house pays a win at even money. (See Circle K in Figure 9-3.)

- **Dozens:** This bet is on the first, second, or third dozen numbers, excluding 0 and 00. The dozens are 1 to 12, 13 to 24, and 25 to 36, and each dozen contains six red and six black numbers. If the ball lands on one of the numbers in your dozen bet, the house pays the win at 2 to 1. (See Circle G in Figure 9-3.)

- **Columns:** This bet is on one of three columns of a dozen numbers, excluding 0 and 00. If the ball lands on a number in your column bet, the house pays the win at 2 to 1. Note that Column One contains six red and six black numbers, Column Two has four red and eight black numbers, and Column Three has eight red and four black numbers. (See Circle H in Figure 9-3.)

Reciting Roulette Etiquette

Roulette attracts a polite, dignified gambler who enjoys a laid-back, casual game, as opposed to the frenzied atmosphere of, say, a craps game. (For a sense of how crazy craps can be, check out Chapter 8.) And, as with any table game, understanding a few social niceties helps you fit right in with the suave roulette crowd. This short section provides key points you need to remember when playing roulette.

- Place your money on the table when asking for chips — the croupier isn't allowed to accept it directly from your hand. Like many casino games, roulette isn't a *touchy feely* endeavor.

- Bet with regular casino chips if you aren't going to play very long, especially on the outside bets, where plenty of room exists for lots of chips. If you want to make inside bets with casino chips, make sure to keep track of them so that another player doesn't claim them in case of a win. In the case of a dispute, the croupier may call the pit boss to resolve the matter (see Chapter 2 for more on the pit boss).

- Wait until the croupier removes the win marker from the layout — the signal that you can begin betting again. Placing new bets before the croupier finishes paying off bets from the previous spin is easily the biggest gaffe that new players make.

- You can join a game anytime after the ball has landed and the croupier has finished paying off the winning bets.

- Remember that favorite numbers, such as birthdays, anniversary dates, children's ages, high school boyfriends' IQs, and so on, possess no magical powers for winning, although they can make gambling more fun.

Improving Your Odds

Remember to stay realistic about the long odds on this popular game of chance. Approach roulette with the sober realization that, with a house advantage of 5.26 percent on the American wheel, roulette is among the worst bets in a casino. Despite the odds, you can still use some simple strategies to stretch your roulette bankroll and enjoy the thrill of the spin. This section contains a few tips that can help you improve your chances of winning.

Roulette is a drain on your wallet simply because the game doesn't pay what the bets are worth. With 38 numbers (1 to 36, plus 0 and 00), the true odds of hitting a single number on a straight-up bet are 37 to 1, but the house pays only 35 to 1 if you win! Ditto the payouts on the combination bets. This discrepancy is where the house gets its huge edge in roulette.

Starting with the basics

Strategy is critical if you want to increase your odds of winning. The first time you play roulette, the players sprinkling the layout with chips may look as if they're heaping pepperoni slices on a pizza. You can make many different bets as long as you stay within the table's maximum limits. Consequently, few players make just one bet at a time.

Of course, the more bets you make, the more complicated and challenging it is to follow all the action. Here are two possible plans of attack to simplify matters:

- ✔ **Stick to the table minimum and play only the outside bets.** For example, bet on either red or black for each spin. This type of outside bet pays 1 to 1 and covers 18 of the 38 possible combinations.

- ✔ **Place two bets of equal amounts on two outside bets: one bet on an even-money play and the other on a column or dozen that pays 2 to 1.** For example, place one bet on black and one bet on Column Three, which has eight red numbers. That way, you have 26 numbers to hit, 4 of which you cover twice. You can also make a bet on red and pair it with a bet on Column Two, which has eight black numbers. Again, you cover 26 numbers, and 4 of them have two ways to win. Pairing a bet on either red or black with Column One (or on one of the three dozens) covers 24 numbers, and 6 numbers have two ways of winning. Spreading bets like this won't make you rich, but it does keep things interesting at the table.

Playing a European wheel

If you happen to find a single-zero European wheel, you greatly improve your odds: The house edge is half that of roulette with the American wheel — only 2.63 percent. You may see a European wheel at one of the posh Vegas casinos, such as Bellagio, Mirage, or Caesars Palace. If you can't find one on the floor, it's probably tucked away in the high-limit area along with the baccarat tables, so you may need to ask. You can also find the single-zero wheel at some other upscale casinos around the country.

Because casinos set aside the European wheel for high rollers, you're likely to find a higher table minimum, say $25. But because the house edge is half that of a double-zero wheel, the European wheel is the better roulette game to play for bigger bettors.

Your chances of winning get even better if the casino offers an advantageous rule called *en prison*. Sometimes available on the European wheel, the en prison rule lowers the house edge even further to a reasonable 1.35 percent. The rule applies to even-money bets. For example, say you have a $10 bet riding on black. If the ball lands on zero, your even-money bet doesn't win or lose but remains *locked up* for one more spin. If the ball lands on black on the next spin, the house returns your original bet of $10, but you don't win anything. If the ball lands on red, you lose. And if the ball repeats the zero number again, your bet stays imprisoned for another round.

Three-billion-to-one odds

Any discussion of European casinos and the graceful game of roulette would be remiss without a mention of James Bond. Sean Connery is the Scottish actor who made Agent 007 famous for his debonair style and willingness to take a risk. Apparently the many times Bond so easily beat the house in the movies rubbed off because Connery reportedly bet on the number 17 (and won) three straight times on a roulette wheel in an Italian casino, walking away with more than $30,000 in winnings.

The odds against that actually occurring are an astronomical 50,000 to 1. Yet author Barney Vinson says he witnessed the roulette ball landing on the number 7 *six times in a row* at Caesars Palace in Las Vegas in the summer of 2000. The odds of six consecutive hits of the same number are more than 3 billion to 1! Vinson reported that the players at the table were in disbelief that the lucky 7 would strike again. The casino lost a mere $300 during the ministreak.

Avoiding Strategies That Don't Work

Again, roulette is a game of chance — and in such games, you're at the mercy of the fates for the most part. Although you can follow some simple steps to stretch your money and improve your odds (for more, see the preceding section), no magic system can turn you into a consistent winner at roulette. Steer clear of falling into these traps.

Basing your plays on history

Each spin of the roulette wheel is completely independent, or unrelated, from the past, so don't let previous numbers influence you. Most roulette tables have a lighted scoreboard that displays the numbers that have hit over the last 20 rolls in two columns: red and black. However, players who try to guess what color will come up next by relying on history are wasting their time. The information means absolutely nothing. The wheel has no memory, and, although streaks of red or black for six or ten spins may occur, these streaks are no indication of the next result.

Blaming wheel bias

You don't have to watch for *wheel bias* — the casino beats you to it. The house regularly balances and checks and then rechecks roulette wheels for any suspected favoritism to certain numbers.

The man who broke the bank at Monte Carlo

What happens when an engineer spots a biased wheel? The casino pays dearly for its sloppy maintenance — which is just what happened at the Monte Carlo Casino in 1873 when an Englishman named Joseph Jagger identified a wheel in which nine numbers hit more frequently than random results would indicate. Jagger pounced, and before the casino bosses figured out what was going on, he walked away with winnings of £350,000, an enormous sum for his day.

Sometimes a wheel becomes *biased* because the mechanical wear and tear results in a less-than-random play. After all, the wheel consists of metal and wood. And certainly, after a quarter-million spins every month, all that activity may cause the wheel to wear down in certain strategic points. For this reason, casinos inspect roulette wheels routinely and monitor the results statistically with software. This close inspection wasn't always the case, leading to one of the greatest gambling stories of all time. (Check out the sidebar "The man who broke the bank at Monte Carlo" for an interesting story about wheel bias.)

Buying into betting systems

The roulette table attracts the largest number of players attempting to apply a betting system. The most prominent progressive betting system is the Martingale system, in which you double your bet after each loss. Another popular one is the Reverse Martingale, in which you cut your bet in half after each win. (Check out Chapter 3 for more about different wagering systems.)

I don't recommend using any progressive betting system, because a streak of four or five bad spins can cripple your bankroll in less than ten minutes.

Despite all the systems advertised for sale, no magic bullet can help you beat a roulette wheel. Books on roulette systems are scams to separate you from your money. Why does someone want to share her amazing supersecret strategy with you? If you'd written such a system, wouldn't you prefer to just make a quick fortune, buy a small island, and retire? So beware of roulette *pros*. They make money by selling books, not by divulging a consistently winning roulette system.

Chapter 10

Not Just For High Rollers: Baccarat

In This Chapter

▶ Understanding the basics of baccarat

▶ Getting a feel for formal and minibaccarat

▶ Playing step by step

▶ Staying away from time-wasting strategies

*T*he camera pans through a luxurious casino in London and then zooms in on two high rollers at the chemin de fer table (a European version of baccarat). A gorgeously dressed woman turns to the dapper-looking gentleman in a tuxedo and says, "I admire your luck, Mr. . . . ." "Bond," he replies as he coolly lights his cigarette, "James Bond."

1962 was the first time the viewing public saw Sean Connery as Ian Fleming's secret agent in *Dr. No,* and, even today, people still know baccarat as James Bond's game. With all its mystique and opulence, baccarat has become *the* game for millionaires, princes, celebrities, and, of course, those in the espionage business.

If you haven't tried baccarat, I can guess why: You think that because you're not a millionaire, royalty, a movie star, or a spy, you don't deserve entree into the glamorous game. The tuxedoed dealers, the chandeliers, and the thick, red-velvet ropes that seem to warn "Commoners, keep out" can intimidate many a player.

Don't be cowed, though. The formality is just for show, and behind its elegant veneer, the game itself is surprisingly easy to play — and offers some of the best odds in the casino. Baccarat isn't so much a game of skill as a game of luck. Playing baccarat is sort of like betting the red or the black on a roulette wheel or hitting the *spin* button on a slot machine — except that if you bet evenly and consistently, your bankroll lasts much, much longer.

In this chapter, I coach you through the game of baccarat and explain just how you can bet evenly and consistently. I identify the two most common versions of baccarat, explain the odds, and offer plenty of tips to help you convince everyone at the table that you're as suave and sophisticated a player as the world's most beloved secret agent.

Counting Down the Baccarat Basics

Baccarat is a simple card game: In the regular version of baccarat (also called *formal, traditional,* or *big baccarat*), the *croupier,* or dealer, deals only two hands, no matter how many players are seated at the table — and as many as 14 can play. One hand is the *player's hand,* and the other is the *banker's hand.* The object of the game is to bet on which of the two hands will come closest to a total of 9 points, also called a *natural* (a total of 8 points is also a natural, but it loses to 9). Players make all bets before the croupier deals the cards, and unlike blackjack, you can't make additional bets, such as doubling down, splitting, and so on. You have only three bets to choose from in baccarat. You can bet on

- ✔ **The player's hand:** A winning bet on the player's hand pays *even money* (1 to 1). So a winning bet of $10 would receive another $10.

- ✔ **The banker's hand:** A win on the banker's hand also pays even money, *minus* a 5 percent commission (the casino charges a commission on this bet because the banker's hand has a better mathematical chance of winning, so the 5 percent commission helps even up the odds between the two bets, although even with the added commission, the banker's hand is still the best of the two bets). The dealer keeps track of these commissions (they aren't actually taken from each bet) and settles up either at the end of the shoe or when you're ready to leave. So a winning bet of $10 would actually end up netting only $9.50. However the croupier only charges this 5 percent commission on winning bets.

- ✔ **A tie:** A winning wager on the tie bet pays 8 to 1.

The tie bet isn't a smart bet because the house has more than a 14 percent advantage (meaning the casino wins approximately $14 for every $100 you bet), and one that sober people shouldn't even *think* about making. However, at some clubs the house pays 9 to 1 on tie bets, which reduces the edge to less than 5 percent, but it's still not a wise bet.

Both hands start with just two cards, and depending on the starting total, the banker or player hand sometimes draws one more card. Whichever hand comes closest to nine wins. Because 9 is the highest score, any amount of 10 or more automatically subtracts ten points; ten is actually worth 0, 11 is 1, 12 is 2, and so on. After the total reaches 10 or more, simply drop the first digit, and that's the score of the hand. That's actually a pretty cool feature — ensuring that you can't bust out like in blackjack.

Can you say "baccarat"?

Pronouncing the name of the game may just be one of the most difficult things about baccarat. But you don't need to speak a foreign language to play this game. The name is simple to say. Don't pronounce the "t" at the end, and let it roll off your tongue; just say *bah*-cah-rah and not back-uh-rat.

The history of the game is a little unclear. Some think baccarat evolved from Tarot cards or the

French game of vingt-et-un (a forerunner of blackjack). Whatever its roots, baccarat spread from Italy to France to Great Britain between the 15th and 19th centuries. Its appearance in the New World is far more recent; it has only been a staple of American casinos for the last 40 years.

Remembering the following pointers about baccarat basics can improve your chances of winning:

- ✔ Two hands are dealt — the player's hand and the banker's hand.
- ✔ Each hand starts with two cards.
- ✔ Whichever hand has the closest to a total of 9 wins.
- ✔ Each *pip card* (cards 2 through 9) is worth its face value; the 2 equals two points, the 5 equals five points, and so forth.
- ✔ Aces count as one point.
- ✔ Tens and royals (kings, queens, and jacks) are worth nothing. In fact, the name of the game is similar to the Italian word *baccara,* meaning *zero.*
- ✔ Suits (clubs, spades, diamonds, and hearts) are meaningless.

With the exception of blackjack and certain bets in craps, baccarat is one of the best table games to play in a casino. The house edge on the player's hand is 1.24 percent and 1.06 percent on the banker's hand!

Of course, more nuances distinguish the novice players from the pros in baccarat. When you step foot in a casino and decide to try baccarat, you need to know that you can play two types of baccarat in most casinos in the United States: formal baccarat, also referred to as *traditional* or *classic* baccarat, and minibaccarat. Although both games follow the same set of rules, each has its notable distinctions. The following sections explain the main differences.

Formal baccarat: High stakes, high rollers

Many high rollers are more interested in testing their luck than exercising their math skills. So baccarat is often the high-stakes game of choice for the wealthiest gamblers. Minimum bets vary greatly from club to club, but posted maximums are typically $2,000 to $4,000. However, the larger casinos often extend higher limits to premium players, and the maximum bet can reach six figures — depending on the high roller's credit line and how much risk the casino is willing to take.

Playing in a room apart

In the biggest games, you find a cast of characters that could populate the *Dr. No* film set — and their wagers reflect their glittering diamonds and gold cigarette cases. Because of the large amounts of money bet on baccarat, the game is sometimes played in an area that's private (open only to premium players or VIPs) and tucked away from the noise and crowds of the casino. This seclusion also allows the casino to provide a measure of security for its high rollers. Sometimes millions of dollars change hands each night at the high-stakes baccarat tables in the biggest casinos.

Setting a table for 14

Baccarat's upscale clientele isn't the only aspect that sets it apart. Play takes place on a large table that seats from 1 to 14 players, as Figure 10-1 shows. (You may notice the absence of seat 13 in this illustration; most casinos skip that unlucky number at their tables.)

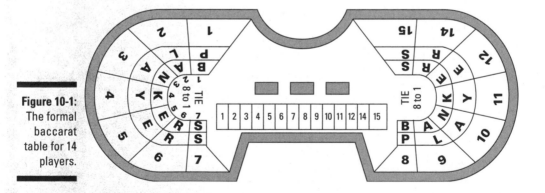

Figure 10-1: The formal baccarat table for 14 players.

Dressing to the nines

Because of the elegance of baccarat, most players honor its tradition and dress accordingly. Of course, the level of dress varies from casino to casino and is becoming less formal, but you're safe to assume that baccarat is the place to wear that long-neglected tuxedo or parade that sparkling evening gown.

A whale of a win

Baccarat is very profitable for casinos, although the slim house edge (see Chapter 3 for more on house edge) combined with big bets may seriously affect the earnings of publicly traded gaming companies if a few *whales* — extremely wealthy gamblers who risk, lose, and win in the millions — have a hot streak at the tables.

The heavyweight of baccarat, Aussie billionaire tycoon Kerry Packer, damaged the bottom line of the quarterly financial report at the MGM casino in 1997 by winning $20 million over several days of play. Giddy over his big win, Packer, *the* whale among whales and one of the greatest bettors of all time, tipped one cocktail server a house (he paid off her mortgage).

Dealing and calling

Three croupiers serve the formal or regular baccarat table. The caller, one of the three croupiers, handles the game and announces the card totals and the winning hand. He may also use an elongated paddle to move cards and chips around the table. The two others stand on either side of the caller and pay off winning bets, collect losing bets, and post commissions (on bank hands).

Banking on the house

Most casinos use an eight-deck shoe to deal the cards in regular baccarat games. And you and other players are part of that ritual! Every player gets a turn at handling the shoe and acting as the banker or dealer. You continue to deal as long as the banker's hand is winning; when the banker finally loses, a different player deals the cards.

You're the banker in name only, because dealing offers you no additional risk or advantage; it just makes the game more sociable. You can choose to participate in the ritual or decline and pass the shoe to the next player.

When you're acting as the banker, you're expected — but not required — to bet on the house (banker's hand). If you'd rather bet on the player's hand, custom dictates that you allow the shoe to pass to the next player. But no matter which hand you bet on, you must be involved and have a wager for the upcoming hand (if you want to deal).

Minibaccarat: Less glitz, lower stakes

Is your tuxedo at the cleaners? Or is your betting bankroll a little low these days? If the formality and high stakes of the regular baccarat table isn't to your taste, then minibaccarat may be the game for you. With lower minimum bets ($2 to $5), this condensed version gives low rollers or the uninitiated a taste of baccarat. It also offers the same low-house advantage of regular baccarat.

Shills: Catching flies with honey

Baccarat is one of the few games where casinos employ *shills*. Shills are people (usually attractive, well-dressed women) the casino pays to sit and play at the table. Although they typically make small bets (with house money),

their presence adds greatly to the ambiance of the baccarat tables. Shills are also a great inducement to lure single men to the table — and get them to bet more and longer than they normally would.

Distinguishing differences

Minibaccarat follows the same rules as its upscale cousin, formal baccarat. The following are the main features that distinguish minibaccarat from regular baccarat:

- ✔ Play takes place on a smaller, semicircular table with places for only seven players, but just like regular baccarat, the game can begin with only one player.

- ✔ Just one *croupier* (called a dealer at this table) is present instead of three.

- ✔ The dealer handles all the cards and deals them face-up.

For specifics on how to play formal baccarat and minibaccarat, check out the next section.

Relaxing at minibac

In most casinos, you find the minibaccarat, or minibac, tables nestled in with the blackjack tables. And picking up on the relaxed and informal tone won't take you long. You can feel right at home at minibaccarat even if you're dressed in shorts and flip-flops. Figure 10-2 shows you what a typical minibaccarat table looks like.

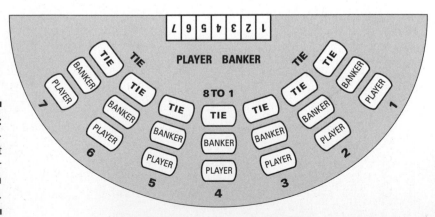

Figure 10-2: The minibaccarat table for seven players.

When playing minibac — or formal baccarat, for that matter — tipping the croupier is perfectly acceptable. Just place a bet for the dealer as you do at other table games.

Stepping into Baccarat

Whether you play minibaccarat or decide to dust off your evening wear and head for a high-stakes formal game, don't worry about any pressure. Baccarat is a no-brainer. But in case you're nervous and need to build your comfort level, the following section walks you through a game one step at a time.

Positioning yourself to play

Feel free to sit in any open seat at the table — your position won't help or hinder your game in any way, nor does it matter how many people are playing. Then observe the unique aspects that distinguish a baccarat table (formal and minibaccarat) from any other gaming surface:

- ✔ **A number outlined on the felt before each player.** The numbers indicate each player's position and run from 1 through 7 in minibaccarat and 1 through 15 in regular baccarat; most casinos skip the unlucky number 13.

- ✔ **Three designated boxes.** These boxes or circles are located on the felt above each player's number. Closest is the *player* bet box. Next is the *banker* bet box, and farthest away is the *tie* bet box. Check out Figures 10-1 and 10-2 to see how the boxes may appear on both a formal and a minibaccarat table.

On the formal table, you also see a boxlike device called the *shoe,* which houses the cards. At the beginning of a game, one of the three croupiers gives the shoe to a player, who acts as the banker and deals the cards from the shoe.

Betting the banker (or the player)

Before the banker deals the cards, the caller asks you to place your bets. So there you are — you haven't received your cards, and yet you must decide the winner: the player or the banker. Or will you have a tie?

As I explain earlier in this chapter in "Counting Down the Baccarat Basics," you're betting on which hand — the player's or the banker's — you think will come closest to nine, the highest possible score, or if you think you'll have a tie. Baccarat is simply a matter of luck. No skill or card counting or complex mathematical formula can beat the house, but knowing that the odds favor the banker's hand can give you an edge.

Betting on the banker's hand offers the best odds (–1.06 percent) because of the simple fact that the banker acts after you each round. Baccarat rules are designed to provide a calculated split between the two hands. Statistical analysis shows the odds of the player's hand winning are about 44.6 percent, the banker's hand winning around 45.8 percent, and ties winning about 9.6 percent. Even after factoring in the house commission (5 percent on winning bets), the banker's hand is still your best bet. For example, if you bet $10 on the banker's hand, you'd push two $5 chips out into the second box or circle in front of you (the one marked Banker or Bankers).

Dealing the hand

If you're playing regular or formal baccarat, as soon as the caller announces, "No more bets," the player with the shoe (known as the banker) deals out four cards. If you're the banker, follow these steps:

1. **Deal two cards, sliding one card face-down to the caller for the player's hand and slipping the second face-down under the corner of the shoe for the banker's hand.**

   Repeat this process with the third and fourth cards.

2. **Take the two cards you dealt for the player's hand and place them face-down in front of the player with the largest bet.**

   This player gets the privilege of taking the first peek at these cards and then turns them over. No advantage actually exists to seeing the cards first — just part of the pomp.

3. **Hand the caller the banker's hand when she requests you to do so.**

   Before you receive this request, the caller places the player's hand face-up in the center and announces the value.

   Then the caller places the banker's cards face-up in the center and announces the total.

Le petit is a natural of 8 points; a natural of 9 is *le grande.* If either hand draws a point total of 8 or 9 on the first two cards, the le grande wins. If the hands have equal value, then you have a tie. Either way, the game is over.

When the player or the banker draws a total of 8 or 9, the hand stands, and the round ends. This rule is the *natural rule* and overrides all the other rules.

Drawing for another card

If neither hand has a total of 8 or 9, an additional card may be drawn on one or both hands, depending on the amount in the hand. The rules for drawing are clear-cut. Neither the player's hand nor the banker's hand has discretion but must follow predetermined rules. The following sections explain the rules.

Following the player's rules

To draw an additional card, the banker's hand is dependent on the total of the player's hand — the reason these rules are known as the *player's rules.* For example, the player's hand has two face cards, which equal 0. The banker's hand has a 9 of hearts and a 10 of diamonds, giving it a point value of 9, a natural. The banker's hand wins based on the natural rule, and the game is over. There are no gray areas, no decision making, no folding, no passing, no bluffing. Just the rules.

Don't worry if you can't remember these rules — the caller (and dealer in minibaccarat) directs all the action. Table 10-1 shows the three possibilities.

Table 10-1	Player's Rules
Value of Player's Hand	*What to Do*
8 or 9	Stands on a natural
6 or 7	Stands
0 to 5	Draws a card

The banker's hand follows these same player's rules as long as the player's hand does *not* draw a third card. If the player's hand draws a third card, the situation gets a little more complicated, and the banker's hand must follow special *banker's rules.* The following section explains what happens when the player's hand draws a third card.

Baccarat by any other name

Whether formal or minibaccarat, the game I explore in this chapter is American, or Nevada-style, baccarat. Some also call it *punto banco,* where *punto* means player, and *banco* is the bank.

Another variation of baccarat is *chemin de fer,* played mainly in France. This form of baccarat differs from the American game in that you can often choose whether to take a third card. In this version, the casino has no stake in the game because the players bet among themselves, and the house makes its money from taking a 5 percent commission on winning bank hands.

Adhering to the banker's rules

The banker's rules apply only to the banker's hand, and only in those situations when the player's hand draws a third card. These third-card rules are consistent for all variations of baccarat around the world. Table 10-2 shows the banker's rules.

Table 10-2	Banker's Rules (When the Player's Hand Has Three Cards)
Value of Banker's Two Cards	**Banker's Action**
8 or 9	Stands on a natural
7	Stands according to player's rules
6	Draws if player draws a third card and player's new hand total is 6 or 7
5	Draws if player draws a third card and player's new hand total is 4 through 7
4	Draws if player draws a third card and player's new hand total is 2 through 7
3	Draws if player draws a third card and player's new total is 0 through 9
0, 1, or 2	Draws a card

Neither the player nor the banker will ever have more than three cards in hand, but the goal is simple— whichever hand has the higher total wins.

Knowing when the banker follows the banker's rules

Once again, unless the player draws a third card, the banker must adhere to the player's rules for the two-card total. Only when the player draws a third card do the banker's rules come into play.

You can refer to Table 10-3 as a resource for when the banker draws. In this table, the numbers across the top, zero through nine, represent the player's hand total. The banker must stand or draw, depending on the player's hand point total and the banker's starting two cards.

Table 10-3	When the Banker Can Draw After a Player's Third Card									
Banker's Score	**Player's Total**									
	0	1	2	3	4	5	6	7	8	9
7	S	S	S	S	S	S	S	S	S	S
6	S	S	S	S	S	S	D	D	S	S
5	S	S	S	S	D	D	D	D	S	S
4	S	S	D	D	D	D	D	D	S	S
3	D	D	D	D	D	D	D	D	S	D
2	D	D	D	D	D	D	D	D	D	D
1	D	D	D	D	D	D	D	D	D	D
0	D	D	D	D	D	D	D	D	D	D

S = STAND D = DRAW

Having trouble memorizing all these variations? Don't strain your brain! Remember that as a player you don't have to remember any of these rules — the dealer does all the work.

Avoiding Baccarat Time Wasters

I've said it before, and I'll say it again: Baccarat is a game of luck. I know, I know — if a smart guy like James Bond played it, then it has to require some brains or skill, or at least a good sense of fashion flare, right? The truth is that most of the advice I can give you has more to do with how to increase the enjoyment of your baccarat experience than how to improve your winnings. But consider following these last bits of advice — about what *not* to do.

Wagering on ties

Don't *ever* bet on the hands to tie. Even though the payoff when you win is far better (8 to 1 instead of even money), ties occur only about once every 9½ hands, making the reward not worth the risk (house edge is a whopping 14.36 percent). This bet is a waste of your hard-earned money.

Because a tie hand is a *push* (neither the player nor the banker wins), your bet on either the player or the banker is also a push — and you won't lose any money for that hand.

Note taking and keeping score

Taking notes is a waste of time. Because of superstitious or misinformed players, casinos routinely stock score cards and pencils at baccarat tables for players to keep track of how the hands are running. The past dozen or so hands are no indication of how future hands will play out, so the pencil and paper are more useful for your grocery list.

Counting cards

No successful card-counting system exists for baccarat. Even though some studies have shown that the low cards favor the player's hand and high cards favor the banker's hand, statistically speaking, the margin is so small that card counting really offers no advantage.

Relying on instinct

Some people think they were born under a lucky star. They believe they have the uncanny ability to predict whether a coin lands on heads or tails with accuracy. Or perhaps their instincts at the tables tell them when a hot streak is about to begin . . . or end.

But my opinion on this matter falls into the rational and scientific camp: You have no way to turn negative odds into a positive expectancy game. Although baccarat is definitely one of your best bets because the slow pace (especially in the formal version) and slim house edge combine to make it a good value for you, over the long run, you end up a slight loser despite the amount of mojo you think you have working for you. You may win in the short term, but no amount of guesswork can swing the odds in your favor.

Don't even try to rely on your instinct. Just drink in the pageantry and ambiance of this elegant game and enjoy the ride. And remember: Don't be intimidated by the posh crowd. You have every right to sit down next to the billionaires and try your luck at this historic game.

Chapter 11

Tackling the "Riskier" Table Games

Savvy gamblers wisely warn against the *gimmick* games. That's good advice, but how exactly do you tell which tables have the highest risk? These tables usually don't have neon lights above them flashing "Welcome to everyone who wants to lose money!" This chapter helps you to decide to sit down and play or keep walking.

Several new games offer an easy way for you to try a table game without risking intimidation by card sharks. A few examples of these new offerings are Caribbean Stud poker, Let It Ride, and Three Card poker.

I can't sugarcoat the news: The odds of these games are *not* in your favor. They all come with a hefty house edge (see Chapter 3 for more on house edge). Although several of the new games are fun and popular, my advice is to stick with the time-tested table games, such as craps (see Chapter 8) and blackjack (see Chapter 7), if you want any chance at all of walking away with some winnings.

In this chapter, I examine some of these riskier casino games and provide a few secret dos and don'ts to help you if you decide to try them.

Cruising for Caribbean Stud Poker

Starting out as a hot draw aboard cruise ships, Caribbean Stud poker has caught on in casinos around the world. Gamblers love Caribbean Stud poker because it's simple to play, incorporates elements of regular poker, and has a *progressive jackpot* that can reach $100,000 or more. (A progressive jackpot is one that continues to increase until somebody hits the jackpot.)

When playing Caribbean Stud poker, the key objective is to beat the dealer's five-card hand with your five cards — you play against the dealer only, not the other players. The winning hands are the same as in poker (check out Chapter 6 for the specifics on poker), but this game exhibits some unique quirks that seem to charm its growing following.

Playing the game: An overview

Up to seven players can sit in on this game, which you play at an oval-shaped table similar to that of blackjack (see Figure 11-1). Even though the term *poker* is used for this game (and also for Pai Gow poker and Three-Card poker), all the games in this chapter are located in the same pit with black-jack and craps, rather than in the poker rooms. The following step-by-step overview can help you understand the game's basics:

1. **You place the required *ante* bet, or wager, in the designated area in front of you.**

   The minimum bet is typically $5.

2. **You may opt to deposit a $1 bet in the progressive jackpot, a slot in front of you. (See "Betting progressively" later in this chapter.)**

3. **The dealer provides you and each player with five cards, face-down, from the automatic shuffler.**

4. **The dealer places his cards, four face-down and one face-up.**

5. **You pick up your cards and evaluate your hand and the dealer's upcard.**

6. **You choose to *fold* (withdraw from the hand) or *call* (continue playing).**

   If you fold, you lose your ante and progressive bet.

   If you call, you place a bet in the designated area in front of you. You must bet twice the amount of the ante bet.

7. **The dealer turns over his four remaining cards.**

8. **The house pays all remaining players *even money* (1 to 1) on their ante if the dealer's hand doesn't qualify.**

   The dealer's hand doesn't qualify if his hand doesn't contain an ace-king or higher (see the following section, "Qualifying the dealer's hand").

9. **If the dealer's hand qualifies, you compare your hand to the dealer's hand.**

10. **If your hand is higher than the dealer's hand, you win on both the ante (even money) and bet (payout dependent on value of winning hand).**

11. **If your hand is lower than the dealer's hand, you lose both bets.**

12. **If your hand ties with the dealer's hand, then you win nothing.**

For example, if your two pair beats a dealer's qualifying hand, you win $5 on your $5 ante (even money) and $20 on your $10 call bet (2 to 1). You originally wagered $15 and ended up pulling $40 back for a profit of $25.

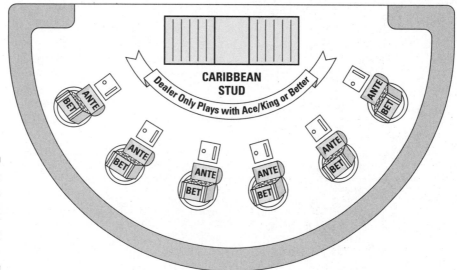

Figure 11-1:
The
Caribbean
Stud poker
table for six
players.

Caribbean Stud poker really is a straightforward game — that's part of its allure. However, I still want to flesh out a few of the terms that may help you if you decide to play this game. The following sections explain a few of the important concepts you may encounter when playing Caribbean Stud poker.

Calling all poker studs

In Caribbean Stud poker, you can't draw more cards, so you must play the hand you're dealt. As a general rule, call with any hand that contains either a pair or a hand of ace-king-jack or better.

If you think your hand has a chance of beating the dealer's hand, call by placing a wager in the bet box that equals twice the amount of the ante bet. For example, if you bet $5, which is normally the table minimum, you must place a $10 bet to call, making your bet total $15.

Remember to keep it simple: If you don't have at least an ace-king-jack, then fold 'em and hope for better cards on the next hand.

Qualifying the dealer's hand

In order for you to beat the dealer and win, the dealer's hand must first qualify by containing an ace-king or higher, such as any pair, straights, flushes, and straight flushes. This is determined after the dealer turns over his four down cards. If the dealer doesn't qualify with at least an ace-king or higher, the house pays even money to you and all other players who are still active for their ante, but your call bet is a *push,* or a tie, neither winning nor losing, and that bet is returned to you.

Betting progressively

The ante is a required wager, but in Caribbean Stud poker you also have the option to place a $1 progressive bet in the drop slot on the table. After you place all bets, the dealer pushes a button that drops the progressive bets into a collection box, where they're added to a running total. At the table, a red light turns on, indicating which players are eligible for the jackpot (anyone who made the bet). Table 11-1 shows how the progressive jackpot generally pays out (the exact amounts vary by casino).

Table 11-1	Caribbean Stud Poker Progressive Jackpot Payout
Hand	*Payout*
Flush	$100
Full house	$100
Four of a kind	$500
Straight flush	10 percent of the jackpot total
Royal flush	Entire progressive jackpot

Although those huge payoffs are enticing, keep in mind that the house edge can be a whopping 20 percent. (Caribbean Stud translation: Good luck, *mon!*) So if you want to try the progressive jackpot once or twice just for the fun of it, go for it. Just don't waste too much money on it.

Assessing your odds

So what's the likelihood that you'll be a winner at Caribbean Stud poker? The house has an advantage of 5.2 percent, making it one of the worst games in the casino. And because of the *qualifying* criterion for the dealer, the game can be extremely frustrating — especially when you finally get that monster hand and the dealer's hand doesn't qualify. In that case, even if you hold a cool-looking flush, you get no bonus payout. You win even money only on the ante and push on the bet, so be sure and carry plenty of aspirin with you.

Betting in Circles with Let It Ride

Shuffle Master, Inc. invented Let It Ride poker, basing it on Five-Card Stud poker. This invention was part of a shrewd marketing ploy designed to draw slot players to table games, which, of course, created more demand for Shuffle Master products — automatic card shufflers and table games.

At first glance, the game looks complex because of its three betting circles. But it's actually uncomplicated because you aren't competing against the other players or even the dealer. In fact, this game is one where you're *hoping* the dealer has an excellent hand!

Playing the game: An overview

You play Let It Ride on a blackjack-style table with a standard 52-card deck (see Figure 11-2). The object of Let It Ride is to make a hand containing a pair of 10s or better and qualify for one of the posted payouts. If your hand is weak, you have the ability to remove up to two of the three bets as the game progresses or to keep your bet in place and *let it ride*.

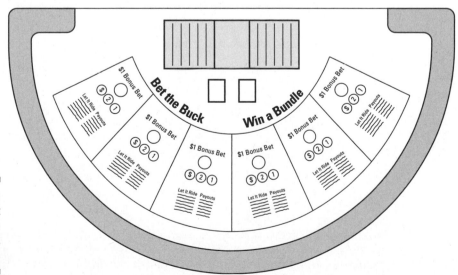

Figure 11-2:
The Let It Ride table for six players.

The cards are ranked according to the normal rules of poker, and suits count toward flushes. You receive three starting cards and use the two face-up community cards to make a five-card poker hand. The higher the value of your hand, the more you win.

Mastering the fundamentals of Let It Ride is easy. The following list walks you through a typical game.

1. **You make three equal bets in the circles indicated as *1*, *2*, and *$* on the table in front of you before the dealer deals the cards.**

   The minimum bet is typically $5.

2. **You may opt to place a $1 side bet for a bonus payout.**

3. **The dealer deals three cards face-down to every player.**

4. **The dealer places two *community cards* (used by everyone at the table for their hands) face-down in front of herself.**

5. **You examine your hand and evaluate whether the two community cards (unknown at this point) added to your three cards may result in a good poker hand.**

6. **You *let it ride* if you hold a payout-worthy hand (two 10s or a better pair) — or the strong potential for a worthy hand — keeping your bet in Circle 1 by placing your cards under that circle.**

7. **If your hand is weak, you scratch your cards on the table, indicating you wants to take back your bet from Circle 1.**

   Touching your chips after they're in the betting box is a table taboo, so always wait for the dealer to push your money back to you.

8. **The dealer turns over the first of the two community cards.**

9. **You again decide whether to take back your bet in Circle 2 or *let it ride* based on how the first community card fits into your three-card hand.**

   You aren't allowed to look at other players' cards, nor should they be peeking at yours. The reason? The card you need (to make your straight flush, for example) may be in the hand of the guy next to you, and it can affect your betting — or his. Not surprisingly, the house is nervous about you getting an extra edge from this practice and possibly taking back your bet after you see other players' cards.

10. **The dealer turns over the second of the community cards and then pays out or collects based on the value of the players' hands.**

The challenge is anticipating whether your starting hand of three cards is solid enough to keep your bets in play or take them back. I offer you some pointers later in the section "Implementing some simplified strategy." The best-case starting scenario is that you hold a pair of 10s or better. After the deal, you just tuck your cards under the $ Circle, which tells the dealer that you're letting all three bets ride and won't be making any more decisions. But if your hand is on the road to nowhere — after the deal or the turning over of the first community card — you scratch, and the dealer pushes back your chips from that circle.

A common mistake beginning players make is thinking they can take their second bet back only if they forfeited their first bet. But your decision on the second bet is totally independent of your first bet. Even if you let your first bet ride, you can still take down the second bet or vice versa.

Understanding the payout

The basis of Let It Ride is similar to Caribbean Stud poker or video poker. The premium hands (such as a royal flush) receive the biggest payoffs. A standard payout schedule (check out Table 11-2) determines your winnings.

Table 11-2	A Typical Pay Table for Let it Ride
Hand	*Payout*
Royal flush	1,000 to 1
Straight flush	200 to 1
Four of a kind	50 to 1
Full house	11 to 1
Flush	8 to 1
Straight	5 to 1
Three of a kind	3 to 1
Two pairs	2 to 1
A pair of 10s or better	1 to 1

Now that you know the rules and the typical payout for Let It Ride, assume that you have an ace of clubs, a king of diamonds, and a 4 of hearts. This is a marginal hand, and you correctly decide to give up your first bet of $10. Now the dealer turns over the first of the two community cards —another ace. Suddenly your hand becomes an automatic winner. So you let your second bet ride. The dealer reveals the last community card, a king. You start whistling "Happy days are here again" as the dealer turns over your hand.

Because you end up with two pair, your payout is 2 to 1 on all your remaining bets — you can't collect from Circle 1 because you forfeited that bet. The good news is that you receive $20 on each of your remaining two bets, yielding a profit of $30 ($40 minus the losing $10 bet).

Implementing some simplified strategy

Let It Ride has a house edge (3.5 percent) that is almost ten times worse than blackjack, but you can still cut your losses with a little strategy. The smartest tactic is to determine whether your cards are good enough to let it ride or whether the hand contains only junk and you need to pull back your bets and live to fight another day.

The buck stops at the third circle; you can never pull back the bet in the $ Circle, no matter how bad your hand is.

On the first bet, the only times to *let it ride* are when the three cards you hold are

- ✔ Any paying hand (10s or better)
- ✔ Any three cards to a royal flush
- ✔ Three suited cards in a row, except 2-3-4 and ace-2-3
- ✔ Three to a straight flush (containing a gap) with one high card of 10 or greater
- ✔ Three to a straight flush (containing two gaps) with two cards of 10 or greater

On the second bet, the only times to *let it ride* are when the four cards you hold are

- ✔ Any paying hand (10s or better)
- ✔ Any 4 to a royal flush, straight flush, or flush
- ✔ Any 4 to an outside straight
- ✔ Any 4 to an inside straight with four high cards (10 or higher)

Of course, you can win even if your cards stink — the last community card may pair up and pay the whole table. But that type of wishful thinking is what pays the light bill at most casinos. You're far better off folding your weak hands and being patient enough to wait for better starting cards.

Avoiding a side bet

The potentially huge payout of the game's $1 side bet (see Table 11-3), usually referred to as a *bonus bet,* seduces many players. The optimal strategy for participating in the side-bet option is simple: Don't. However, you can try it once just for fun and hope that you get lucky with the high payouts. But don't waste too much time or money, because the side bet has a house edge in excess of 25 percent — definitely not good for your pocketbook.

Table 11-3	Let It Ride Pay Table for $1 Side Bet
Hand	*Payout*
Royal flush	$20,000
Straight flush	$2,000
Four of a kind	$400
Full house	$200
Flush	$50
Straight	$25
Three of a kind	$5

Two pair or less doesn't qualify for a bonus. These payout amounts aren't standard and may vary from casino to casino.

Picking Up on Pai Gow Poker

Pai Gow poker is a hybrid of Seven-Card Stud and a Chinese dominos game. (The Chinese call it *Heavenly Dominos*). That odd combination of celestial paradise with gaming tiles may sound confusing, even to Confucius. But if you're familiar with poker hands, you'll pick up the gist of Pai Gow quickly (pronounced *pie now*), especially because the game is played at an easy, relaxing pace.

What else distinguishes this game? You turn a seven-card hand into two poker hands, you play against the dealer, and you can employ strategy to improve your chances of winning. Also, some casinos allow you to participate as the *banker* (the house), which increases your winning percentage dramatically.

Playing the game: An overview

You play Pai Gow with a standard 52-card deck plus a joker on an oval table similar to a blackjack table, with spots for six players and the dealer (check out Figure 11-3).

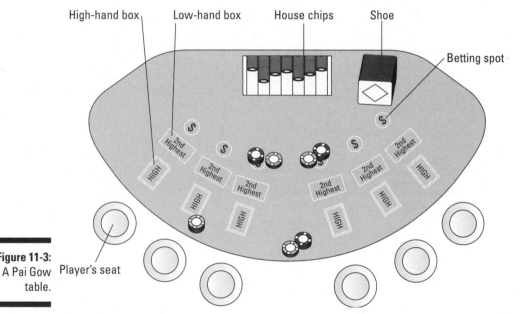

High-hand box   Low-hand box   House chips   Shoe

Betting spot

Figure 11-3:
A Pai Gow   Player's seat
table.

At some casinos (but not all), the role of banker rotates from player to player. This means each player (and the dealer) takes a turn at being the banker for that hand. If you want to be the banker, you have to have enough money to cover the bets of all the other players at your table. But you can decline this option, in which case the dealer takes your turn as banker for that hand. The reason that you may pass on being the banker is because of the additional financial risk involved.

A roll of the dice by the dealer determines the first player dealt. (Or, more commonly today, a device at the table randomly generates all table positions from one to seven to determine the first player.) The following overview of the game walks you through its typical progression:

1. **You place a wager — most casinos have low minimums— in the betting circle in front of you before the dealer deals the cards.**

2. **The dealer hands out seven sets of seven cards, regardless of whether the table is full.**

3. **The dealer ceremoniously removes the cards from the vacant places after she deals the cards.**

   (Hey, I know it sounds odd, but why buck tradition?)

4. **The dealer places a white plastic marker, called a *chung*, in front of the player acting as banker.**

   The dealer is part of the rotation when the casino acts as the banker.

5. **You *set* your cards, splitting the seven cards into two poker hands: a five-card hand (called the *high* or *back hand*), and a two-card hand (called the *low*, *front*, or *second-highest hand.*)**

   (See the following section, "Setting the hand," for more.)

6. **You place your two hands face-down in the designated areas on the table, marked *highest* and *second-highest*.**

   After placing your cards in the boxes in front of you, you aren't allowed to touch them again.

7. **The dealer turns over her cards and sets them into two hands, high and low.**

8. **The dealer turns every player's hands over, one by one, and compares them to the banker's two hands (high versus high and low versus low).**

9. **If both of your hands beat the banker's hands (in most cases the banker and the dealer are synonymous terms), you win even-money minus a 5 percent commission.**

10. **If you win one hand and lose the other (it doesn't matter which one), you have a *push* and win nothing, which happens 40 percent of the time.**

11. **If one of your hands is the same as the banker's, a *copy* occurs and the house wins that specific hand (no ties).**

Setting the hand

To win at Pai Gow, your high hands and low hands must have a higher poker ranking than the banker's high and low hands. (To review poker hand rankings, see Chapter 6.) So setting your hands with some skill is critical. (Remember that you don't get any second chances — as soon as you place your hand in the appropriate box, you can't change it.) When you first pick up your seven cards, get into the habit of looking for a flush or a straight first rather than pairs. However, suits and straights don't count for the two-card, or low, hand.

Be careful when setting your cards because the two-card hand can't have a higher value than the five-card one. If the two-card hand does, you automatically *foul* and lose the bet. For example, if you place two aces in the low hand and your high hand consists of a smaller pair (such as two jacks), the hand is disqualified.

Playing with the joker

Remember that the Pai Gow deck includes the joker, which changes the ranking of the hands. Five aces is the best hand, and a *wheel* (ace-2-3-4-5) is the second-highest straight. But you can only use a joker as an ace or as a wild card to complete a flush, straight, or straight flush.

Calculating your odds

Aside from Let It Ride, Pai Gow poker is the only other game in this chapter that allows you to exercise some degree of skill. If you play correct basic strategy, you can trim the house edge down from 2.84 percent to 2.54 percent. (Check out the next section for trimming the house edge.)

Implementing some strategy

The best opportunity for taming the dragon in Pai Gow poker is to be the banker because the banker wins all copies. But not all casinos allow you to take a shot at being the banker. If that isn't possible, keep these few tips in mind (you can find a more complete strategy at www.wizardofodds.com).

- ✔ If you have no pair, put the highest card in the back hand and the next two highest in the front hand.
- ✔ If you have one pair, place the pair in the back hand and the next two highest cards in the front hand.
- ✔ If you have two pair, most of the time you should split them and put the lowest pair in the front hand.
- ✔ If you have three pair, always place the highest-ranking pair in the front hand and the two lower pairs in the back hand.

One of the best ways to learn Pai Gow poker, as well as Caribbean Stud and Let It Ride, is to go to www.bodog.com/blackwood. At this site you can practice for free and improve your play, and I highly recommend figuring out these games on your computer before taking them on in a casino with a loaded wallet.

Tripling Your Fun with Three Card Poker

Derek Webb, a professional poker player from England, invented Three Card poker in 1995. He got the idea from the British game, *brag*, and the American game, *guts*, both ancestors of poker. The game was an immediate hit with players because of its simplicity and attractive payouts.

You play this quick-paced poker variation, which is actually two games in one, with just three cards. You may play against the dealer, or you can bet that your hand will be a pair or better. Similar to Caribbean Stud poker, Three Card poker features three wagering circles at each player position: ante, play, and an optional betting circle called *pair plus*.

Playing the game: An overview

You play Three Card poker with a standard 52-card deck on a blackjack-style table with up to seven players. The outlines of three betting boxes appear on the table in front of each other player. The first box is marked *Play*, the middle *Ante*, and the top one *Pair Plus* (a bet on whether you will have a pair or better). (See Figure 11-4 for an example of a Three Card poker table.)

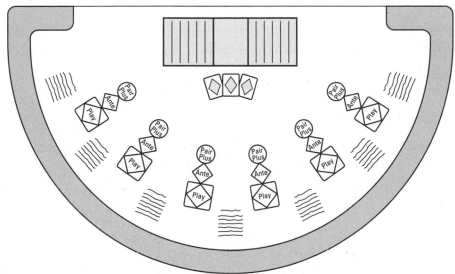

Figure 11-4:
The Three Card poker table for six players.

As I mention above, Three Card poker is actually two games in one. The Ante and Play circles are for betting that your hand will beat the dealer's hand, while the Pair Plus circle is for betting on whether your hand will be a higher pair (you win or lose regardless of the dealer's hand). The following list walks you through a typical game:

1. **Before the cards are dealt, you bet by placing chips in the Ante spot or the Pair Plus circle.**

   You may place bets in both spots, and the amounts don't have to be the same.

2. **The dealer deals all players (including herself) three cards face-down.**

3. **You evaluate the strength of your hand and choose to *fold* (withdraw from the game — at which point you lose your ante bet) or stay in the game and place another bet equal to your ante in the Play circle.**

4. **The dealer turns over her cards as well as the cards of all players still active (those who didn't fold).**

5. **If the dealer's hand doesn't qualify (doesn't have a queen high or better), the house pays all remaining players even money on their ante bets.**

   However, the play bet is treated as a push, and that bet is returned to the players.

6. **If her hand qualifies (does contain a queen or higher, including pairs, straights, flushes, and so on), the dealer compares the rank of her hand to your hand.**

7. **If your hand beats the dealer's hand, you win even-money for both the ante and the play bet.**

8. **If the dealer's hand beats your hand, you lose both your ante and play bets.**

9. **If you have a straight, three of a kind, or a straight flush, you earn a bonus on your ante bet — no matter what the dealer's hand shows.**

   Bonus payouts are typically 1 to 1 for a straight, 4 to 1 for three of a kind, and 5 to 1 for a straight flush.

10. **The dealer settles the Pair Plus bet.**

    If you don't have a pair or higher, you lose your bet in that circle. But if you do have a pair or higher, the dealer pays you according to the pay schedule in the next section.

Tallying up your pair-plus payouts

To win in Pair Plus, the payout depends on the rank of your three-card hand, which must have at least a pair or better (*Pair Plus*) in order to win. You're not playing against the dealer in this wager, so this bet is simple to make for habitual slot players who want to step across the aisle and try a *hands off* table game. The outcomes and payoffs for the hands are as follows:

- A pair pays 1 to 1.
- A flush pays 4 to 1.
- A straight pays 6 to 1.
- Three of a kind pays 30 to 1.
- A straight flush pays 40 to 1.

For the ante and play bets, my only strategy recommendation is that you have a hand of queen-6-4 or better to continue to play. Otherwise, fold and wait for greener pastures.

No strategy is possible in Pair Plus, so it's a nice game if you have a propensity to pound down drinks while you gamble.

Ranking Three Card poker

In Three Card poker, the hands are ranked according to the highest card in each hand, then the second highest, and then the third highest. For example, a hand of queen-8-7 beats queen-8-6. The following list shows the hand rankings for Three Card poker from highest to lowest:

✔ Straight flush

✔ Three of a kind

✔ Straight

✔ Flush

✔ Pair

✔ High card

Reckoning your odds

The house advantage on the Pair Plus bet is 2.3 percent and 3.4 percent on the ante wager. Although these odds still aren't as good as those of blackjack (typically .5 percent or less — see Chapter 7), or baccarat (1.06 percent — check out Chapter 10), they're better than plenty of other games in the casino.

Avoiding the Riskiest Table Games

Casino gambling is all about taking risks. But you need to know the difference between taking a calculated risk and flushing your money down the toilet. Based on my experience, I think the following five games should come with the label "Warning: This game may be hazardous to your wealth." With their astronomical house advantage and the overall lack of skill or strategy they require, these games are definitely unhealthy for your bank account. If you're curious, try them out for a few minutes. Otherwise, stay away from them unless you're ready to donate to the casino's bottom line.

✔ **Big Six Wheel:** Some people know this game as the *Wheel of Fortune* or *Money Wheel*. But if you spend any time losing money at Big Six Wheel, I'm sure you'll come up with a more colorful name for this carnival contraption. The large, upright wheel sports 54 spaces designating six possible bets ($1, $2, $5, $10, $20) and two other slots (the joker and the casino's logo, each for $40). The lower denominations have more slots on the wheel, while the higher payouts have fewer chances to win. You make wagers while sitting at a table. The dealer spins the wheel. When it stops, the flap at the top rests in one slot. If you bet on that symbol, you win.

Are you wondering about strategy? You don't need no stinkin' strategy. You employ no skill and master no rules. Just place a bet before the wheel spins and start praying — er, I mean *playing*.

The casino edge *starts* at 11 percent on the $1 spot and increases substantially, all the way up to 24 percent on the joker and logo. This game clearly has some of the worst odds in the entire casino.

✔ **Red Dog:** Red Dog (also known as *Acey Deucy*) is a rapidly disappearing card game. The object is to bet on whether a third card to be drawn will fall between the values of the first two community cards already dealt. You start by betting an ante, and the correct strategy is to raise the ante if the spread is seven or more (for example, when the first two cards are 2 and 9). This tactic lowers the house edge to less than 4 percent, but those odds are still bad; the best strategy is to pass on this game.

✔ **Sic-Bo:** Sic-Bo is the ancient Chinese game of dice that requires no strategy and carries a huge casino advantage. You play it on a table that has a layout of 50 possible bets, with payouts ranging from even-money to as high as 180 to 1. The object is to bet on the specific number or the three-number combination rolled by three dice.

If you can't resist the pull of this game, your best bet is to wager on the *small* or *big* combinations, which pay 1 to 1, giving the house an advantage of 2.78 percent. All other bets are progressively worse, with most falling in the 10 percent to 19 percent range, making Sic-Bo one of the silliest bets in the casino.

✔ **Spanish 21:** Spanish 21 is a confusing game. The game looks like blackjack, smells like blackjack, plays out like blackjack — but it's not really blackjack. The big difference is that all the 10s (but not face cards) are absent from the six-deck shoe. You play with 288 cards instead of 312, so the chances of getting dealt a natural (ace-10) or a 20 (10-10) aren't quite as high.

The unusual rules and options that spice up play may lure you to this game. For example, hitting 21 with six cards pays 2 to 1, and hitting 21 with seven cards pays 3 to 1. And a dealer's natural blackjack doesn't push your natural — you still win 3 to 2. You can also *double down* (double your original bet and receive one more card) on any number of cards and surrender bad hands. (See Chapter 7 for more about these terms.) Spanish blackjack even has a super bonus: If you're lucky enough to have a suited 7-7-7 against the dealer's upcard of 7 and you wager $5, the bonus pays you $1,000.

Spanish 21 is far better than any of the other gimmick games in this section because skillful play can reduce the house edge to less than 1 percent. But that is still far worse than regular blackjack, and the strategy for Spanish 21 is harder to master. So if you want to play 21, I suggest you stick to regular blackjack (check out Chapter 7) and save your Spanish for your next trip to Mexico.

✔ **War:** War is an easy game to play — just your one card against the dealer's one card. Higher rank wins even money, and suits don't matter. If the two hands tie, you wage *war*. You have the option to either surrender and forfeit half your bet or play one more hand (and make an additional bet) to see who wins.

If you win the ensuing battle, the house pays you 2 to 1 on the second bet (but the first bet is a push). If you tie again, the house pays you 3 to 1. A side bet on the tie is available, but avoid it. The only strategy in this game is to always go to war in case of tie hands. The house edge for this popular children's game is at least 2.8 percent and can be much higher for inexperienced players. That edge is stiff enough to put most gamblers on the warpath.

The real cost of playing gimmick games

All of the table games in this chapter have grown in popularity in recent years, particularly Caribbean Stud poker. Unfortunately, that popularity isn't reflective of the games' player profit potential. Each of these games has a negative win expectancy. Here's what your average loss looks like after one long day of play (400 hands of $10 bets):

Game	Odds	Expected Loss
Caribbean Stud poker	5.2 percent	–$208
Let It Ride	3.5 percent	–$140
Pai Gow poker	2.5 percent	–$100
Three Card poker (ante)	3.3 percent	–$132
War	2.8 percent	–$112
Red Dog	3.8 percent	–$152

To put those numbers in perspective, the same amount of play at baccarat yields an average loss of $42, and blackjack sets you back about $20. You don't have to be Einstein to do the math on that comparison.

Part III
Beyond the Tables: Slots, Video Poker, Sports Betting, and More

In this part . . .

In this part, I provide helpful guidelines and optimal playing strategies for slots (Chapter 12) as well as video poker (Chapter 13) and keno and bingo (Chapter 14). Slots are the biggest cash cow for casinos, yet many myths and misconceptions abound about them. I offer practical, no-nonsense advice on which ones to play and, more importantly, which ones to avoid. Furthermore, Chapter 15 shows you how to navigate the complex high-tech sports books in order to place a bet on your favorite team. Chapter 16 gives the rundown on the sport of kings — horse racing.

Chapter 12

Mastering the Machines: Slots

From its Wild West roots in San Francisco, the slot machine has evolved into one of the most diverse and high-tech games in the casino. In fact, slots are now the most popular feature in a casino, enticing players with an endless variety of colors, shapes, types, and styles. Yet, for all their gadgets and gizmos, slot machines are blessedly easy to play. You merely yank the lever or (more often than not) press the button. That's it — and that just may be the reason behind their popularity.

Even though slot machines are cash cows for casinos (generating nearly two-thirds of the revenue in most casinos), they're far and away the most popular game for gamblers. And, although there are several reasons for this appeal, the main one is spelled J-A-C-K-P-O-T! The chance to win life-changing money is the rainbow that draws many eternal optimists back to these machines, trip after trip, push after push (or yank after yank), ever searching for their own pot of gold.

In this chapter, I focus on the most important facts about slots: how to play them and recognize different types, how to understand the odds and stretch your bankroll, and how to take advantage of the comps. After you read this chapter, you'll be ready for the one-armed bandits.

The birth of the slot machine

German immigrant Charles Fey developed and created the first slot machine in San Francisco in the late 1800s. The metal box, which he named *The Liberty Bell,* stood on cast-iron feet and displayed three metal reels through a window.

The first machines took a nickel to play and displayed ten different symbols, creating 1,000 possible combinations. You won a whopping jackpot of ten nickels if you lined up three Liberty Bells (compelling some happy winners to sing *America, the Beautiful*).

Back when Bugsy Siegel laid the foundation for Las Vegas gambling in the 1940s, slot machines were an afterthought, a distraction to keep the wives happy while their husbands played craps or blackjack. Slots were considered *one-armed bandits* because of their poor odds. Now, a generation later, slots have turned the tables on the more popular games, and the widespread appeal of slots drives today's casinos.

Understanding How to Play the Slots

The design of slot machines remained the same in the early years, except for one detail: The reels expanded to 20 symbols, increasing the possible combinations from 1,000 to 8,000. By creating so many more ways to win, this new version stirred up greater excitement and promised a much bigger jackpot.

Although modern machines present several new twists and updates to the original game, the goal for gamblers remains the same: to line up identical symbols in a row. Machines vary: They may have five reels instead of three. They may have multiple paylines. They may have more options than one-coin-a-pop. They may have buttons to push rather than a handle to pull. But the concept hasn't changed — line up a row of identical symbols, up–down, left–right, or diagonal, and call yourself a winner.

Low maintenance and high profit: A casino's dream

Slot machines make the perfect employees. They require no wages, tips, workmen's comp, or insurance benefits. They never call in sick, show up late, or have to leave early. Slot machines are also easy to play, they're available 24/7, and their computerized operating system allows gamblers to pump coins in at a frantic pace — producing a high profit margin for the house. (Now, if only the casinos could build robots to deal at the blackjack tables or cyborg cocktail servers to deliver drinks!)

This section shows you how to play slots and what you need to know about the inner workings of a slot machine. I also cover the all-important payouts and how technology has changed the way you play slots.

Playing the game: Easy as pushing a button

Although hitting a jackpot is the biggest attraction for slot fans, the machines are popular for other reasons. One of the biggest pluses is their simplicity. With most machines, you don't have to master a complicated strategy or decipher some finicky rules. You simply put in your money and watch the reels spin. You could even play blind-folded because the machine automatically pays you on every winner — whether you realize it or not. Figure 12-1 shows you how popular slot machines are.

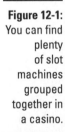

Figure 12-1: You can find plenty of slot machines grouped together in a casino.

© Louie Psihoyos/Corbis

Several buttons on the machine allow you to streamline your playing (translation: drain your wallet faster). Look for the following:

- ✔ **Money slot:** Most machines accept coins or bills. There is usually a slot for the coins and a bill receptor for your paper currency. When you use bills, the machine shows a credit for the amount of cash you inserted.

- ✔ **Bet One:** Press this button when you want to wager just one of your credits.

- ✔ **Bet Max:** This button permits you to play the maximum number of credits that the machine allows per spin (each machine has an established max) and saves you the trouble of hitting the Bet One button several times.

> ✔ **Change:** Push this button when you want to summon a slot attendant.
>
> ✔ **Cash/Credit:** Ready to cash out and move on? Just press here to receive any unused credit.

Dissecting the innards: How slots work

Novice slots players may wonder if there is any strategy to pressing the button or pulling the lever that increases the likelihood of a win. Unfortunately no strategy exists. You can press lightly or forcefully. You can blink three times, click your heels together, or say a little prayer. It makes no difference. After you make your move, the outcome is preordained.

The computerized *Random Number Generator* (RNG) chip determines the outcome of each spin. The RNG is always at work, cycling through millions of random numbers, even when the machine isn't being played. The moment you press the spin button, the generator freezes the current numbers and their corresponding stops on the reels.

Because of RNG technology, nothing can be done to predict or change the outcome. Even if you play on an interactive machine that allows you to make some decisions, slot machines are cold creatures that can't be influenced by anything you do.

On newer machines, your eyes just see a representation of the old-fashioned spinning reels. The RNG chip has predetermined the outcome — the images flashing before you on the machine are just for show.

Each spin is completely independent of any previous results. As its name suggests, the RNG is *random*. There is no pattern or cycle that repeats after it has run its course.

Getting wise to virtual reel-ality

Although the RNG is random, it does allow for some tweaking of individual machines. For example, although the machines *appear to have* only 20 different symbols on each reel, the RNG creates virtual reels that *actually have* many more possibilities. This option creates bigger jackpots, but it also allows casinos to adjust the odds (or payback) for each machine. So, two identical machines can sit side by side, yet their odds for winning can be different.

But don't misunderstand. The casino doesn't change the payouts at will. There is no magic switch that allows an evil slot supervisor behind the green curtain to crank back the odds when the casino is losing. Reprogramming the RNG chips requires a great deal of paperwork and effort, so this adjustment is rare after the machines are on the floor. The manufacturer usually sets the exact payback before shipping the machine to the casino.

Entering the coinless age: Cashout tickets

Coin-operated slot machines are quickly disappearing from casinos as the new paper ticket technology, called *TITO* (ticket-in, ticket-out), takes hold. This change has revived penny and nickel slots because gamblers don't have to carry rolls of coins and a $20 win doesn't require hauling 400 coins to the cashier's cage. (Refer to Figure 12-2 for an example of a payout ticket.)

Figure 12-2: A typical payout ticket is a bar-coded voucher.

Wow Casino   Las   Vegas,   NV
Slot   Id   142411   Floor   Location   042390

CASHOUT   TICKET

SAMPLE

INSERT THIS SIDE UP

INSERT THIS SIDE UP

00-5104-3214-3100-0929

VALIDATION   00-5104-3214-3100-0929
05/14/2006   01:14:05   TICKET # 3007
ZERO DOLLARS AND TEN CENTS

$0.10

TICKET VOID AFTER 30 DAYS.   MACHINE #

Typical cash ticket

TITO also cuts down overhead and employee costs for casinos because they no longer have the hassle of refilling machines with thousands of pounds of coins. Here's another important feature for the casino: Players can spin more reels per hour on a coinless machine because they don't have to stop and feed coins into the slot. The result? Higher profit. Talk about a win-win for the casino!

TITO slot machines accept both cash and machine tickets to start play, so there's no need for a coin hopper (metal bin to catch coins). For psychological effects, however, the machines still provide that irresistible sound of clinking coins when a player hits a jackpot (that lovely *Dink! Dink! Dink!* as if real coins were pouring through the trough).

The ticket also gives you, the player, more flexibility. For example, if you've played six or eight spins on a machine without hitting anything, you can move to another machine by *cashing out* (pressing the cash/credit button). The machine prints a new ticket with your remaining credit balance so you can take it to another machine, even one that uses a different denomination. After you're done playing, redeem your ticket at the cashier's window.

Don't throw away or lose your ticket — make sure you cash it in before you leave. Some tickets are valid for up to six months. Just be sure to turn it in before it expires. Casinos earn hundreds of thousands of dollars a year on the revenue from unclaimed tickets (even though most of them are under $1).

Identifying Differences in Slot Machines

You may have cut your gambling teeth on traditional slot machines, such as *Double Diamonds, Red White & Blue,* and *Blazing 7's,* but the brave new slot world of the 21st century means you no longer need to settle for plain vanilla. Every conceivable flavor, shape, and color is now available to tempt gamblers. Literally hundreds of new designs reflect the public's insatiable appetite for video slot machines, especially those with interactive touch screens. Some machines are so versatile, they let you change the type of game without leaving your seat! Just make sure you check the payout schedules for the winning combinations and for any special quirks that particular game has.

Anyone can play a slot machine — no wonder it's a favorite indoor sport. This section takes a look at the basic types of slots that you may encounter in your friendly neighborhood casino.

Increasing wagers with multipliers

On most machines you're looking for identical symbols to come up on one line (cherry, cherry, and . . . cherry!). On a typical machine, you can play just one credit/coin, or you can play up to five credits, meaning you're *multiplying* — increasing — your wager. However, there is no advantage to betting more credits because the payout is proportional. For example, hitting three cherries may pay $50 if you played one coin, $100 if you played two coins, $150 if you played three coins, $200 for four coins, and $250 for five coins.

A variation is the *bonus multiplier*, which offers a bonus when you play maximum coins and hit the jackpot. For example, for the same three cherries, the bonus multiplier may pay $50 for one coin, $100 for two coins, $150 for three coins, $200 for four coins — but $500 for five coins (twice the normal multiplier). This type of machine encourages players to wager the maximum number of coins, and they have odds similar to those of regular machines. If you play a bonus multiplier, you should always play max coins to take advantage of the bonus.

Zigzagging for multiple paylines

Both traditional reel-spinning slots and newfangled video machines offer *multiple payline* games, which can pay on dozens of different lines. These lines may appear as straight or zigzag patterns on the screen. Each line bet you make — and you can make multiple selections — corresponds to one line on the screen: up, down, or diagonal.

If you want to play just one line, you can still bet one coin, but if the machine displays a winner on one of the lines you *didn't* bet, you don't win. Multiple paylines are very common on lower-denomination machines, such as the penny and nickel machines that are popping up all over the casino floor. (Check out Figure 12-3 for an example of a multiple payline machine.)

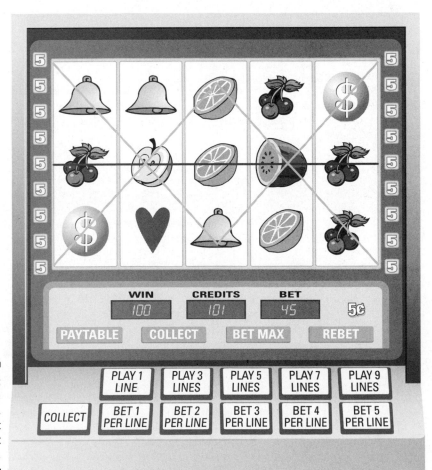

Figure 12-3: The multiline, multibet video slot machine.

Tuning in to theme machines

The hottest trend in slots links the game to popular TV shows (such as *Bewitched, Beverly Hillbillies,* and the *Wheel of Fortune*), traditional board games (such as *Monopoly, Yahtzee,* and *Battleship*), movies, cartoons, and so on. These *theme* machines rely on familiarity and popular branding to entice loyal fans.

But in most cases, I suggest you skip these theme machines, even if you're a big fan of Vanna White or Jed Clampett. The reason is simple: These machines have bad odds. Typically, the casino must agree to share the revenues from any slot connected to a celebrity, show, or cartoon. (You don't expect Vanna to let them use her face for free, do you?) Consequently, the pie has more slices — and smaller paybacks.

Working the progressive slots

The *progressive* slot machines are typically grouped together in a *bank* or a *carousel* with a large jackpot tally spinning feverishly above them. The progressives can be linked to slots in one casino or multiple casinos. (The Megabucks game, for example, is linked to several casinos throughout the state of Nevada.)

The jackpot is based on a small percentage of the money played at each machine in the group. Because progressive slots are linked together on a network, the jackpot grows, little by little, each time a player feeds the beast. The question is: Should you play a regular machine with its paltry little jackpot, or should you gamble at the neon-flashing progressive machine with the shiny sports car spinning on the platform above the slot carousel?

The answer depends on your goals: If modest wins are fine, then you have much better odds of hitting a small jackpot on a regular machine than winning the big jackpot on a progressive machine that has as many as four or five reels and thousands of potential combinations. But some players aren't satisfied with a lot of small wins — they want to go for the glory. *Note:* The odds are long, and the winners are few at the gigantic progressives.

Engaging in interactive machines

The new *interactive* slot machines have become enormously popular with gamblers. Interactive means the player gets to make some decisions (usually done with a touch screen) during the game. However, other than blackjack slot machines, most interactive slot machines have few (if any) choices that allow skill to enter into the equation.

Megabucks hits . . . and misses

Less than a year after the Megabucks progressive slots were introduced, Californian Terry Williams made slot history by winning almost $5 million at Harrah's Casino in Reno on February 1, 1987.

(In case you ever wondered, the large cardboard check that winners struggle to hold up is just for camera time. Most MegaJackpots are paid out in 25 annual installments, with the exception of the Elvis Presley, Party Time, and Slotopoly machines, which are paid in one lump sum. Can you say, "Viva, Las Vegas"?)

On the other end of the spectrum, consider one of the saddest moments in gambling: A player miraculously hit all three symbols on a machine but failed to play the maximum credits needed to win the big jackpot. This life-crushing experience happened to Kirk Tolman on March 14, 2001. Distracted by a friend while playing in Wendover, Nevada, Tolman popped just two coins instead of three into a Megabucks machine. Sure enough, the three reels lined up for the jackpot. Although the 22-year-old won $10,000 for his two-coin play, he lost the chance to collect the $7.96 million prize, just because he was a buck short.

The moral of the story: If you want a jackpot, play max credits — every spin, every session.

But even if these interactive machines don't change the odds, they're still extremely popular. They're fast and fun to play, but they're also mesmerizing, seductive, and hard to tear yourself away from. They hypnotize you with their subtle chant: "Must. Have. Your. Last. Dollar." And they usually get it.

The advantage of interactive slot machines is that the manufacturers get really creative. These games often have increasingly challenging levels, and each step up the ladder offers more money to make the game interesting and the journey worthwhile.

Most players are hoping to reach these bonus rounds — where the fun really begins. For example, on one version the reels disappear, and animated characters pop up as the game progresses. You choose between several images and click on one to reveal the bonus hidden behind the icon. The object is to win additional credits before clicking on a character with no credits, which ends the bonus round.

The total amount you win in the bonus round depends on the number of coins you play, so it's important to play the maximum coins allowed on interactive machines. Some bonus rounds also award bonus spins, where you can double or triple your winnings and win additional free games.

One pull can change your life. Twice.

Although I personally feel that playing progressives is a waste of time (check out "Working the progressive slots" in this chapter), lightning *can* strike and make people rich overnight. And occasionally it may even strike a second time: On September 19, 2005, a Las Vegas resident became the first person ever to win a Megabucks Jackpot — *twice!* Elmer Sherwin won $21.1 million while playing at the Cannery Casino in North Las Vegas. But unlike everyone else, he already knew the thrill of winning big — he'd won a $4.6 million jackpot in 1989 at the Mirage Casino. At 92 years young, Sherwin's bio should place him alone atop the slot player's pantheon because the odds of winning the Megabucks a second time are pretty much incalculable.

Getting a Handle on Slots Odds

Before you decide to drop your quarter, nickel, or penny into a slot machine, you first need to understand the odds. Sad but true, coming up with a strategy to beat the odds — when they favor the house so strongly — is impossible. (Check out Chapter 3 for more on house odds.)

The payout of slot machines generally falls somewhere between 90 and 95 percent. That means for every $100 you put into a machine, your average return is $90 to $95 (a loss of $5 to $10). This hefty house edge makes slots one of the worst games in the casino. When you factor in the speed of the games, you start to understand why slots are so profitable for modern casinos.

 If you're serious about slots, check online for the most up-to-date slot payout information at sites such as www.wizardofodds.com. These watchdog sites post names of Las Vegas casinos with their observed rates, and they breakdown the odds of winning per coin played. The results show that nickel slots tend to be the *tightest* (worst odds) machines, returning about 91 percent, while $1 and $5 slots are the *loosest* (best odds), returning about 94 to 95 percent.

 Generally, you find the best machines and odds where the competition is most fierce. Try the Las Vegas Strip, where casinos are clustered closely together, each of them vying equally hard for your gambling dollar. On the other hand, playing slots on the water often leaves you all wet. Because cruise ship casinos aren't under the jurisdiction of U. S. gaming laws, some have payouts as low as 80 percent. Consequently, you're better off tucking your money back into your purse or wallet and waiting until you're on dry land.

Stretching Your Money at the Slots

With literally hundreds of machine choices, perhaps the most difficult decision is which one to play. You want to choose the game that offers the highest theoretical return. Unfortunately, finding the best machine in a sea of slots can be a difficult task — and a bit like comparing apples to oranges. For example, one machine may pay 5,000 coins for its jackpot while another pays only 1,000. But the jackpots are only part of the equation: Your total return also depends on the other winning combinations and how frequently they hit.

Although you can't do much to change the odds of hitting the jackpot, you can take steps to extend your gambling bankroll. Think of it this way: When you make your money last longer, you're maximizing the value of your entertainment dollar at the slots. This section helps make your slot experience more memorable by explaining what you can do to make your money last longer.

Reading the paytable

The *paytable* (located on the top glass of each machine) provides the most valuable information about a slot machine. Be sure to read (what combinations will win, how many coins are required, and so on) and understand the paytables before you start playing. (Check out Figure 12-4 for an example of the glass-panel payout information.)

		1ST COIN	2ND COIN		
ONLY HIGHEST WINNER PAID ON CENTERLINE	7 7 7	400	5000	7 7 7	ONLY HIGHEST WINNER PAID ON CENTERLINE
	7 7 7	50	100	7 7 7	
	B2R B2R B2R	25	50	B2R B2R B2R	
	ANY 3 MIXED 7 7	18	36	ANY 3 MIXED 7 7	
	B1R B1R B1R	8	16	B1R B1R B1R	
	🍒 🍒 🍒	4	8	🍒 🍒 🍒	
	ANY TWO 🍒	2	4	ANY TWO 🍒	
	ANY ONE 🍒	1	2	ANY ONE 🍒	

Figure 12-4: The glass panel gives the payout information.

Machines that display a higher paytable usually have a greater number of symbols on each reel. For example, the older, three-reel slot machines have 20 symbols with 8,000 possible combinations ($20 \times 20 \times 20$), which means your odds of hitting the jackpot are 1 in 8,000. Likewise, a four-reel machine has odds of 1 in 160,000. The odds increase even more dramatically on a five-reel video machine: With 20 symbols, your chances of hitting the highest jackpot are about 1 in 3 million!

Having more reels and symbols doesn't necessarily make a machine any better or any worse. It just creates more potential combinations. You hit the jackpot more frequently on the three-reel machines, but the amount of money you win is typically much less than a jackpot on a five-reel machine. So which type of machine should you play? In the long run, it hardly matters. The casino has a sizeable edge over you on every slot machine in the house.

Choosing the type of machine

If you feel a need for speed, then you may want to try the traditional three-reel machines. These machines usually spin faster than video machines, which means you get more plays in an hour — and more opportunities to lose money. On the other hand, video slot machines have those cool bonus rounds that come up several times in an hour; they can slow down the pace, stretching both your bankroll and your enjoyment.

The final decision is yours. You can try them both and then select the one you like the best.

Choosing the denomination you bet

Slots are the only game in the casino where the odds depend on your bet. The higher the machine's denomination, the higher the potential payback — normally.

However, returns vary from casino to casino, so the exact amount of payback (such as 91 percent for nickel machines and 95 percent for $5 machines) can be quite different depending on where you play. When a casino advertises that its dollar machines pay back 97 percent, for example, it usually means it pays *up to* 97 percent on *some* machines. These qualifications make a big difference because most casinos only have a couple of machines with the loosest payouts. The average for all the dollar machines is typically much less (usually around 93 percent), and there is no way to know which *special* machines are set to pay out at the higher rate (97 percent).

The color of money

To avoid that "kid-in-a-candy-store" confusion around slot machines, you need to know what kind of "candy" you want, right? Well, keep this point in mind: The big light on the top of a slot machine is called a *candle,* and the rim color of the light tells you the denomination of the machine. In most casinos, you can check for the following colored candles to decipher the denominations of each machine:

✔ $1 machines are blue.

✔ Half-dollars are gold.

✔ Quarters are yellow.

✔ Nickels are red.

✔ Pennies don't have a standard color.

By knowing these colored candles, you can instantly spot the denomination you want to play when you look across a casino.

Even though a dollar machine may pay back 95 percent and a nickel machine only 90 percent, you still lose less money with the nickels in the long run because you risk less money each spin.

Here's the math with five coins per spin: Dollar machines cost you 25¢ per pull ($5 times the house edge of 5 percent), and nickel machines cost you less than 3¢ per pull (25¢ times the house edge of 10 percent). So even though the house edge is twice as high on the nickel slots (10 percent versus 5 percent), the nickel slots are easier on your wallet (you only lose a few cents a spin on the nickel slots versus 25¢ each spin on the dollar machines).

Other potential budget-busters are the multibet, multipayline video slots that are so hot today — they can cost you a lot more money than normal machines. A nickel machine may cost a mere 5¢ for a single coin spin, but if you go with a max bet of 45 credits, your game actually costs $2.25 per spin. Some machines allow up to 90 credits, meaning you'd be betting $4.50 per spin! Surprisingly, even the max credit on the lowly penny slots can be 300 coins, or $3.

Even at the lowest denomination, max betting can rapidly drain your gambling stake, and you may soon find yourself feeding another $20 bill into the penny slot machine — not what you intended. When coin options are sky-high, you're better off playing a dollar machine for one or two coins than a low-denomination max bet with worse odds.

Hitting an empty casino

If you're a sun-worshipper, you probably pursue your slot jackpot in the evening because you prefer to spend your afternoons at the hotel pool, sipping your favorite drink. But what's the best time to play the slots? Actually, the drowsy hour just before dawn is the deadest time in a casino. Light sleepers can grab an early morning cup of coffee and hit a nearly empty casino to enjoy a relatively peaceful playing time with the widest array of machines available. However, the odds never change on these machines, so don't expect to find looser slots just because they're lonely and looking for players.

Playing full credits on progressive games

When playing a progressive machine, you need to keep one hard-and-fast rule in mind: Always play the maximum number of coins or credits each spin. If you don't, you greatly dilute your odds because a big part of the payback in progressive machines is predicated on hitting the jackpot with max coins. If you don't have the bankroll to play the maximum number of coins, then play a non-progressive machine where the payback is unaffected by the number of coins played. See the section "Increasing wagers with multipliers" for more information.

Playing max credits does have its downside, though. Proficient players can easily get in 600 spins an hour on most machines. If you play the max number of coins each time, your money can vanish darn fast. An average loss can be $100 an hour — or more — at many dollar machines, which makes for a pretty expensive hobby.

If you're new to slots, your safest bet may be to stick to two-coin, single pay-line machines. Although they don't offer a large jackpot, they at least stretch your bankroll, enabling you to play longer and enjoy more of that one-armed bandit euphoria you sat down to experience in the first place.

Maximizing your fun

As a seasoned casino gambler, I'm fairly negative about slots. These machines carry a high price tag for their fun. But I can't ignore the fact that there's something addicting to those whirring, humming sirens. And the fact that they're so simple to play makes them irresistible to most casino guests. So if you can't say *no* to slots, I suggest you keep the following tips in mind to enhance your relationship with these aptly named one-armed bandits:

- ✔ **Leave your myths and superstitions at home.** Rid yourself of any myths or hunches about hot and cold machines.

- ✔ **Do some investigative work.** Find out which casinos have the best paybacks on their slot machines before you take your trip. A good way to do your homework is by subscribing to *Casino Player Magazine* or *Midwest Gaming and Travel.*

- ✔ **Stay within your means.** Never play a game that you don't understand or one that requires larger bets than you planned on making.

- ✔ **Remember the odds.** Slot machines are *negative expectation* games. The longer you play, the more you lose. So take frequent breaks and pace yourself and your bankroll.

- ✔ **Be realistic.** The odds of hitting the Megabucks jackpot are much worse than your chance of getting hit in the head by an asteroid.

- ✔ **Slow down.** Savor your jackpots and enjoy the journey. Because of the high house odds, the faster you play, the more you lose.

- ✔ **Double-check your payouts.** On your big wins, always make sure you get paid correctly *before* rushing to the next spin. Also, be careful to cash out all your credits and scoop up every last coin before you leave the machine.

You also want to make sure you bring your ID. You must have a valid driver's license or government ID to get paid on any large jackpot ($1,200 or more). And while you're at it, comb your hair. You want to look good for the paparazzi when they snap a photo of you holding your oversized cardboard check.

Honing Your Slot Etiquette

Etiquette in slots? You think I'm joking, right? Actually, even though playing slots is a solitary activity, a few little courtesies can ensure that you keep the peace with the blue-haired lady to your left. This section focuses on the main do's and don'ts of slot-machine etiquette.

Saving a machine

How can you tell if a machine's been saved? Well, it doesn't shout, "Hallelujah, I've seen the light!" But, trust me, you definitely want to know if the seemingly unattended machine has been claimed by someone else. Otherwise, the wrath you incur just might feel like Judgment Day. There's no quicker way to turn a kindly old grandmother into the avenging angel than by *stealing* her favorite machine (especially when, after only a few coins, you magically win *her* jackpot).

It's common practice in casinos for a player to save a machine for a short while when she needs a break. The length of time you can hold a machine varies, depending on the casino and whether you're a high roller; 10 to 15 minutes is rarely a problem. But expecting the machine to remain exclusively yours while you chomp down crab legs in the buffet for an hour may be pushing it. You can save a slot by placing an inverted coin cup on the handle or over the coin hopper, by leaving your coat on the chair, or by asking a slot attendant to hold the machine.

Playing two machines at once: Double trouble

Many avid slots players like to play two machines at once. They do so by sitting in one seat and reaching back and forth between two machines. In those cases, you may think a machine is available because the seat is empty. Beware: Before you get a chance to pump in your first coin, you will get a stinging rebuke from the serious "I can't lose my money fast enough, so I play two machines at once" gambler in the next stool.

Minding your manners

Slots may be a solitary game, but you're still playing in an open environment, so be sensitive to your neighbors to your right and left. Consider these helpful tips for being a polite gambler and keeping the peace.

- **If you aren't actually playing, stay out of the way.** If you're watching a friend or spouse play, make sure you aren't in the way of another player. Just like at the table games, nonplaying guests must give up the seat to a player who wants to play.

- **If you find a slot card, in a machine you want to play, be careful.** (Check out the next section for more on slot or club cards.) If the player is nowhere in sight, feel free to remove the card and play. But don't toss it in the trash or give it to an attendant; just put the card on top of the machine. Chances are, the player is already headed back to retrieve it and will be grateful for the gesture.

- **Never covet thy neighbor's jackpot.** Slots are different from table games like poker. You're not competing against each other; everyone is competing against the house. So don't sulk when an adjacent machine hits a big winner. Cheer him on and help him enjoy the moment. Being a good sport won't change your luck, but it makes the overall gaming experience more enjoyable.

Playing for Comps

One of the best incentives for slot players is the generous comps that casinos bestow on them. Typically, the more you play, the more freebies you receive (comped meals, entertainment tickets, cashbacks, and other perks). There's just one drawback to playing for comps — it can become too enticing. Just like some people go crazy over frequent-flyer miles and take extra trips to get to the next level, some gamblers play longer and for more money just to score a comp to the buffet.

Slots can be very entertaining, but those free meals can end up being very expensive. Always stick to your budget when gambling, and never chase the comps. But hey, as long as you're there, feel free to enjoy the great side benefits that come your way.

This section focuses on how to take advantage of slot comps, including how to sign up for a slot club and cashing in. You can also check out Chapter 21 that addresses important tips to keep in mind concerning comps.

Taking advantage of the comps

Today's casinos use club cards to keep track of how much individual gamblers bet and how long they play. Slots are the perfect vehicle for this system because the machine automatically tallies every wager you make. The longer you play or the more you bet, the more club points you accumulate.

The main reason you should want a club card is to turn those points into *comps*. Comps come in many shapes and forms, from free hats to penthouse suites. But the premise is the same for all gamblers, whether high rollers or nickel slot players — the amount of time you play and the average amount you bet is tabulated to determine what comps you receive. A comp is truly a great benefit and can help defray your losses. Although formulas vary among casinos, the basic principle is this: A percentage of your theoretical loss is returned to you in the form of comps (such as free meals, shows, or complimentary hotel accommodations).

You don't get comps only when you lose. The casinos never care whether you win or lose in the short run — they only want to see some action from you. Because they're *always* the favorite, they know they're going to win in the long run.

Some comps are immediate, although others may accrue over a few trips to the casino and finally bring you up to a new level, such as an invitation to a special event or a tournament. Because casinos want to develop a loyal customer base, they aggressively reward their best customers with little extras to keep them coming back.

Signing up for a slot club

Casinos strongly encourage new players to sign up for the slot club, and they make it simple. With just a few minutes of your time and a valid ID, you receive a shiny laminated card with your name on it (and usually a handy little key chain to fasten the card to your body.) Also, be sure and ask if there are any sign-up perks. Many casinos offer special deals to attract new players.

When you play the slots, simply insert your card into a card reader on the machine; the computer automatically tracks how long you play and how much you bet.

If you ever lose your card, which is very easy to do, just go back to the desk where you first signed up and ask for a duplicate. Or you may want to ask for an extra card to begin with, especially if your spouse also wants to play under your account or you intend to play two machines at once.

Cashing in on cash rebates

What's even better than free meals? Free cash! Many contemporary casinos offer cashback programs (up to 1 percent) in addition to their generous comps. Of course, casinos can afford to be generous because slots are so profitable for the house.

Casinos normally figure your comps and potential cashback rewards on a point system. The more points you accrue (based on the machine denomination and how many hours you play), the larger your perks. Also, just like with grocery store coupons, you can get double or triple points on certain days of the month, putting you on the fast track to cashing in. Points are usually nontransferable and often have an expiration date.

Your cashback typically comes in two flavors:

- You receive the cashback the same day you earn it.
- You're mailed a cashback certificate, good for your next trip to the casino. This program is called a *bounce-back*.

  Bounce-back programs typically require you to return within a certain time. If your favorite casino is within a short drive, that isn't a problem. But if you have to fly across the country to cash it in, your certificate becomes much less valuable.

Chapter 13

Scoring Big in Video Poker

*V*ideo poker burst onto the scene in the late 1970s and revolutionized the casino industry within a few years, propelling the economic shift from table games to slots. In fact, video poker quickly became the game of choice for many gamblers. Today, it's so popular that some pundits label it the *crack cocaine* of gambling.

Although you must approach all games of chance cautiously, video poker offers a number of positives that make it one of the few casino games I heartily recommend to anyone who wants to explore the world of casino gambling.

In this chapter, I explain the fundamentals of video poker and investigate its allure. I also discuss the game's low house edge and share some simplified basic strategies that can help you improve your odds and possibly take your game to the next level if you so desire.

Poker? Slots? Characterizing Video Poker

Video poker is a game like no other. Gamblers often describe this game, which was designed to attract a crossover crowd, as a blend of slot machines and poker. But what really defines this popular game is how it's *not* like slots or traditional poker.

In this section, I look at what video poker really is by comparing it to slots and traditional poker. I also briefly look at why video poker is so trendy in today's casinos.

Contrasting video poker and slots

At first glance, video poker machines may look and act like most other traditional slot machines (check out Chapter 12 for more on slots). You often find video poker machines in the same location in the casino as regular slot machines. Furthermore, both slot and video poker machines have a coin slot or bill acceptor, a slot-club card reader, and a payout hopper. That's about where the similarities end.

People sometimes describe video poker as the *thinking* man's slot machine because you actually need some skill to play. Your understanding of poker strategy improves your odds of winning. Instead of mindlessly pulling a handle and praying for three cherries to line up, *you* call the shots.

What separates video poker from other slot machines is your ability to choose — both the cards you want to play and the types of machines you play on — because different versions of video poker offer different payouts. Your fate in slots lies in the cold, calculating microchip called the *random number generator,* or *RNG.* Although the RNG determines your five starting cards in video poker, your outcome has more to do with which of the starting cards you choose to hold or discard than the whims of a microchip's brain. This decision distinguishes video poker from slots. Your choices make video poker a game of skill — a game that gives you more control over your destiny.

 Not only are your choices in playing your cards critical to your success in video poker but also your choice in machines affects your odds. Some machines have better payouts than others — so you definitely want to know how to identify machines with higher payouts and stick with them. (The section "Putting Your Money on the Best Machines," later in this chapter, spells out how to choose the optimal machines.)

Distinguishing between video and traditional poker

Success at video poker requires some skill, specifically a cursory knowledge of poker. Video poker most closely resembles Five-Card Draw. (For some poker pointers, check out Chapter 6.) As soon as you receive your randomly dealt five starting cards, *you* choose what moves to make in order to win.

Although you need some basic poker knowledge to play video poker, remember that video poker differs quite a bit from the traditional table game. Video poker is a game between you and the machine rather than between you and other players. Because you're not interacting with other players, you can leave your sunglasses at home — no need to hide your reactions, attempt to bluff, or try to *read* your opponents. You don't need to beat anyone but the machine. Figure 13-1 shows you an example of a video poker screen.

Check out the following characteristics of video poker that distinguish it from traditional table poker:

- ✔ **You play at your own pace.** Other players can never rush or intimidate you.

- ✔ **You have no need for deceptive tactics.** Forget about using tactics such as bluffing, checking, and raising in video poker. You have no opponent to bluff.

- ✔ **Each hand has a fixed cost.** You never lose more than you put into the machine, which isn't the case in traditional poker.

- ✔ **An ace is *not* the most important card.** For example, three aces pays exactly the same as three 5s.

- ✔ **Video poker machines are always ready to take you on, 24 hours a day.** Live poker requires real opponents, and finding a game isn't always possible.

- ✔ **Guesswork is absent from the equation.** You never have to deduce what your opponent has because you're playing only against the payout table.

- ✔ **A royal flush is more than the best hand; it's a gold mine.** Although a royal flush is the best hand for both games, it's exponentially better in video poker because of the jackpot payouts. For example, if you hit a royal flush at a dollar machine playing max coins, you win at least $4,000 (more with a progressive jackpot). In contrast, if you make a royal flush in a regular poker game, you rarely win much more than a normal pot (typically about $50 in a $5- to $10-limit game).

- ✔ **You never lose with a good hand.** In video poker, you always get paid when you make certain hands. In regular poker, a miracle straight flush may beat your full house, leaving you steaming for hours over your bad beat.

Understanding the allure

Video poker is a popular game in casinos, but what makes it so alluring? Video poker offers a near-unheard-of low house edge, especially when you're savvy about some basic playing strategies and other factors, including choosing the right machine. (Check out the next section, "Playing the Game," for more info on the low house edge.)

Video poker provides a bit of solitude when you want a break from table games. When you play video poker, you don't have to worry about a pushy dealer intimidating you or obnoxious players harassing you. You can play at your own pace, focusing only on the screen and the flashing cards in front of you.

Playing the Game

If you decide you want to try video poker, this section can help you with all the ins and outs of playing the game. You can usually locate the video poker machines in carousels in the same section of the casino as slot machines. Like slots, almost every modern video poker machine takes bills, which it converts into credits. So you use those credits instead of hand-feeding coins for each play. Video poker machines also have buttons similar to slot machines, which you use to start the game process.

Making your bet

On most machines, you can play from one to five coins at a time. In other words, you can increase your bet — and winnings — based on how many coins you play per game. Most video poker machines are either quarter or dollar machines, but they're also available in denominations from a nickel to $100. Some machines are even multidenominational, and you can pick which level you want to bet. Machines have a Max Bet button if you want to bet five coins every time. If you want to bet more than one coin but fewer than five, you simply press the Bet One button the appropriate number of times.

The benefit to playing the maximum five coins? You qualify for the royal flush jackpot available only in the five-coin line.

Stretching your bankroll

Video poker's high return is based on hitting a royal flush, but that only happens about once in every 40,000 hands. So patience is important. A royal flush usually takes a long time (80 hours on average), and you need a hefty bankroll to ride out the swings, so I recommend starting off with quarter machines rather than dollar machines. Unfortunately you can go several trips without hitting a royal flush.

The minimum bankroll I recommend for tackling the quarter machines is $1,000. For dollar machines, that figure jumps up to $5,000. Seems steep? I'm actually scaling down the amount for beginning gamblers and weekend warriors. You can still play video poker with a smaller bankroll, but your chance of surviving long enough to hit a royal flush diminishes accordingly. Remember that you can play up to 500 hands an hour, so be prepared for some crazy swings to your bankroll.

Making your best hand in one draw

After you feed your money into the machine (or play credits) and hit the Deal button, five cards pop up on your screen, dealt from a standard 52-card deck. After you receive your initial starting cards, the game closely resembles Five-Card Draw poker. You can push any of the five buttons — one for each card — on the front of each machine to *hold*, or keep, any cards. You have three options available with each hand:

- ✔ Hold all your cards.
- ✔ Discard all your cards.
- ✔ Hold some cards and toss others.

 After you receive your first five cards, many machines automatically highlight winning hands for you on the payout table, and some even suggest which cards to hold. Following the machine's suggestions can prevent you from accidentally throwing away a big winner. The pay scale rewards the better hands and uses standard poker rankings. If you're unsure of the poker hand rankings, check out Chapter 6.

The machine replaces whatever cards you throw away with new cards from the remaining 47 cards in the deck. Because you have no other opponents to beat, your objective is to make the highest poker hand possible with your one draw.

 After you're happy with your selections, press the Deal/Draw button to receive your new cards. You can change your mind on the Hold buttons by pressing them again at any time before you hit Draw. For example, hitting the Hold button a second time reverses the action and throws away the card you were going to hold.

 Some older machines may have sticky buttons (too many people playing while eating cinnamon buns, I guess), so always make sure you're discarding the correct cards, especially when you have a great hand. I've lost some big payoffs because of malfunctioning buttons when I inadvertently broke up four of a kind or a straight.

Collecting your winnings

The machine pays you in coins or credits. After your hand is finished and you're done celebrating, simply press the Deal/Draw button, and the entire process starts over. When you're done playing, hit the Cash Out button, and the machine either spits your coins into the hopper or prints a cash-out ticket for you to redeem at the cashier's cage.

Putting Your Money on the Best Machines

The most important decision you make in video poker isn't what to hold or discard but which machine to play. Video poker comes in a wide variety of machines, such as

- All American Poker
- Deuces Wild
- Double Bonus
- Double Double Bonus
- Jacks or Better
- Joker Wild
- Triple Play

Many of these games look alike to the untrained eye, which can be a problem. The strategies for different machines can get quite complex, and frequently new versions of video poker come and go with the wind. Some very profitable games (for the players) have become extinct, and newer games that are profitable only for the house have replaced them. Despite their similarities, the machines may offer returns for players that vary dramatically. For example, over four hours of play, you lose (on average) approximately $50 playing max coins on a dollar Jacks or Better 9/6 machine, but that loss jumps up to $500 for the same scenario on a Jacks or Better 6/5 machine.

Holding out for the highest payout

You want the video poker machine with the best —*highest* — payout schedule, which is reflected in the numbers separated with a slash. These numbers are based on the payout for a full house and flush for anyone playing a single coin. For example, in a 9/6 machine, one coin pays out nine coins on a full house and six on a flush, while an 8/5 machine pays out only eight coins for a full house and five for a flush.

The small difference in the pay structure from a 9/6 machine to a 8/5 machine may not seem like much, but your expected return drops from 99.5 percent (for 9/6) to 97.3 percent (for 8/5). ***Translation:*** Your bankroll gets chewed up about six times faster with the lower payout because your return is only $97.30 for every $100 played. A typical weekend playing 9/6 (12 hours of play with max coins on a dollar machine) costs you about $40, but with 8/5, that loss swells to about $240.

TIP

Avoid video poker machines in places such as airports and convenience stores. These machines usually have some of the lowest payouts.

Comparing short-pay and full-pay machines

When a casino offers a lesser-paying version of a video poker machine, it's called a *short-pay* rather than a *full-pay* machine. Jacks or Better offers several examples, starting with 9/6, then 8/5, 7/5, and even 6/5. Anytime the payouts are reduced, your wallet is hurt. But another variable (progressive jackpots — see the next section) sometimes comes into the equation to offset the lower payouts.

Table 13-1 shows some examples of percentage returns on some of the more popular video poker games. The percentage is how much the casino returns to you (on average) for every dollar wagered. In most cases you lose (such as when the return is 99.5 percent), but some video poker games actually offer you a positive return (100.2 percent).

Table 13-1 Returns on Video Poker Games

Game	*Percentage Return*
Deuces Wild (Full-Pay)	100.8 percent
All-American Poker	100.7 percent
10/7 Double Bonus	100.2 percent
9/6 Jacks or Better	99.5 percent
9/6 Double Bonus	97.8 percent
7/5 Jacks or Better	96.2 percent
6/5 Jacks or Better	95 percent
Deuces Wild (Short-Pay)	94.3 percent

Down the toilet with a royal-flush myth

Many people mistakenly think that the longer they play, the more likely high progressive jackpots are to hit. But the odds don't change even if the machine hasn't hit a royal flush since Donald Trump's last divorce. Every new spin is completely independent of any previous results. Video poker machines *do not* run hot or cold.

Hitting one royal flush doesn't mean you won't hit another one for 40,000 hands. A few years ago, I got invited to a VIP promo at the Flamingo

Hilton in Reno. The casino gave an invited group of high rollers seven minutes of free play on any dollar slot machine.

Naturally, I chose video poker and hit a royal flush on my third spin. Later that same weekend, I hit another royal flush. So at times, luck may seem to follow you around, but it's just that — luck — not a sign from the video poker gods that you're hot and need to bet more.

Advancing to progressive machines

When choosing a video poker machine, you also can consider playing a progressive machine. *Flat-tops* are video poker machines that have fixed jackpots. Their maximum payout for a royal flush never changes. However, many video poker machines are *progressive,* meaning their jackpot increases a certain amount from every coin played that doesn't hit the royal flush. These progressive machines usually are grouped together in the casino in a bank of machines all tied to the same meter.

Even though your chance of hitting a royal flush doesn't increase with progressive machines, the payoff grows and a losing game can turn into a profitable situation if the jackpot gets high enough. However, most progressive jackpots are tied into the lower-paying machines (such as 7/5 instead of 9/6), so, unless the progressive is very high, you're usually better off playing flat-tops.

Playing Jacks or Better: The Best Bet for Beginners

When first starting out in video poker, concentrate your energies on one type of machine: 9/6 Jacks or Better. Jacks or Better is one simple version of video poker that's been around since the beginning of video poker and is considered the industry standard. It's also one of the safest bets in a casino. What's with the name? You need at least a pair of jacks to get paid.

This section looks more closely at Jacks or Better, including the payout and some strategies you can use to improve your odds.

Analyzing the payout

Jacks or Better is fast, fun, and very simple to understand. But even more importantly, it offers some of the best odds of any game in the casino. With optimal playing strategy, a 9/6 Jacks or Better machine offers a 99.5 percent return, which means the house has a very small edge. When you factor in *cashback* programs from the slot clubs and a few comps, you're often breaking even or ahead of the game. (Cashback programs give cash back to you based on how long and how much you play. You can check Chapter 4 for more on these types of programs and other comps.)

Table 13-2 shows a pay table from 9/6 Jacks or Better.

Table 13-2	Payout for 9/6 Jacks or Better				
Hand	*1st Coin*	*2nd Coin*	*3rd Coin*	*4th Coin*	*5th Coin*
Royal flush	250	500	750	1,000	4,000
Straight flush	50	100	150	200	250
Four of a kind	25	50	75	100	125
Full house	9	18	27	36	45
Flush	6	12	18	24	30
Straight	4	8	12	16	20
Three of a kind	3	6	9	12	15
Two pair	2	4	6	8	10
Pair of jacks or better	1	2	3	4	5

Table 13-2 shows only the number of coins you get when you win, not the dollar amount. So if you're playing quarters (25¢ machines) and hit a max coin royal flush, you win $1,000 (4,000 coins), not $4,000.

Table 13-2 shows that the higher-ranking hands offer the largest paydays. And the amounts rise in equal proportion to the number of coins you play — with one exception: The royal flush is the jackpot you and every video poker player shoot for, and the return jumps dramatically when you play five coins (the maximum amount).

Because of the jackpot potential on the royal flush with max coins, always play five coins at Jacks or Better. Otherwise, you dilute your expected return by about 1.5 percent.

Table 13-2 also includes your original wager. If you put one coin in the machine and get two jacks, your win pays you back one coin, which is really your original bet. So you only break even. But, hey, breaking even is better than losing — and hitting one pair is by far your most frequent win.

Adding strategy to the equation

Although most of the decisions that come up in Jacks or Better video poker are fairly intuitive, the game has enough complexities to turn it into a losing venture. Many gamblers usually don't know the correct strategy for some of the difficult hands. Instead, they rely on their gut when deciding which cards to hold or discard.

Fortunately, just like blackjack, video poker has a correct strategy for each and every hand. Because video poker doesn't hold the unknowns that traditional poker does (strength of opponent's hand, bluffing, and so on), you can determine the optimal play for all conceivable decisions.

Some people find the full-fledged version of video poker strategy a little daunting to memorize, but two easier options are available:

- ✔ **Buy a strategy card and keep it with you as you play.** A strategy card is permissible and can keep you from making mistakes, though it slows your pace as you stop frequently to check the card. You can purchase these in many places, including casino gift shops.

- ✔ **Study a simplified strategy.** I focus the next section on using a simplified strategy that can help you in your video poker endeavors.

Using a simplified strategy

Michael Shackleford, the gifted mathematician called The Wizard of Odds, uses the following simplified strategy. With this strategy, you lose very little in accuracy, and your return drops to only 99.46 percent. Additionally, his Web site, www.wizardofodds.com, is a great place to find out more about video poker or to practice before your next trip. Figure 13-1 shows the strategy.

Michael Shackleford's Simplified Strategy for Jacks or Better Video Poker

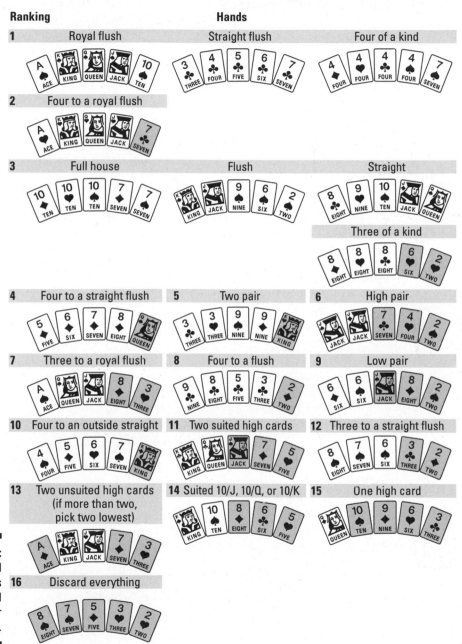

Figure 13-1:
Michael Shackleford's simplified strategy for video poker.

The hands in Figure 13-1 are in hierarchical order, the best hands with the highest payout first. For each starting hand, you simply try to find the highest option available and play accordingly. The following pointers clarify a few items:

- *High cards* and *high pairs* are jacks, queens, kings, or aces.

- *Low pairs* are 2s through 10s.

- An *outside straight* is open-ended and can be completed at either end. For example a 5, 6, 7, 8 becomes a straight with either a 4 or a 9.

- An *inside straight* has a hole in the middle (A, K, Q, 10), and only one card makes a straight. (Only a jack can make this a straight.)

The first eight options on the strategy chart in Table 13-3 are fairly straight-forward. When you're dealt a flush or a full house, most players understand that they should stand pat and not draw any additional cards. However, over-looking numbers 2 and 7 (four to a royal flush and three to a royal flush, respectively) is sometimes easy.

You get only a few chances at a royal flush each session, so make sure you don't overlook these plays (numbers 2 and 7) and miss a shot at hitting the jackpot.

Conquering the mundane hands

When playing Jacks or Better, most strategy battles take place in the trenches with commonplace hands (see numbers 9 through 16 in Table 12-3). Here's where the strategy gets a little more complex and may not be quite as obvious.

Suppose you have Figure 13-2 as your hand.

According to Table 12-3, the top three plays are as follows:

- Keep four to a flush (number 8).

- Keep the low pair (number 9).

- Keep the two suited high cards (number 11).

Figure 13-2:
A sample hand in Jacks or Better.

Because four to a flush is highest on the strategy chart (No. 8), it's the best play, so discard the ♥3.

Some plays can be difficult for new players, such as keeping a high pair over four to a flush and keeping four to a royal flush over a *made flush* (being dealt five cards of the same suit).

Sticking to the strategy is critical to your long-term success with Jacks or Better, even if your gut tells you to make a different move. The following tips can help you when you're playing Jacks or Better:

- ✔ **Never keep three cards to a regular straight or to a regular flush.** The exception is if they're all high cards, such as K, Q, and J.

- ✔ **Whenever you have four cards to a royal flush, always draw for the royal flush regardless of what the other card is.** For example, if you are dealt the hand in Figure 13-3, break up the two aces by discarding the ♦A and go for the royal flush with the four hearts.

- ✔ **Always play max coins.** Your total return is diluted unless you play max coins.

- ✔ **Never keep a *kicker* (a high card in addition to your pair).**

- ✔ **Break up a high pair only if you have four to a royal flush or a four-card straight flush.**

- ✔ **When you have both a four-card flush and a four-card straight draw, play for the flush.**

Figure 13-3: A sample hand in Jacks or Better.

Sticking to the system. . .no matter what

Very few casino games offer such high paybacks as video poker. But just because the payback is close to 100 percent doesn't mean you always break even. Even with ⅞ Jacks or Better, you can swing wildly on both sides of the bell curve on most trips, rarely finishing close to even. Only over the long run does fluctuation level off so you end up near your expected return.

Because of the financial gyrations involved in video poker, many players give up on the prescribed strategy and start playing by the seat of their pants again, especially when they're losing. But take my advice: Be patient and stay the course. Don't let short-term results discourage you. Video poker is a great game, and if you play correctly, you do well over time.

A great way to ingrain the strategies for video poker into your brain is to practice at home on a computer (check out Chapter 17). Several excellent software programs are available to teach you the proper strategy for any video poker game. And because your computer screen looks so similar to the video poker screen, you can feel very comfortable when you play for real.

Investigating Other Video Poker Machines

Plenty of other video poker machines are available in casinos to attract your attention — some with potential payouts of more than 100 percent. But weighing against the attractive payouts are some challenges, such as more-complex strategies. After you master Jacks or Better, you may be ready for more challenging play — and better returns! This section looks more closely at a few other machines that you may want to consider.

Walking on the wild side

Deuces Wild demands a strategy of a different sort, but it rewards you well for your homework because the full-pay version returns more than 100 percent!

Deuces Wild uses the standard 52-card deck, but, as the name implies, deuces (2s) are *wild* (meaning you can use them like a joker and take the value of the best possible card in the deck). Because having wild deuces may create stronger hands, the payout table changes dramatically. With Deuces Wild, you need at least three of a kind to win one coin. Table 13-3 shows the payout table for the full-pay version of Deuces Wild.

The addition of wild cards makes Deuces Wild a popular game, both for tourists and for pros. But the game is much more volatile than Jacks or Better. Because much of your edge comes from either hitting a royal flush or a hand with four deuces, many times you end up throwing away all five of your starting cards in pursuit of a big payday.

Table 13-3	Payout for Full-Pay Deuces Wild
Hand	*Payout for One Coin*
Royal flush	800
Four deuces	200
Wild royal flush	25
Five of a kind	15
Straight flush	9
Four of a kind	5
Full house	3
Flush	2
Straight	2
Three of a kind	1

Keep the following points in mind when playing Deuces Wild:

✔ Avoid the short-pay versions of this game at all costs.

✔ Never throw away a deuce.

✔ If you're dealt two pair (without a deuce), throw away one pair (which one you throw away doesn't matter).

✔ A pair is better than four to a straight or four to a flush.

✔ Always hold five of a kind.

✔ Never keep a single jack, queen, king, or ace.

The strategy for playing Deuces Wild is slightly more complicated than for Jacks or Better, but you can still master it if you're diligent and disciplined. If you're lucky enough to find a casino that offers Full-Pay Deuces Wild video poker, I suggest you first go to www.wizardofodds.com and study up on the strategy for this unusual game.

Multitasking with Multi-Game Play

A new variety of video poker — Multi-Game Play — has become quite popular, and for good reason: You can play out several games instantaneously with the same starting hand. But be prepared; the first time you try Multi-Game video poker, such as the trendy Triple Play version, you may think your alcohol consumption is affecting your eyesight. The multiple images on your video screen have nothing to do with the number of margaritas you've downed.

Triple Play lets you play three separate hands at once and is available in many popular versions of video poker, including Jacks or Better and Deuces Wild. When you start, you usually have several options of games available. You simply touch the screen to choose the type of game and the denomination you want to play.

Playing three hands helps even out the fluctuations because you have three separate shots to hit a winner. Even though your overall payout and results don't change, the time you take to hit a royal flush is much less because you probably hit one about every 30 hours.

The following list details the sequence of a typical Triple Play game:

1. **The machine deals the normal five starting cards to you.**

2. **You pick which cards you want to hold and which you want to discard.**

3. **The cards you keep pop up in two additional hands.**

4. **You hit Draw.**

5. **The machine deals all three hands new cards from different 52-card decks.**

6. **The machine pays each winning hand.**

    Ending up with a mix of winners and losers among the three hands is common.

The downside of Triple Play: You can eat through your bankroll three times as fast as regular video poker. If, for example, you're playing a dollar machine, you must bet $15 rather than $5 to play all three lines at max coins.

Multiple-play video poker machines are also available. These machines operate the same way as Triple Play but offer options of playing 5, 10, 50, even 100 hands at once. These options seem rather over the top to me, but if you're an action junkie, these new machines may be just the ticket to keep you happy.

Exploring other machines

Judging a book by its cover is hard to do — a saying that's especially true with the myriad of video poker games available. Many new machines may look flashy, but if you're unsure how they work or what their payout is, the best rule is to avoid them. If you're eager to try one, I suggest you do so once and then focus on the video poker games in this chapter that have better odds. However, if do you want to try some other video poker machines, just remember that these games have lower payouts and odds than Jacks or Better, Deuces Wild, or Triple Play. In fact, even their names can be deceptive.

Chapter 14

Striking the Mother Lode: Keno and Bingo

. . . .

In This Chapter

▶ Uncovering keno basics

▶ Strategizing at keno

▶ Reviewing the fundamentals of bingo

▶ Discovering some winning bingo moves

. . . .

*U*nless you're already a keno or bingo aficionado, you may be a little amazed by the large crowds that swarm around these two simple games at casinos (not to mention bingo halls and churches) throughout the gambling world.

Keno and bingo have tons in common. The following are just a few of their major commonalities:

✔ People have played them for centuries.

✔ They're games of pure chance.

✔ They're super simple to play.

Keno is familiar to most casino goers because it's so visible. Anywhere you wander in a casino, you're bound to find a big, flashing keno board in view. Part of keno's appeal is that it's so accessible and convenient. And although keno offers some pretty dismal odds, its leisurely pace affords you a reasonably slow way of losing money — while still dangling the hope of a payout for a relatively small wager in front of you.

Bingo attracts millions of people every day around the world. In fact, you'd be hard-pressed to find a person over the age of 6 who *doesn't* know how to play bingo. Most bingo playing actually occurs in bingo halls, churches, and synagogues rather than in casinos. The fact that some casinos do offer bingo may surprise regular gamblers.

So are you ready to get the balls bouncing and the numbers calling? This chapter covers the basics of keno and bingo and provides some strategies that can help you succeed (or at least survive) at these two popular games.

Catching On to Keno Basics

In many casinos, keno operates 24 hours a day, and a new game starts about every ten minutes. (However, most cruise ship casinos and some smaller casinos don't have keno.) In fact, *keno runners* — whose job is to zip throughout the casino gathering bets — make betting at keno while you're playing the slots or having a drink at the bar possible. Keno is a "need-not-be-present-to-win" game. So whether you choose to play in the comfy keno lounge, where cocktail servers are at your beck and call offering free drinks, or you flag down a keno runner while eating breakfast, you're bound to find a keno game within easy reach.

Before you can play, you need to know where to go and what to do. This section provides you with the essentials: how to play, how to mark your card, and how to gather your winnings (if you're so lucky).

Playing the game

Gambling doesn't get much easier than keno. Each keno game is a *race*. When playing keno, your goal is to guess numbers drawn from a large hopper that vaguely resembles an oversized popcorn popper. From 80 balls marked with numbers, the machine randomly shoots up 20 balls — the winning numbers — into a long gooseneck. (Some casinos, however, have modernized and now use a computer to pick the numbers.) The *caller* announces each winning number. Here's how you play:

1. **Choose your numbers.**

   Mark your selected numbers on a keno card with the special little crayon. (Check out the next section, "Filling out your ticket: X marks the spot," for more specifics.) I still haven't figured out why casinos provide crayons instead of pens or markers, but perhaps crayons are appropriate considering that the game requires no more than a kindergarten education. You usually are asked to pick anywhere from 1 to 15 numbers, or *spots,* on one card.

2. **Make your wager on the keno card.**

Keno wagers are among the lowest the casino offers. You find brochures explaining the rules and payouts for each type of bet in the keno lounge and in the casino's restaurants. The typical keno bet is $1 per race, but some games are even lower. You may also bet $2 or $5. You indicate the amount of your wager on the keno card.

3. **Give your card to the keno runner or go to the counter yourself to place the bet.**

   After you mark the card with all your favorite numbers, give the card and your wager to the keno runner. She takes it to the keno counter and brings you a printed receipt confirming your number selections. Or if you need the exercise, take the card directly to the counter in the keno lounge yourself. You may want to take the card to the counter if the game is about to begin; keno runners usually are the last in line to place wagers at the counter and sometimes they don't get the bets in on time.

   Don't lose your receipt! You must have it in order to collect your winnings.

4. **Follow the numbers on the board.**

   As the race is in play, the 20 numbers appear one at a time on the keno boards throughout the casino. You can tell when the game is over — the last number picked flashes repeatedly on the screen.

Or you can take the easy route. If you find picking a handful of random numbers an overwhelming task, you can choose the "Quick-Pick" option and have a bunch of numbers selected for you. You can also tell the keno runner that you want to play the same numbers you did before, which saves you the time of filling out a new card.

Filling out your ticket: X marks the spot

Keno is probably the easiest game in a casino. Mark a few numbers with an X, and cross your fingers as the keno board fills up. But you do have a few betting variations when playing keno, in addition to the standard way to play, which is called a *straight ticket*.

This section identifies the different ways you can fill out your keno ticket as well as the important areas on the actual ticket that you need to fill in.

Tallying your ticket

When filling out a keno ticket, you have many options. The following list identifies all the most common ways to fill out a ticket:

✔ **Straight ticket:** This ticket (check out Figure 14-1) allows you to mark up to 15 numbers, and if any of them are drawn, you win an amount according to the payout table. You can bet the minimum (usually $1) or any multiple of that for each ticket (the price per ticket is irregardless of how many numbers you play). Each ticket is classified according to how many numbers are played. For example, if you played four numbers, that is called a 4-spot ticket. The more numbers you pick, the more numbers are required to hit in order to win any money (refer to "Winning and collecting," later in this chapter). The straight ticket is considered the standard play and is definitely the easiest way to play — especially for the beginner.

✔ **Split ticket:** This ticket is simply two or more straight tickets that you play on the same card. In essence, you're playing two games on one card. You designate which numbers go with which game by either circling or separating them with a line. (See Figure 14-2.)

The drawback of playing a split ticket: You can't use the same number in both games.

✔ **Way ticket:** With this option (see Figure 14-3), you play two or more sets of numbers in the same race. You need to circle each set to differentiate it. Many people play the way ticket to qualify for the *fractional rates* — depending on the casino, you can play for as little as 25¢ per way instead of the $1 you need to bet on a straight ticket. But remember that the payout is lower as well if you split your $1 bet into fractions.

✔ **Top/bottom ticket:** In this bet, you mark the ticket "T" for top or "B" for bottom and bet the 40 numbers in either half. This ticket is a "casino special" and costs $5 to wager. If 13 of the 20 numbers drawn fall into the half you select, you win.

1	2	3	4	5	6	7	8	9	10
11	12	13	14	15	16	17	✗	19	20
21	✗	23	24	25	26	27	28	29	30
31	32	33	34	35	36	37	38	39	40
41	42	43	✗	45	46	47	48	49	50
51	52	53	54	55	56	57	58	59	60
61	62	63	64	65	✗	67	68	69	70
71	72	73	74	75	76	77	78	79	80

NUMBER OF GAMES — 1
PRICE PER GAME — $1.00
NUMBER OF SPOTS — 4

Figure 14-1: Marking a straight ticket.

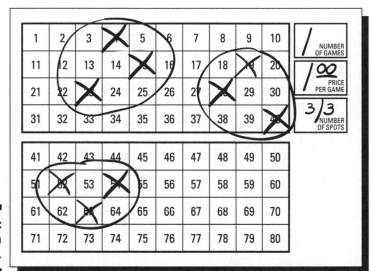

Figure 14-2:
Marking a
split ticket.

Figure 14-3:
Marking a
way ticket.

The top/bottom ticket is a terrible bet. You have a better chance of scoring a big payout if you stick that crayon in your ear and sue the casino for damages.

The easiest way to start is by betting the minimum of $1. But if you want to be a keno high roller, you can play multiples. In order to do so, for example, you can bet $3 on a straight ticket and win three times the $1 payout rate. Just remember that if you do get real lucky, most casinos cap the maximum payout to an aggregate of $50,000 per game.

Don't let the variations of keno bets overwhelm you. You don't *have* to get fancy: You can simply stick to a straight ticket. If you have any problems with figuring out how to wager, ask the keno runners, who are happy to help you.

Working your way down a card

This short section is a quick keno shorthand lesson for entering the betting information in the right-hand column of your ticket, also known as the *conditioning* area. If you want to play a combination ticket with, for example, a 4-spot in the top group of numbers, a 4-spot on the bottom, and play the entire ticket as an 8-spot, write the following in the margin:

$3	1/4	1/4	1/8	$1

Filling out your card this way means the terms of the wager you're betting are as follows:

$3 is the total price for your ticket.

1/4 is keno-speak for a *one 4-spot* bet.

1/8 means *one 8-spot*.

$1 indicates you're making a $1 bet on each combination.

Just be aware that if you bet $2 on the two 4-spots and *all eight numbers* come up, you win the two four-number bets — but you do *not* win the 8-spot payout because you didn't bet that option!

Winning and collecting

A *catch* is any number that you mark and is one of the 20 numbers the house draws. But whether you win depends on how many numbers you hit in relation to how many you originally marked. The brochure available in the keno lounge spells out the house rules and payouts — and payouts do vary from casino to casino. But, basically, the size of the payout depends on the following two factors:

✔ The number of spots you select

✔ The number of spots you catch

For example, if you mark only one number and bet $1, you win $3 if your number comes up. But the more numbers you mark on a $1 ticket, the lower your winnings will be if you have only a few catches. If you bet $1 and mark six numbers (which you call a *6-spot ticket*) and hit three of them, you win $1, which is really only your original bet returned. But if you hit *five* numbers, your payout increases to $90. And if lightning strikes and you catch all six numbers, you win $1,500.

The origin of keno: An ancient Chinese secret

Keno is an ancient lottery game that originated in China during the Han Dynasty (around 200 B.C.). Since that time, merchants, peasants, and emperors have played it for more than 2,000 years. The name of the old game was "kino," and according to legend, an emperor used it to help finance the building of the Great Wall of China. Chinese laborers who came to the United States to work on railroads in the 1800s introduced the game in the American West, where keno parlors quickly became the rage.

Refer to Table 14-1 for a better idea of the various plays and payouts to expect.

Table 14-1		A Typical $1 Keno-Payout Chart								
Catches Marked										
1	*2*	*3*	*4*	*5*	*6*	*7*	*8*	*9*	*10*	
1 $3										
2	$12									
3	$1	$43								
4	$1	$3	$125							
5		$1	$15	$700						
6		$1	$4	$90	$1,500					
7			$1	$20	$400	$8,000				
8				$5	$100	$1,800	$25,000			
9				$5	$30	$300	$5,000	$50,000		
10				$1	$20	$150	$1,000	$8,000	$50,000	

As you can see, the more numbers you mark, the more hits you need to collect for a payout, and, consequently, the longer your odds. A great example of this principle is the 10-spot card. Hitting all ten numbers scores you a nice $50,000 payday, but the chances of hitting ten out of ten is about 9 million to one.

At some casinos in Nevada, if your ticket wins, you have only until the start of the next game to cash in. After that, the ticket is worthless. So if that is the case, check your numbers against the display board to see if you hit, and then quickly go to collect. If you place your wager through a keno runner, redeeming your ticket and bringing you back your winnings is her job. But the best advice is to always check in advance to find out the particular casino policy for cashing in winning tickets.

Exploring keno variations

Live keno is the keno you play in casinos, based in the keno lounge and broadcast on the large keno boards throughout. Although it's quite convenient and accessible, live keno still requires you to be in the casino to track the results and claim your prize if you win. But other versions of keno offer even more flexibility. This section covers a few of those more popular versions.

Cashing in later with multirace keno and keno to go

If you want to avoid rushing like a madman to cash in your winning ticket before the next game begins, you can play *multirace* keno, in which you can bet 20 games or more on one ticket and cash in any winning tickets at the last game.

In some casinos, you must submit your tickets after the last game ends — and before the next game begins — or you forfeit your winnings. Once again the best policy is to always ask when you're purchasing your ticket so you don't miss the window of opportunity for cashing in your winners.

And if you don't want to be in the casino but still want to play, another option many clubs offer is *keno to go.* In this version, you can play a larger number of games — up to 999 games in some casinos — and have up to a year to cash in your winnings. Check at the keno counter to review the rules concerning multigame tickets.

Seeing is believing with video keno

Video keno is played on slot machines in the slot area of casinos (see Chapter 12 for more on slots). Video keno is a faster and more exciting version of the live game and is easy to play: Simply touch the screen to select your numbers, choose the number of coins or credits to bet, and press Play. The machine then picks 20 numbers randomly and displays them on the screen. A color change indicates if you catch any of the numbers, and the casino credits winnings to your total just like when you play a slot machine.

You can play video keno for stakes as low as 5¢ to 25¢ per draw, and payouts can be very attractive — up to $2,000 for hitting eight out of eight.

Your odds are actually better with video keno (a more attractive 8 to 10 percent house edge due to better pay tables) than regular keno (which can be close to 30 percent). But because video keno plays so much faster, your losing rate (cost of playing per hour) is actually much higher. Regular keno has a game every ten minutes; but you can make 100 bets on a video version in the same amount of time.

If you play a machine that offers a *progressive jackpot* (a jackpot that increases until it's finally hit), be sure to bet the maximum credits required and the maximum numbers. For example, if the game requires you to bet ten numbers, don't bet eight. Be sure to study the payout chart on the machine carefully to determine your best shot at the jackpot.

Improving Your Odds at Keno

If you're familiar with any type of lottery or lotto game, you probably have a good understanding of keno. No strategy is needed for the game because it depends entirely on chance. And although you can't strategize a win, you can take steps to regulate the amount you lose by following these few simple guidelines:

- **Stick to a betting pattern that works for you, such as straight tickets.** (For more on straight tickets, see the earlier section "Tallying your ticket.")

- **Look for a good payout table for both live and video keno, and restrict your play to those casinos that offer the best odds.** Just remember that the odds of hitting your numbers never change, only the payout tables.

- **Keep your bets small in keno.** The house edge in live keno varies wildly depending on how many numbers you bet and where you play, but it's always high. The house edge usually starts at 25 percent and can be as high as 40 percent, which means the casino keeps up to $40 for every $100 wagered. This game is fabulous for casinos — just look at how much floor space they devote to it.

- **Don't waste your money on bets with astronomical odds.** Hitting 15 out of 15 numbers is nearly impossible, so don't even try.

- **Opt for live over video keno.** Live keno takes a lot longer to play than video keno, which means you lose money at a much slower rate.

You can see why keno isn't a good bet, especially with so many other games in the casino to choose from. Yet keno does have an upside — most people play for only a $1 per game, and with only a few games running per hour, keno can take a long time to drain your wallet. And the game has one more plus: At most casinos, when you sit around the keno lounge with a crayon in your hand, cocktail servers cheerfully bring you free booze until you're not sure which side of the crayon is the business end.

Figuring Out the ABCs of B-I-N-G-O

Like keno, bingo is a numbers game that has been around for centuries, slowly evolving into its present form. Originating in Italy in the 1500s, bingo is very popular worldwide — not just in casinos and on cruises, but at churches and other religious institutions as a way to raise funds. Arguably one of the most familiar forms of gambling, the game of bingo may need little explanation — you play it virtually the same way whether you're at a second-grade birthday party or in an Indian-reservation casino.

Setting the scene: The cast, crew, and props

At most casinos and bingo halls, bingo involves a few constant components and a familiar cast of characters. This section focuses on the people and the props you need to know.

Bingo worker bees

At any bingo session, you're likely to find two key characters who facilitate the games. The *caller* announces the letter-number combinations that come up. The floor persons, or *checkers* (their number depends on the size of the crowd), check when someone declares a bingo that the caller has indeed called all the winning numbers.

Bingo balls

In the past, casinos used a large, metal cage or big, plastic blower that housed bingo's 75 small plastic balls, each with a unique letter-number combination. The blower "whooshed" the balls around, and the caller chose them randomly one by one. The caller announced the letter-number combination. The result was also immediately posted on a large flash board.

However, that system is becoming antiquated, and most modern casinos use computers to generate the random bingo numbers and automatic card scanners to validate winners. Some clubs (such as John Ascuagua's Nugget near Reno, Nevada) have taken bingo into a truly high-tech era. They have play stations that players can rent to keep track of their games, which allows patrons to play up to 90 cards at a time!

Bingo cards

As the caller announces the letter-number combos, you mark them on one or more bingo cards (which are often laid out on sheets rather than on individual cards). These cards (see Figure 14-4) spell out B-I-N-G-O across the top of five columns, and under each letter are five numbers, giving a selection of 24 out of 75 possible numbers. One free space is in the middle of the card.

Bingo cards don't randomly distribute the 75 numbers used in bingo but spread them out evenly over the five letters, as follows:

✔ **B column:** 1 to 15

✔ **I column:** 16 to 30

✔ **N column:** 31 to 45 (the center spot is always free)

✔ **G column:** 46 to 60

✔ **O column:** 61 to 75

Figure 14-4:
A standard
bingo card.

B	I	N	G	O
2	17	31	51	●
6	20	38	●	67
7	22	●	54	69
12	●	39	57	72
●	27	44	60	75

If the cards are individual (rather than printed en masse on sheets), two main types of bingo cards are available when you play:

✔ **Flimsies:** Paper throwaways.

✔ **Shutter cards:** Plastic permanent cards. Their name comes from the fact that these cards have little window shutters that you use to cover a called number and that you can reset for the next game.

Bingo markers

When using the paper cards, you mark them with a special ink bottle or pen, known in bingo lingo as a *dauber*. If you instead use sheets (rather than individual cards), then punch-out options and markers aren't used. Sheets typically come with either 3, 6, 9, or 12 games preprinted on them.

Playing B-I-N-G-O down the line

You typically play bingo in a session consisting of several games. One great feature of bingo is that every game has a winner! An individual game may only last ten minutes or so, but the entire bingo session typically lasts a few hours. The following steps show how you play bingo:

1. **Before the start of a bingo session, purchase bingo cards, usually sold in packets of three to six cards, or sheets (which have a fixed number printed on them).**

   The purchase of your bingo cards is your admission charge to the session. In many bingo casinos and halls, you must buy a minimum number of cards. An average price is 25¢ to 50¢ per card, but games can go for as little as a nickel or dime and as high as $1. You can't bring in your own bingo cards or unused cards from another session.

2. **The bingo game starts when the caller yells "Eyes down."**

3. **The balls start popping, and the caller begins selecting and announcing the letter-number combinations.**

4. **With each call, you check your cards to see whether you have the called letter-number combination and, if so, you mark it on your card or do the punch-out on the sheets.**

   The object of the game is to cover a specified pattern on a card before any other player. The most familiar pattern is the *line*, with five numbers in a row, running in one of the following directions:

   • Diagonally

   • Horizontally

   • Vertically

5. **When you find you have a winning pattern, you shout "Bingo!" to alert the caller to stop the play.**

   Typically, most wins occur within 12 to 14 calls.

6. **A checker rushes to your side and reads off the letter-number combos in your winning pattern to verify that you're a winner.**

   If another player calls bingo at the same time, you both win, and you split the prize money.

   To stop the game, you must loudly call out "Bingo" as soon as your last number comes up. If you don't attract the attention of the checker and the play continues with the next ball called, your bingo won't be honored. For example, if the caller announces I-19 and then B-12, I-19 is no longer a winning number! The I-19 is a *sleeper* and isn't a valid bingo. So be extra alert if you're playing multiple cards — or limit yourself to one card until you pick up some speed. After the game is over, a new game begins with everyone keeping their same cards or sheets, but starting over (a clean slate).

Spicing up cover patterns

Not all bingo games play the traditional line pattern of five covered numbers in a row. To keep bingo from getting boring, you can play dozens of different cover patterns. Some commonly used patterns include

- **Four corners:** You cover the four corners of the card.
- **Checkers:** You cover alternating squares — like a checkerboard.
- **Letters:** You cover squares to create the shapes of letters, such as "E," "S," and "T."

Some of these complex patterns are more challenging to track if you're playing multiple cards. As an aid, the rules of the game allow you to premark your card with a different colored marker or a pencil — just sketch or outline the pattern you need in order to win. Then use the regular blotter to mark the called numbers. And always remember to mark your free square before you begin every game! However, the newer computerized versions of bingo typically display the current game pattern on a big screen behind the caller. So if you're ever confused, just snatch a quick peek there for reference.

If that still sounds too challenging, then I suggest you throw away the marking pen and go to a club that offers newer high-tech versions of bingo. For example, the Nugget Casino also has computer monitors as an option for players. These monitors automatically track all of your games, mark the numbers as they're hit, and alert you when you win. It also has customized options to increase the fun, such as using diamonds or hearts to mark your numbers, or allowing you to watch TV or play solitaire on the screen while the computer keeps track of all your Bingo games.

Uncovering bigger prizes with coverall

Special bingo games, such as *coverall* — in which you must cover all 25 spaces on the card to win — offer larger prizes. Frequently, the big cash pot goes unclaimed because the coverall game limits how many numbers are drawn (usually 48). Why a limit of 48? It's good for the house. The odds are 1 in 799,399 that the caller announces all 24 numbers on your card among the 48 balls drawn. With each additional number drawn, the chance of covering all the numbers increases substantially: 1 in 212,085 with 50 numbers and 1 in 715 with 60 numbers.

If no one wins the coverall prize in 48 draws, the eventual winner receives a smaller consolation prize, and the unearned prize money goes into a progressive jackpot that keeps growing. Some casinos (and bingo halls) run a progressive jackpot game for the session's finale, which is what bingo vets wait for!

Calling Forth Winning Bingo Strategies

Bingo is another one of those games of chance. Although you have no sway over which numbers the caller announces, and no amount of skill or troll dolls, rabbit's feet, or lucky tokens can change the outcome of the draws, you can take steps to improve your odds of winning.

Seeking the ideal bingo venue

The most important strategy is to select a place to play that offers the optimal conditions that favor your chances of winning, which you can do by following these tips:

- **Choose a casino or bingo hall that lets you select your own cards.** If you play two or more cards, you don't want to have duplicate numbers. Otherwise, if the number doesn't come up, neither card can win (if you were playing coverall for example). When you play several different cards without duplicate numbers, you're able to cover almost all 75 possible numbers, which increases your chances of winning.

✔ **Play with the fewest number of people possible.** You have better odds of winning with fewer players. Ask the crew at the casino or bingo hall what time of day and which day of the week is the least busy. If the payouts are guaranteed, your potential return can increase, particularly if a snowstorm hit and most regulars stayed home.

✔ **Look for casinos and bingo halls that offer a progressive jackpot.** Unearned winnings accumulate throughout the session and often build up to attractive amounts that the winner of a final game receives.

Winning at bingo: Odds aren't all that bad (sometimes)

You may be surprised, but casino bingo sometimes has excellent odds! Unlike keno's steep 25 to 40 percent house advantage, casino bingo has a much lower house edge and can be as low as 1 to 3 percent. The game isn't a big winning proposition for casinos, but they offer it as one more way to bring in the crowds that they hope hit the slots before (and after) the bingo sessions. Unfortunately, if you're cruising for a mean bingo game in Vegas, you won't find it on the Strip. But you can find one at some of the older casinos downtown.

Does bingo drive you crazy?

Toy salesman Edwin Lowe brought bingo to the masses when he designed "Lowe's Bingo" in 1929, back in the days when players covered numbers with beans and shouted "Beano!" when they covered a line. Lowe saw potential in the game and went to Columbia University math professor Carl Leffler to ask him to develop cards. In 1930, long before the days of computers, the professor wrote 6,000 bingo-card combinations with nonrepeating number groups. You can print 1,474,200 unique bingo combinations on a 24-number bingo card, which may explain why Leffler spent the rest of his life in a mental hospital.

Chapter 15

From the Cubs to the Bears: Sports Betting

Some men and women think about it every seven minutes. They dream about it at night, and it often hampers their productivity at work. Just talking about it gets their hearts pumping like jackhammers.

Am I talking about sex? Heck, no. I'm talking sports, Baby! And nothing makes this passion burn brighter than placing a bet on a favorite professional or college team. Whether you're a basketball, baseball, football, hockey, boxing, or tennis fan — or you just love to bet on sports events — sports betting may be the perfect outlet for someone who loves to heighten the thrill of the competition with the challenge of the wager.

Although the odds are bad (the house usually has a 4.5 percent edge), sports betting in Nevada casinos offers great entertainment value. For a small wager, you can buy hours of enjoyment while watching your favorite team. For many fans, this wager is a paltry price to pay in order to crank up the excitement quotient of watching a big game. And even if your team doesn't win the game, you still may beat the spread (see "Defining point spread" later in the chapter).

Beating the spread, reading the line. . . I explain these phrases and more in this chapter on sports betting — a business that isn't just recreational for some people. In this chapter, I spell out the circumstances in which sports betting is legal. (Believe it or not, even your office pool for the NCAA Basketball Championships isn't quite aboveboard). I also offer an overview of the major sports you can bet on in Nevada casinos, and I serve up the strategies and logic behind analyzing numbers and match-ups.

Defining Sports Betting: The Legal Kind, That Is

Sports betting is the wagering on the outcome of sports events, from pro teams to college tournaments, from football to boxing to basketball. A *sports book* is the facility that operates the betting arena. A sports book may be a stand-alone establishment, one that operates within a casino, or one that exists ethereally in cyberspace. Think of the sports book as the legal form of your local bookie, without the insults, the phone calls in the middle of the night, and, of course, the baseball bats.

Before you draw up plans for the office Super Bowl pool, be aware that, except in specific circumstances, sports betting is illegal in the United States. In 49 states, Nevada excluded, a relationship with the local *bookie* can land you in jail.

Sports betting is aboveboard in two situations, so don't despair. One situation requires you to do some traveling (unless you live in Nevada). You can indulge in the other from the comfort of your couch (as long as it's within reach of your phone and computer). The two legal ways to make a sports bet are as follows:

✔ **Betting in Nevada.** Within the United States, sports betting is legal only in the state of Nevada, although the Oregon State Lottery allows limited wagering on sporting events. Nevada is home to more than 150 licensed sports books in casinos. So if you're seeking to bet on the next big game in the cozy ambiance of a casino, you'd better pack your bags and head for the Silver State.

Can you call or e-mail your bets to Nevada sports books? Only if you're within the state when you make contact — the casinos aren't allowed to accept out-of-state wagers (via telephone or Internet). You must also be 21 to place a sports bet in Nevada.

✔ **Betting on the Internet.** Several hundred offshore Internet sports betting Web sites gladly accept your wagers, regardless of where you live. The legality of betting online is still somewhat murky, so check your local laws before taking the plunge.

You can place the same types of bets you make in a casino sports book online with just a few clicks of the mouse and be done in less than a minute. Additionally, Internet sports books are open 24/7, and because of the fierce competition for your gambling dollar, they offer some of the best betting opportunities.

Online betting has its potential pitfalls. In the past, a few crooked sports books refused to pay winners, or they closed up shop and ran off with the money. (Check out Chapter 17 for more on online gambling.)

To avoid being scammed, be sure to deal only with a reputable online casino. Two sites I highly recommend are the Greek Sports Book and Bodog Sports Book. Both of these are honest, dependable companies with great long-term track records for good customer service and prompt payments.

Betting on a wide world of sports

Sports betting in the United States encompasses a spectrum of sporting events, although professional and college ball games are the most common. While in Nevada, you can make your wager on the following sports and sporting events, listed in order of popularity:

- Football
- Basketball
- Baseball
- Boxing
- Hockey
- NASCAR
- Golf
- Tennis
- Special events such as the Indy 500 or Olympics
- International events such as World Cup soccer matches

Because the rest of the world's taste in sports is quite different from that of Americans, an online sports book offers an array of events that may seem strange when viewed through red-white-and-blue–tinted glasses. If you broaden the betting net to include events accessible online or overseas, you can bet on

- Bicycle racing
- Cricket
- Dog racing
- European football
- Motorcycle racing
- Rugby
- Track and field

Making money for the house

Sports bets aren't even-money bets like most other casinos games. In sports betting, you normally wager $110 to win $100 (often known as an 11/10 wager). This wager is the industry standard, but you can bet any amount to suit your bankroll (within the minimum and maximum bets the sports book allows).

On first glance it may seem like casinos make $10 on every $110 wagered (or around 9 percent), but fortunately, that's not true. For example, you and a friend each bet $110 on opposing sides of the same game. Your team wins, and you cash in your ticket and get back your $110 plus an additional $100, totaling $210. However, your friend loses his entire $110 because his team played like high school chess players in football pads. The net result for the casino is a profit of $10: $220 in and $210 out.

This net $10 is, in essence, the casino's commission, also known as the *vigorish,* or *vig* for short. The vig may not sound like much, but this small advantage (4.5 percent) wins $45 for the house for every $1,000 wagered, and that adds up to a very profitable sum over time.

But the casino's 4.5 percent win is only guaranteed if there is an equal amount of bettors on both sides of a game. How, then, does the house keep everyone from betting on the heavy favorites? When Notre Dame plays North Dakota, for example, what's to prevent every bettor from picking the Fighting Irish and bankrupting the casino? Read on; I explain it all in the next section.

Leveling the Betting Field with Lines and Point Spreads

How does the casino get you to bet on an underdog, such as North Dakota in a game against Notre Dame? With all due respect to North Dakota, the Sioux probably don't have much of a chance in a football game against the Fighting Irish. Great disparities between teams exist throughout the world of sports competition. If everyone bet on the favorites, casinos would have a hard time making money. Thus, sports books employ one of two systems, commonly called *lines,* to level the playing fields between the Davids and the Goliaths — at least in the betting arena.

The casino doesn't care who wins the game. Its primary concern is to get an equal amount of wagers on both sides in order to ensure its vig.

In this section, I discuss how a casino determines point spreads and money lines. This section explains how the lines are set, why they move, and how they affect the way you bet.

Setting the money line

A money line is just a fancy way of saying *odds* for a sports event. Like any other odds, a money line is a ratio: what you bet to what you get paid. The only confusing part about the money line is remembering the amount $100, because it's not listed with the odds, it's only implied. The following is an example of a money line listing that could count for any sport:

–300 Cougars

+240 Pumas

In this instance, the Cougars are favored to win against the Pumas. The Cougars are listed at –300 (you would say they are "minus three hundred"), which means that bettors must bet $300 in order to win $100. That's just a ratio; you don't actually have to bet that much. You could bet any amount you wanted to and it would be calculated the same way: $3 bet for every $1 won.

The weaker team — the Pumas — is listed at +240. Again the $100 is implied. But for the underdogs, the implied $100 is the amount you bet, not the amount you win. If you bet $100 on the Pumas and win, you get paid $240 or 2.4 to 1. Again, you need not actually bet that much; it's just a ratio. If you bet $20, you get paid $48 (2.4 × $20) for a win. The casino makes a profit because it takes in more money from the losing bettor than it pays to the winning bettor.

A common misconception is that the money line reflects the actual difference between the strength of the two teams. In reality, the line reflects how casinos *think* the public will bet. In a money line wager, whether the game is close or a blowout doesn't matter. The only factor that counts is which side wins.

Money-line bets are most common in baseball, boxing, soccer, and hockey. Baseball betting lines, for example, look something like this when they appear in the newspaper:

ATLANTA   6:5   Houston

Atlanta is the home team and the favorite. The first number (6) means you need to bet $6 in order to win $5 on the favorite. The second number (5) means you need to risk $5 to win $5 on the underdog.

Defining point spread

A more popular method of betting is using a *point spread* for the bets rather than a money line. The point spread method for balanced betting focuses on the actual difference in the score rather than simply which team wins. Point spreads are the most common way to bet football and basketball games.

The point-spread is a value that bettors must add or subtract from their team's score when they place an even-money sports bet. Favorites have negative point spreads, and underdogs have positive point spreads. For example, look at the listing for the AFC Championship Game played in January 2006:

> Steelers
>
> Broncos   —4

The point spread in this game was Broncos minus 4. The minus sign means the Broncos were favored over the Steelers. (You could also say that the point spread in this game was Steelers plus 4, even though +4 doesn't appear next to the Steelers.) Point spreads are sometimes listed in 1/2 point increments.

What does all this mean? Bettors on the Broncos have to subtract 4 points from the final score to determine the result of their bet. If, after subtracting 4 points, the Broncos still outscored the Steelers, the bet on the Broncos is a winner. Steelers bettors get to add 4 points to the Steelers' score at the end of the game. Even if the Steelers lost the game on the field, bettors still won the bet if the difference in the game was less than 4 points.

When a team wins against the point spread regardless of the on-the-field result, it's said to have *covered the spread*. Should there be a point spread tie (for example, if the Broncos had won 28-24), the bet is called a *push,* and most casinos refund your wager.

Every sports book assigns its own initial point spread, also known simply as *the spread* or *the line* (not to be confused with *the money lines* mentioned in the previous section) to each game before it's played. The big books have their own handicappers; other books subscribe to line-making services, such as the Las Vegas Sports Consultants. (Check out the nearby sidebar "Las Vegas Sports Consultants: The wizards behind the curtain" for more info about these wizzes). There is no single official point spread, although most casinos tend to be within a point or two of each other.

Being a total winner

Almost as popular as betting on the point spread are *over/under* bets. Instead of picking a team in a game, the bettor determines whether the combined score of both teams will be above or below a *total* number. Casinos determine totals the same way they do point spreads; their goal is to split the betting evenly between the under and the over. Totals are usually listed next to the underdog team in the point spread like this:

> Steelers   42.5
>
> Broncos   —4

Over/under bets are common in professional basketball, baseball, and football games. They're also usually available on the most popular college football and basketball games.

Moving the line

When the lines are first set and posted by the casinos, they're most vulnerable to *smart money* (from professional bettors). Because these lines aren't true reflections of the exact difference in point spreads between two teams, the pros armed with computer models sometimes find a line that's off and bet aggressively. When these pros hammer the early lines, the casinos respond by *moving the line.* For example, a Super Bowl game may open with Miami as a seven-point favorite, but the line may change to nine or ten points by kickoff.

Occasionally, lines move because of player injuries, but, in most cases, lines move because you and other bettors are wagering a disproportionate amount of money on one team. Because the casinos' goal is to evenly distribute the betting, they move the point spread up or down to attract more action on the opposing team. Moving the line makes sports betting a true democracy because the lines respond to how you *vote*.

Las Vegas Sports Consultants: The wizards behind the curtain

The process of setting money lines used to be a mystery. In the past, point spreads were as mysterious as the workings behind the curtain in *The Wizard of Oz*. With the advent of the computer age, the business of setting the lines has changed dramatically. Now most casinos use the services of a group called Las Vegas Sports Consultants (LVSC) to set their odds and betting lines. LVSC has several knowledgeable odds makers assigned to each major sport. These experienced analysts consider the various strengths of the two opposing teams and factor in recent injuries and form.

Every Sunday night during the NFL season, these experts gather in the offices of LVSC to determine the early lines of next Sunday's football games. They use a combination of subjective information (injuries, travel schedules, weather) and objective information (win and loss records and the cold, hard data of computer power rankings). These experienced prognosticators juggle all of these variables and then reach a consensus on where to set the lines for each game.

LVSC experts then send out numbers to the various casinos and sports books that subscribe to LVSC. Most sports books immediately post these lines on their boards, although they retain the prerogative to modify the numbers to suit their own clientele.

Eyeing the exotics (bets, not dancers)

There's more to sports betting than simple wagers. *Exotic bets* offer the sports fan an opportunity to make higher-risk, higher-reward wagers. Like other sports bets, exotic wagers have posted odds in the casino that move up and down depending on how heavy the betting is. The following list identifies some typical exotic wagers available at almost every sports book.

- **Parlays:** By far the most common exotic bets, parlays involve placing a single bet that involves multiple games.

- **Teasers:** These wagers are similar to parlays in that they are a combination bet involving multiple games. But when you *tease* two or more teams, the point spreads are moved in your favor for every game. It's not all good news though; the payouts are less than parlays.

- **Propositions:** These are those zany bets you occasionally hear about where bettors put money on who will win the coin toss or some other single (and sometimes obscure) aspect of a given game. These bets are usually available only in heavily bet events like the Super Bowl.

- **Futures:** If you think you can predict a team's long-term achievements, plunk down some cash on a future bet. You get paid handsomely for betting on something like the World Series champ or the number of wins the Mavericks will have. . .before the season even starts!

Exotics are the kind of bets to avoid for two reasons: First, exotics attract tourists rather than knowledgeable bettors, and second, the odds usually don't compensate for the risk you're taking. (Check out the following sections for more information about exotic bets.)

Multiplying your fun with parlays

With a parlay, you choose two or more teams to win on the same ticket, or parlay card. In order for you to cash in, all your teams wagered on the parlay card must win if it is a money line bet, or all your teams must beat the point spread if the card is based on that.

Because of the multiple games involved, parlays are more difficult to win than single straight bets. You can win a lot, however, with only a small bet, which makes parlays as attractive as the lottery. But the odds can be very bad on parlays, so you pay a fairly high price for the added excitement of a big payday.

Table 15-1 illustrates that the more teams you pick on your parlay card, the higher the house edge. This happens because the true odds for your bet are different from the winnings you receive. For example, with a $100 bet, the chance of picking four random winners is exactly 1 in 16, so the break-even point for the win is actually $1,600. But, based on the 11 to 1 payout odds, you receive only $1,200 for a $100 bet.

Table 15-1	Casino Edge on Parlay Bets		
Parlayed Wagers	*Typical Casino Payoff*	*True Odds*	*House Edge*
2 for 2	13:5	3:1	10 percent
3 for 3	6:1	7:1	12.5 percent
4 for 4	11:1	15:1	25 percent

Teasing your betting bone

A teaser is similar to a parlay because you bet on more than one team on the same ticket, and you must win more than one game in order to collect. Teasers don't offer the long-shot odds of parlays because they pay off like single straight bets. With teasers, however, you typically get 6 or 7 points in your favor on all picks. But even this extra bonus isn't enough to make this type of bet worthwhile. Teasers belong in the gimmick bet category.

Playing parlays close to home

With a parlay, you choose two or more teams to win on the same ticket, or parlay card. The following table shows you an example of a betting a parlay. Suppose I decide to show my regional pride by picking all four Northwest major universities (Oregon, Oregon State, Washington, and Washington State) to win their Saturday football games. I fill out the parlay card by selecting the corresponding numbers on the card for those four schools with the appropriate bet spreads. (Remember, they don't have to win the game, only cover the spread). Here is how the lines look in the newspaper (see the following table). The first team mentioned is always the favorite, and the home team is always capitalized. The number in the middle is the point spread to be added to the underdog's final score.

The weekend starts off great as WSU wallops Stanford on the road 31-14. Then Oregon State hangs on for a wild 28-24 win over UCLA. My luck then continues as Oregon stuns the undefeated USC Trojans 38-31. Ka-Ching! I can almost count my winnings now. Three up and three down. Unfortunately, in the late game, Washington goes down without a whimper and gets shellacked 51-0 by the Cal Bears.

The net result for my mostly successful day? A loss of $100. Despite picking three out of four winners, the whole ticket loses if any team fails to cover the spread.

Saturday's Games

STANFORD	8	Washington State	USC	24	Oregon
UCLA	Pick'Em	Oregon State	CALIFORNIA	33	Washington

If a tie occurs on any of the games in your parlay or teaser bet, it automatically drops down to the next lower number of games. For example, if you have a four-game parlay and one of the games results in a tie, your parlay becomes a three-game parlay and pays off as such. If a tie occurs in a two-team parlay or teaser bet, the ticket is usually voided and your money refunded.

Intriguing propositions

Proposition bets, better known as _prop_ bets, target special events or actions that may occur during a particular game, especially during the Super Bowl. Some examples of prop bets include bets on the longest touchdown of the game, which team makes the first punt, whether a defense or special team's touchdown occurs, and so on. The casino tote board displays the odds and point spreads for prop bets just as for single straight bets.

Proposition bets are great for entertainment purposes, but not so great for winning money over the long haul. In fact, the odds are usually terrible. Nevertheless, placing several proposition bets on a big game gives you something to root for if your primary bets aren't doing so hot. The score could be 48-7, but you'll be cheering like crazy in the fourth quarter as the team lines up to kick the third field goal of the game that puts your proposition bet (over/under on the total number of field goals in the game) into the winner's circle.

Forecasting with futures

Futures are another popular bet. A good example of a future bet is picking the winner of the Super Bowl a year in advance. Or you can bet on how many wins your favorite team will end up with next season. This bet is listed as a total number (such as the Mavericks will win 55 games this year), and you can wager whether the number of wins will be over or under the total amount posted by the casino.

Futures can be good bets, but they do have some negatives. The biggest drawback is that your money for that bet is tied up for several months. And calculating how a team may do over a long, unpredictable season (with unknown injuries) is difficult.

Placing Your Bet in a Sports Book

Your first impression when you walk into a modern, high-tech sports book, whether in Nevada or somewhere outside the United States, is that you've been magically transported into the war room of the Pentagon. Dozens of wide-screen plasma TVs flash images of every conceivable sporting event from all parts of the globe. If this spectacle isn't overwhelming enough, a gigantic board displays an incomprehensible array of teams and numbers. As a first-time visitor, you may feel you need a translator to decipher the secret code of point spreads and money lines (see the earlier "Leveling the Betting Field with Lines and Point Spreads" section).

But sports betting is a fairly straightforward process. The person behind the counter, called a *writer,* takes your money and processes your bet. After the writer finishes, she hands you a ticket with your bet printed on it. Always verify your ticket for accuracy before walking away.

This section includes everything you need to know to make a bet in a sports book, including how to read the board and collect your winnings.

Reading the board

The board in a big sports book can be confusing — after all, it contains a massive amount of information representing all the sports events you and your betting compatriots can place bets on. Check out the earlier section "Leveling the Betting Field with Lines and Point Spreads" if you're not sure of a term on the board. Now you just need to get accustomed to finding the information you want. This section looks at two examples of how you might see games listed on the board — one for football and one for baseball.

Point-spread listing for football

The board always lists the away team first (in the case of the example in Table 15-2, the Seahawks) and the home team second (Jaguars). The point spread or line is eight points, with the Jaguars being the favorite. The number –8 means that you're giving up, or *laying,* eight points if you bet on the Jaguars. Conversely, you're getting, or *taking,* eight points if you bet on the Seahawks.

Table 15-2	Point-Spread Listing for Football			
Time	*Bet*	*Team*	*Line*	*Total*
4:30 p.m.	303	Seahawks		38
ESPN	304	Jaguars	–8	

The easiest way to understand the point spread is by adding the points to the final score. For example, if the final score of the game is Jaguars 21, Seahawks 14, the adjusted score becomes Seahawks 22, Jaguars 21 (after you add 8 points to the Seahawks).

The other number, 38, is the total. You bet that the combined score for both teams in the game is either over or under that number. For example, if you bet *under* with a 21-14 score, the score total is 35, which is less than 38, so you win that bet. If, instead, the final score is Jaguars 28, Seahawks 14, then the *over* bet wins. In totals, the point spread does not factor in.

The odds makers take into account many factors when setting the totals, so don't assume you can get an edge by betting the under when two defensive teams clash. Casinos already incorporate those stats into the line.

Ties result in a *push* (you don't win, and you don't lose), and all bets are returned, which is why many lines have half-points (–4 ½). Half-points ensure that all total bets always have a winner on either the over or under.

Money-line bets for baseball

In baseball, the betting is a bit different than in football. (See Table 15-3 for an example.) The first category shows the game time and whether the game is televised. Not surprisingly, betting is much heavier on TV games because many gamblers like to bet on the games they can watch. The second column is the bet number, which the ticket writer must record in order to properly place your bet. After that, the board lists the two teams playing.

Table 15-3	Money-Line Bets for Baseball				
Game Time	*Bet*	*Team*	*Pitcher*	*Money Line*	*Total*
5 p.m.	905	Yankees	Mussina	+115	8
Fox	906	Red Sox	Wells	–125	

The fourth column is exclusive to baseball because pitchers play such a significant role in the outcome of the game. Most baseball bets are voided if the scheduled starting pitchers don't take the mound.

The money line displays the actual odds on your bet. A minus number always designates the favorite team, and a plus sign always indicates the underdog team. So if you want to bet on the Red Sox, you have to wager $125 to win $100. (The house returns a total of $225 to you with a winning bet). If, instead, you take the boys in pinstripes, you have to bet $100 to win $115. (The house returns a total of $215 to you if you win the bet.)

You may sometimes hear the baseball money line odds referred to as a *dime line* because the absolute difference is $10 between the two bets (favorite and underdog). However, most lines on totals in all sports have a difference of $20 between the two bets, referred to as a *twenty-cent line*.

The last column on the board lists the total number of runs both teams score in the game. In this particular example, the number is eight, which means you can bet on whether the total number of runs will be over or under eight. For this bet to be valid, the game has to go the distance and both listed pitchers must start.

Redeeming your winnings

How do you redeem your winnings? You can redeem your winnings in person by going back to the same counter where the writer handed you your ticket or to the casino cashier's cage. Or you can redeem your winnings by mail. You usually have up to 60 days to cash in your winning ticket.

Treat your ticket like cash. Until the game ends, any ticket can be a winner. However, after the final gun sounds and your team goes down in flames, you may want to toss the ticket into the circular file (otherwise known as a trash can). But if your team wins the game or you cover the spread, you have a winning ticket you can redeem for cash. Without the ticket, you're out of luck.

Rounding Up Sports Betting Differences

Betting activity varies from sport to sport. Remember that football and basketball wagers typically involve point spreads, while baseball uses money line bets. This section looks at the major sports and their unique idiosyncrasies when you make a sports bet.

Tackling football wagers

You can follow both college and professional football games with the highlight being the bowl games and the NFL playoffs. Football is far and away the most popular sport with bettors, so you'll be joining a huge fraternity of people who jump for joy and weep with anguish over something as trivial as a missed extra point.

If you've never bet on a football game before, you need to pay close attention to all the injuries. Everyone knows when the quarterback or a star wide receiver is injured. But football is a team sport, and sometimes obscure injuries to positions out of the limelight (such as a lineman or a safety) can have ripple effects across the entire team.

College football teams are much more prone to emotional highs and lows. For example, an old wives' tale, known as the *goalpost rule*, says you should bet against a team whose win the previous week was so emotional that the student body rushed the field and tore down the goal posts.

Slam-dunking basketball bets

You can wager on both college and professional basketball games. Just as in football, point spreads, parlays, and teasers are par for the course. The one major difference between football and basketball is the number of games. The basketball season (for pros and college) is three to five times longer than the football season, which gives you more opportunities to uncover information that may give you an edge.

Travel is also a much bigger factor in basketball. NBA teams play many games on back-to-back nights and in different cities. The fatigue factor for these road warriors is always a big concern for sports bettors.

Although NBA basketball takes a back seat to professional football in gambling action, those roles are reversed in the college arena. Every March, the NCAA basketball tournament creates true madness in casinos across the country. Except for the Super Bowl, no other sporting event gets the attention and money wagered as the Big Dance that begins every spring to crown the king of college hoops.

Taking a swing at baseball betting

Unlike football and basketball, sports betting on baseball doesn't cover college sports — only Major League teams. But with 162 games in the regular season, plus two rounds of playoffs and the World Series, there are plenty of games to go around.

Baseball is far behind basketball and football in terms of amount wagered per game, but baseball can still be a rewarding venture. The best baseball bettors share characteristics of the average baseball fan: they like the slow, steady rhythm of the game, they appreciate the sport's elegant subtleties, and they don't mind digging into statistics once in a while.

I don't need to tell a baseball fan that the role of the starting pitcher is critical to the game. If you want to beat baseball in the sports book, plan to bone up on your pitchers! Several good books cover arcane topics like left-handed pitchers versus right-handed batters (see Appendix B for sports betting recommendations).

Knocking around some boxing bets

Boxing uses a money line for all its matches. You can also find prop bets, such as how many rounds the fight will go or whether it will end in a knockout. (Check out "Eyeing the exotics [bets, not dancers]" earlier in this chapter for more about prop bets.)

Big fights, however, are few and far between, so this sport, unlike baseball or basketball, has few opportunities for betting. *Handicapping,* or using statistics to predict an outcome, is a challenge, too, because much of the available information is more subjective than statistically based. (See the following section "Understanding Handicapping Basics" for more about handicapping.) And the house vig is generally worse for boxing than for bets on other sports.

Lining up hockey wagers

Hockey usually offers straight money line bets, but it also has a hybrid option, called a *puck line,* which is closer to a point spread than a money line. A puck line adds goals (such as 2) to the underdog and then combines that with a money line for betting. The puck line then adjusts the actual game score to determine the winner, and the house pays out according to the money line. You can also do totals and parlays in hockey.

Understanding Handicapping Basics

Sports betting isn't all fun and games. You have to do your homework — and park your emotions and team loyalties at the door. Successful sports betting involves *handicapping,* or gathering data as diverse as weather forecasts and player statistics to determine the probability of a game's outcome.

There are a few unofficial schools of handicapping that focus on the following:

- ✔ **Fundamentals:** A fundamentals handicapper focuses on one team's strengths against another team's weaknesses. For example, this handicapper may notice that Colorado's receivers are all tall and that Nebraska's cornerbacks are unusually short, creating an obscure but important mismatch that Colorado could convert into a point-spread victory.

- ✔ **Statistics:** Statistics handicappers dig into numbers to find advantages that other bettors may not see. They may track teams with the best rebounding, or they may identify statistical factors that lead to a pitcher's success. They may even invent and track their own unique statistical measurements to evaluate teams or players.

✔ **Technical:** Technicians are all about trends. Like statistics handicappers, they share a fascination with numbers, but trends handicappers are trying to identify general situations where teams tend to do well or not. A technical handicapper looks through reams of past game logs and finds indicators that a team will outperform or perform poorly against the spread.

Many handicappers are a combination of all three types, blending their own unique perspective with methods borrowed from other handicappers. If you're a smart handicapper, you can consistently beat the house. One reason for your success is that you can choose which teams to bet or pass on, which gives you much more control than the house has.

Relying on Strategic Handicapping

Handicapping and overcoming the house edge is hard work. But it can be done if you're disciplined and rely on objective material instead of getting sentimental and betting with your heart. The following strategic tips can help you settle into a winner's betting stride:

✔ **Avoid the exotics.** Bettors wagered millions on football parlays last year, and a large chunk of that stayed in Nevada. Don't make sucker bets — they only help the casino's CEO expand his beach house in Maui.

✔ **Pick your sport.** Being an expert in several sports is hard, if not impossible. Pick one sport and only bet a few quality games at a time. Or increase your odds of success by picking one conference. You just may become the most informed follower of some small college leagues and direct that knowledge into betting success.

✔ **Turn the page.** The only way to be successful in gambling is to quickly get over losses. Don't stew. Pick yourself up and move on.

✔ **Don't chase your losses.** If you have a bad day or two, don't start chasing your losses by betting more and hoping that you'll eventually start to win. You may find yourself heading for even harder times.

✔ **Ignore the tout services.** These so-called experts sell you sure-fire picks for upcoming games. The truth is that very few of these companies surpass the break-even point of 52.4 percent, let alone show a reasonable profit. To compensate for the poor returns, some companies use bait-and-switch tactics (their services aren't really free, as advertised) or other unscrupulous practices to reel you in.

✔ **Disregard trends.** How teams have done on the road, on turf, on grass, or on bye weeks after Monday-night football games with a full moon is usually worthless information. An insufficient sampling exists of these trends to make any mathematical analysis. And team personnel changes so frequently today that how the Bears did over the last four years may have little reflection on this season.

✔ **Lock onto key numbers.** Pay attention to key numbers, especially in football. Two examples are the numbers 3 and 7 in point spreads. A field goal or a touchdown decides many games. So before you bet, look around and see if you can get 4 or 8 points in a different casino for the same game.

✔ **Shop for the best line.** Point spreads vary among casinos and Internet sports books. Additionally, one site may offer lower *juice* (less of a vig). These little differences can add up to big money over a long season, so never be satisfied with the first number you see.

✔ **Manage your money**. Make sure you have enough money to last through the inevitable negative swings of a long season — which translates into at least 50 times the maximum amount you bet per game. (Check out Chapter 4 for more money-management advice.)

✔ **Don't overreact.** Although players' injuries sometimes affect the expected outcome of a game, unless the injury is to an all-pro quarterback, key pitcher, or basketball superstar, the injuries don't have as much impact on the game as you may think. The benchwarmers at the professional level are very capable, and in some sports you find little difference between starters and subs.

✔ **Be a contrarian.** One of the simplest and most powerful strategies is to bet on the underdogs. Because of the public's fascination with the marquee teams, frequently a small edge exists in taking the points and betting on the weaker teams.

Chapter 16

More than Just the Derby: Betting on Horse Racing

....

....

*Y*ou may not associate horse racing with casino gambling, but if you're visiting a casino that allows off-track betting, that perception is about to change. Many of the biggest gaming destinations in several states (such as Nevada, Connecticut, and New Jersey) now offer visitors a full service equine wagering experience. From the Boots and Saddle bugle cavalry call to the photo finish, you can enjoy a day at the races, and you'll never have to leave the comfort of your casino . . . or catch a whiff of horse manure.

If you're looking for both adrenaline-rush action and intellectual challenge, playing the ponies in a casino may just be the ticket for you. Casinos offer steady action for horse racing from January to December via the miracle of simulcast media. Even if Belmont has a blizzard or Santa Anita has a sandstorm, a race is about to start somewhere. And this chapter gives you a fighting chance to pick some winners.

Identifying Different Racing Formats

A horse is a horse, of course. Or is it? In fact all race horses aren't the same. Different racing formats showcase the abilities of specific breeds. This section lists the most common forms of horse racing, along with the horse breeds they feature. (***Note:*** Because Thoroughbred racing is by far the most popular, I focus the majority of this chapter on Thoroughbred wagering.)

✔ **Thoroughbred racing:** Today's Thoroughbred race horse is the product of a low-tech, slow-motion, genetic engineering project that is hundreds of years in the making. These magnificent animals provide by far the most popular horse racing format in the world in terms of attendance, general public attention, horse population, and dollar amounts wagered.

In North America, Thoroughbred races vary between three-quarters of a mile and a mile-and-a-half and take place on flattened oval dirt or grass racetracks. A typical race features 6 to 12 horses running at a *gallop* — a horse's fastest gait.

Successful Thoroughbreds aren't only about raw speed. They must possess stamina, agility, strength, healing ability, and a host of other tangible and intangible characteristics to become winners. The job of the bettor is to spot these champion qualities and capitalize on them.

The Triple Crown (including the Kentucky Derby, Preakness, and Belmont Stakes races) and the Breeders Cup are two of the best-known Thoroughbred events, but that's just the tip of the iceberg. You can find more than 100 tracks in North America alone, and Thoroughbred racing is popular throughout the world as well. Casino visitors with race books enjoy remote access to the most important tracks in North America, such as Churchill Downs.

✔ **Harness racing:** Harness races are run exclusively with Standardbred horses, a stockier and perhaps less fiery breed than their Thoroughbred cousins. In harness racing, a driver (not a jockey) guides the horse from the *sulky,* a small, two-wheeled cart pulled behind the horse. The horses run at either a *trot* or a *pace,* both of which are one gear slower than a gallop.

The driver plays a more important role in this structured race format than in Thoroughbred racing. Therefore, knowledge of the jockey's racing history is more critical for the harness-race bettor. Most harness races cover one mile and are less chaotic (the horses usually settle into two orderly columns) than Thoroughbred races, so driver savvy is vital to winning the race.

Standardbred racing isn't as prevalent as Thoroughbred racing, but it's still extremely popular throughout North America. So most casinos include harness races in the simulcasting schedule, and casino visitors watch and wager on them almost as often as they do Thoroughbred races. For some great tips on picking Harness winners, read *Betting on Horse Racing For Dummies* by Richard Eng (Wiley).

✔ **Quarter Horse racing:** Quarter Horses are built to accelerate and get to maximum speed quickly, but they lack the endurance of Standardbred and Thoroughbred horses. As a result, Quarter Horse races are *sprints* — short (usually a few hundred yards long), straight, and over in a hurry. Casinos normally don't simulcast Quarter Horse racing, but if you want to know more, check out *Betting on Horse Racing For Dummies* by Richard Eng (Wiley).

Keeping horse racing safe and honest

The National Thoroughbred Racing Association (NTRA) guides big-time horse racing in the United States. The association's role is to promote the sport around the country, set standards, and lobby governments on behalf of the racing industry. Beyond the NTRA, each state operates a racing commission that is responsible for regulating horse racing and wagering within its borders. Other agencies, such as the Thoroughbred Racing Protective Bureau, serve lesser roles in maintaining the integrity, uniformity, and safety of the sport.

Betting in a Casino: Inside the Race Book

Why even bet on horses? Well, for starters, the *race book* (officially called the *race and sports book;* it's where casino visitors can place bets and then watch horse races) is one of the few places in a casino where the house doesn't have an automatic advantage over the individual bettor because skill is involved. But success isn't easy, and very few people develop the necessary aptitude to pick the ponies correctly on a consistent basis. You can begin to develop those skills, however, by reading this chapter.

First, you need to maneuver yourself around the race book. Quite a bit of this space is relegated to horse racing — more than you typically find there for other sports — which is a testament to the popularity of horse betting. This section guides you around the race book and points out its unique features, particularly the tote board.

Look for these standard fixtures within the race book:

- ✔ **Betting windows:** You can place your bet at these windows until one minute before a race begins, and then collect your winnings from the same windows when the race is over.

- ✔ **Scratch sheets:** These one-page reference sheets list the day's schedule of races, including horses and odds for each race. Bettors use these daily updates (usually found on a counter inside the race book) to determine their wagers.

- ✔ **Television monitors**: Remote horse wagering is made possible through a technology called *simulcast,* a system that broadcasts races from tracks all over the country in real time. The result is that you get to sit back and watch the race as it happens on big screens from the comfort of a casino race book.

✔ **Tote board:** This electronic display (covering the upper walls of the biggest race books) makes the room look like a cross between the New York Stock Exchange and Grand Central Station. The board covers each race track available for simulcast betting that day and lists the day's races at each track, the race start times, the names of the horses running, and each horse's current odds to win.

Understanding and Reading the Sheets

Successful betting starts by putting on your detective's hat and sifting through tons of information. The information covered on the tote board is duplicated on the casino's scratch sheets and racing forms. But the good news is that basic race information follows a standard format, no matter where it is.

Table 16-1 shows a sample race listing from a fictional track that might appear on a tote board or on a scratch sheet.

Table 16-1	A Sample Tote Board Display			
BELFAST RACEWAY Sunday, January 14, 2007 Race 1 Post 3 p.m., Race 1				
1M BEL 4YO&UP CLM				
1	Fleet-a-foot	8	J Wood	118
2	Lucky Lefty	10	T Greider	118
3	The Real Deal	7/2	J Souder	119
4	Mr. Irish	30	J Strickland	118
5	Tony the Tiger	6	T Favreau	118
6	Super Fast	12	J Hoff	118
7	Maximum Horse Power	16	S Dymale	118
8	Disco Dancer	3	D Ahlsten	120

✔ **Top line:** The name of the track; date and time of the race. The reference to *Race 1* means this 3 p.m. race is the first of the day for the fictional Belfast Raceway. But, unlike other sporting events, most horse races don't have a specific starting time. Race track schedules are based on their *post time,* the start time of the first race on the schedule. After that, races run approximately every 30 minutes.

✔ **Line 2:** Critical bettor information. All those letters, numbers, and abbreviations may appear as gobbledygook at first, but they're surprisingly simple to interpret after you know the code.

✔ **The length of the race:** In this example, *1M* refers to 1 mile. Other common values are *furlongs,* listed as *f* (1 furlong is ⅛ mile) or *yards,* listed as *yds.*

✔ **The racetrack's official abbreviation:** In this example, *BEL* stands for the fictitious *Belfast Raceway.*

✔ **The entry qualifications:** In this example, a horse must be at least 4 years old (*4YO&UP*) to enter.

✔ **The *class* (type) of race:** In this example, *CLM* indicates a *claiming race.* (Check out "Showing a bit of class," later in this chapter, for more information about race classes.)

✔ **Remainder of chart:** The list of horses.

✔ **The first column on the left gives the numbers on the *silks*** (the colorful jockey and horse uniforms that help spectators identify the horses during the race).

✔ **The second column lists the horses' names.**

✔ **The third column contains the early odds.** Unless otherwise noted, the number implies *to 1* odds. For example, Mr. Irish is a 30-1 long shot. This number is only an estimate and won't, in all likelihood, match the actual payoff odds.

In this race, Disco Dancer is the early favorite at 3-1, with The Real Deal close behind at 7/2. (Are you wondering what that means? Check out Chapter 3 on odds and probability. Also read "Sticking to straight bets," later in this chapter, for specific odds on horse betting.)

✔ **The final column lists the jockeys' names and their weights.** Bettors like to know how much weight a horse is carrying because too much weight may slow the horse down.

Placing Bets in the Race Book

Horse betting in the casino can be fast paced and frenetic — multiscreen simulcast monitors keep the adrenaline pumping as bettors rush to place their wagers before the betting windows close. But the more you understand the betting process and various types of bets, the more in control you feel. This section gives you some pointers, including how to employ a winning strategy in your betting choices.

Understanding the system: The feeling is mutuel

Most forms of casino gambling, such as slots or craps, are considered *fixed odds* wagers, which means the payoffs can be calculated in advance, depending on the type and amount of the bet. Knowing their edge in advance assures casinos of the profits they need to keep serving you those free whiskey sours all day long.

Betting on horses is another story: The payoff for a winning wager in a horse race depends on how *other* bettors wagered on the same race. All the money wagered is pooled together and then split up among the winning bettors (after the casino takes its cut). So the greater the number of bettors who picked the winning horse, the smaller their individual payout, because the money has to be shared by more people. That system is the essence of *parimutuel* wagering, and it's why the odds on each horse are constantly changing before the race.

The pari-mutuel environment can be confusing to beginners. Good handicappers not only judge horses but also constantly evaluate betting odds, attempting to get good betting value for their horse. In other words, they look for horses whose payout odds are higher than their chances of winning the race. (For more on handicapping, check out "Getting a Hand on Horse Racing: Handicapping Basics," later in this chapter.)

You must understand certain unusual aspects of pari-mutuel betting in order to be a successful horse bettor.

- **Opening odds are different from closing odds.** A horse's morning odds in a publication or on a scratch sheet have no direct relationship to the amount a horse pays if it wins. The odds are initially estimated by a handicapper a few days ahead of time, and they continue to change until the betting windows close a minute before the race (at which point the payoff odds are locked in).

- **More bets don't make for a bigger payout.** When the popular horses win, they pay out less. (Large numbers of gamblers betting on the same winning horse means less money for each of them.) Consequently, a *contrarian* outlook — finding horses that no one else is betting on — is often wise. This outlook doesn't necessarily mean betting long shots. You're looking for a solid horse that's being ignored by the betting public, resulting in fewer people to share your winnings.

- **Favorites don't equate to winners.** Favorites win about one in every three races, but you can go broke betting on them exclusively because the payout isn't high enough to cover the two lost bets you suffer for every win.

Sticking to straight bets

The most common type of bet is the *straight bet,* where your wager is on a single horse to *finish in the money,* or, more specifically, first, second, or third place. You can place more than one straight bet on the same horse, and betting *across the board* means you've placed Win, Place, and Show bets on one horse.

The smallest amount you can put down on a single straight bet is $2. There are three types to choose from:

- ✔ **Win:** The horse you pick must finish first in the race in order for the bet to pay off.

- ✔ **Place:** The bet pays if the selected horse finishes first or second.

- ✔ **Show:** The bet covers the top three positions in a race. If you bet a horse to show and he finishes first, second, or third, you win.

In pari-mutuel betting, the dollars placed on each type of straight bet go into three separate pools: a Win pool, a Place pool, and a Show pool. After the race is over, the pool money is distributed (after the house takes its cut, of course). To start with, the Win pool dollars are split among the bettors who placed a Win bet on the victorious steed. Then the Place pool dollars are split among all bettors who put a Place bet on either of the top two finishers. And finally, the Show pool money is split among bettors who placed Show bets on any of the three horses that finished first, second, or third.

With this system, the horse that wins the race pays off for all three types of bets. The second-place finisher pays off for Place bets and Show bets. And the third-place horse pays for Show bets only. The amount of money paid to winning bettors is usually displayed in a table like the one in Table 16-2, which lists the numbers and names of the top-three finishers in a fictional race.

Table 16-2	A Sample Race Payoff		
Horse	*Win*	*Place*	*Show*
5-Silver Sheldon	10.80	8.40	4.40
9-Black Butte	—	16.20	6.80
1-T Woods	—	—	4.00

Silver Sheldon won the race and paid off gamblers who bet him to Win, Place, and/or Show. Each number is the amount paid on a $2 bet ($10.80, $8.40, $4.40). Black Butte finished second, so bettors who had him to Win are left high and dry, but they do collect for Place and Show. T-Woods came in third and won $4 for the bettor who had the foresight to bet him to Show.

Experimenting with exotic bets

Casino horse bettors can also place *exotic wagers* (bets involving more than one horse). These bets gained popularity several decades ago when race tracks began offering them to counter a decline in attendance and interest in the sport. They may have seemed strange at the time of their introduction, but today, exotic wagers represent an important option for horse bettors looking to get the most out of their wagering dollar. The following are a few examples:

- **Exacta:** Bettors must pick the first and second place horses in a race in the exact order of their finish.

- **Quinella:** Bettors must pick the top two finishers in the race, but the bet pays regardless of the order of their finish.

- **Trifecta:** Bettors must pick the top three horses in one race in the exact order of finish. This bet can pay off thousands of dollars.

- **Superfecta:** This bet is like a Trifecta except bettors must pick the top four horses in the exact order in a race.

- **Daily Double, Pick Three, Pick Six, and Pick 23:** These bets, when available, require you to pick winners for multiple races. In some cases, the bets are only available for certain races, but sometimes you can select which races you want to include in your wager.

Like all bet types at the track (or the casino race book), multirace bet money is kept in a separate pool. For example, for the Pick Six, prizes often reach into the tens — even *hundreds* — of thousands of dollars because wins are rare and the pools carry over if no one wins.

The same factors that govern payouts on straight bets also govern payouts for exotic wagers, whether they are multihorse or multirace bets. Under the pari-mutuel system, the more popular the bet, the less it pays — no matter what the bet is. For more information on how to take full advantage of exotic bets, check out *Betting on Horse Racing For Dummies* by Richard Eng (Wiley).

Placing your bet at the window

To bet on a horse at a casino, you must give the cashier several pieces of information. Remember to say the name of the track, the number of the race, the number of the horse you're betting on, the type of bet you want to place, and, of course, the amount you want to wager. Make sure to check the ticket for accuracy before you leave the counter. After you walk away, it's yours — win or lose.

Winning strategies for your wagers

Not all wagers were created equal. Many professional horse bettors usually know what kinds of bets to make and which ones to avoid. Here are some tips to help you become an expert in picking winners:

- ✔ **Bet on medium shots.** Sure, you can cash in tickets more regularly if you bet the favorites, but profitable betting means being a contrarian and finding reasons to go against the crowd. See the earlier section, "Understanding the system: The feeling is mutuel," for more on this strategy.

- ✔ **Bet to win.** As seductive as Place and Show bets are, the payoffs are rarely worth it. Find the top two horses that you think have the best chance to win the race, and bet them to Win.

- ✔ **Avoid small fields.** When a race has seven or fewer entries, it usually doesn't have good betting value. Sit this one out.

- ✔ **Use exotic bets wisely.** You don't win many of these bets, but when you do, it's something special. But don't get seduced by the gigantic payoffs. The odds are long for a good reason — exotics are awfully tough to hit.

- ✔ **Have a betting plan for each race.** Don't wait until you get to the window to decide what you're going to do. For starters, you annoy the cashier and everyone in line. Plan your bets and then stick to them.

- ✔ **Spot play.** Limit yourself to races with certain characteristics, such as a specific length or a certain class. (Read up on classes in "Showing a bit of class," later in this chapter.) Specializing is an important tool in getting a leg up on your competition and the first step to becoming an expert.

- ✔ **Take the time to discover more.** Read *Betting on Horse Racing For Dummies* by Richard Eng (Wiley) from cover to cover.

Getting a Hand on Horse Racing: Handicapping Basics

This key section discusses *handicapping* the races, which is the practice of studying, researching, and analyzing the various factors that may influence the outcome of the race. As important as it is to understand statistics, probability, and equine biology, a lot of handicappers bet largely on *gut feel*. For beginners, the key is to discover a little of the science of handicapping so you can gain experience with the gut part.

The good news for novices is that it's worth your time to educate yourself. Learning just a little bit about what makes horses tick and how races work can help you separate yourself from the pack of uninformed bettors. You don't have to be a cigar-chomping, visor-wearing insider to have some fun (and make some money) on the horses.

Digesting the race data: The Daily Racing Form

Handicapping is built upon the generally accepted theory that a horse's past performance plays a key role in predicting future race performance. But the concept of looking backward to see forward didn't become commonplace until the first publication of the *Daily Racing Form (DRF)* in the late 1800s.

The *DRF* is widely considered to be the horse bettors' Bible because it contains a wealth of past performance information on horses and jockeys, along with an ocean of arcane handicapping data. The *DRF* is published several times a week in dozens of regional versions that focus on a cluster of race tracks. Every major race track in North America is covered. You can usually purchase a copy at the casino betting windows. Other horse racing publications cover the same basic information, but the *DRF* is the most common. Your foray into horse betting should begin with picking up a copy.

The *DRF* publishes all that data because there is no simple, all-encompassing formula for success at the racetrack. Picking winners — and identifying losers — is as much an art as a science.

 Expert handicappers say that eliminating losers is as important as picking winners. If you can reject the horses that have no shot at winning and focus your energy on studying the remaining entries, you'll save yourself time and energy.

But conventional handicapping wisdom says that the following four major factors predict a horse's success, along with other minor factors that can be as obscure as track surface and jockey quality. Different handicappers may focus on different aspects of a race, but most pros would rate the following factors as being the most critical. In order of importance, they are

- Speed
- Pace
- Class
- Form

The following sections look closer at these influential factors and provide valuable information that can help you handicap a race, if you so desire.

Assessing the speed factor

In all forms of racing — whether you're talking hooves, feet, skis, or tires — speed is king, and it's the first element any handicapper considers when evaluating a horse. The faster the horse, the more likely it is to win the race. That's why many handicappers focus squarely on how fast horses run as a way to predict race outcomes.

The challenge of speed handicapping is that horses don't run consistently. As a result, the handicapper must identify reasons why a horse may disappoint or outperform on a given day. Thoroughbreds are fickle animals and many factors can affect their speed. For example, the horse may not react well to traveling between race facilities or may not be in shape after a long layoff.

A key concept for beginning handicappers is the *speed figure* or *speed rating*, a statistic derived from a horse's final time in his recent races and adjusted to account for other factors, including track conditions and the track's historical speed average. Longtime handicappers often calculate their own speed figures based on their own closely guarded formulas.

Fortunately for you, Beyer has speed figures covered. This racing system, which appears regularly in the *DRF*, calculates the figures so you can compare horse performances without first performing all the math gymnastics. The higher the Beyer Speed Figure, the faster the horse has performed. (Check out the sidebar "Beyer Speed Figure" for more information.)

Beyer Speed Figures

Beyer Speed Figures have become the standard statistics in North American racing to evaluate a horse's speed. In his landmark 1975 book, *Picking Winners*, handicapper extraordinaire Andrew Beyer introduced a methodology for normalizing speed figures across different distances, conditions, and tracks. Beyer Speed Figures take thousands of races into account to create *par times* for each race distance (that is, a standard that subsequent times can be judged against). Those times are then translated into easy-to-compare speed figures and put into past-performance charts for every horse listed in the *DRF*. The higher the number, the faster the horse. Other speed ratings are available, but Beyer's is the most popular and well known.

Contemplating pace

Pace refers to how race horses apply their speed during a race. Some Thorough-breds are *stalkers* — staying within striking distance of the leaders early in the race and then hitting the gas at the end to compete for the win. Other horses are more adept as *front-runners* — using energy early to get a lead, and then maintaining enough speed to outlast and exhaust their competition.

Horses have different running styles that suit different race lengths, tracks, and competition. You can detect these patterns by looking at a horse's race progression through its recent races (see my earlier section on the *Daily Racing Form*). Does this horse typically gain ground on the leader late in the race? If the race had been longer, could this horse have finished higher in the standings? And if a horse won the race, was it increasing its lead as it crossed the finish line? When you consider pace, you're trying to find the right horse for the right situation.

Showing a bit of class

Class is a general term that refers to different aspects of a horse's maximum racing capabilities. In its most basic sense, class refers to the level of compe-tition. When one *horse* has more *class* than another horse, it means that he has beaten better competition, and all things being equal, should win. This definition doesn't mean that the classier horse *will* win; it just means that the classier horse *should* win.

When one *race* is a higher *class* than another race, it offers a higher winning prize and attracts better and faster horses. *Class handicapping* is evaluating a horse's winning potential, based on the level of competition it has faced. Class handicappers put less emphasis on speed and win/loss records and more emphasis on horses that are likely to perform better against a different class of opponents.

Taking pace to the next level

Advanced pace handicappers perform complex analyses on speed figures, fractional times, track variants, and other statistics to create a detailed profile of the horses in a particular race. With those profiles, experienced bettors can build a model of the entire race from begin-ning to end. They predict which horses will take an early lead, how the rest of the field will react to the speed of the race, and which horses have the potential to finish strong.

If you're a beginner to horse betting, don't make the mistake of believing that race classifications act as a perfect challenge ladder, where a race winner always moves up a level, and a loser automatically moves down a level. Owners and trainers work together to determine the best race for their horse, and their criteria may be different from those of the owner and trainer of a horse with a similar track record.

Thoroughbred racing is broken up into three kinds of races: claiming races, allowance races, and stakes races. They are further broken into distinct levels of competition by restricting entry to horses with certain characteristics, or by offering differing prize amounts.

Claiming races

Regardless of where they end up, race horses start with claiming races, and most toil there forever. Two-thirds of all races in North America are claiming races, whose level of competition is identified by their *claim amount,* a dollar value at which a qualified buyer (usually another race horse owner) can purchase an entrant in that the race.

The higher the claim amount, the classier the race because it attracts better competition. If a horse performs well in one level of claiming race, it would likely be placed in a higher-level claiming race.

Allowance races

Entrants of the middle tier of races aren't for sale, so they have no claim price to guide the bettor on how classy the race is. Instead, these allowance races break down by the size of *prize purses* (money paid to the owner of a winning horse). Allowance races often have special eligibility requirements, such as "horses who haven't won a race other than a maiden or claiming race."

Stakes races

Stakes races, the top class of Thoroughbred racing, make up less than 5 percent of all horse races. They are the pinnacle of the sport. To get into a stakes race, a horse usually qualifies by winning other high-class races. Owners sometimes pay an entry fee for their horse, and, because these races always carry the biggest purses, they attract the best horses. For example, all three legs of The Triple Crown are stakes races.

A bit more about class

Horses who win races are valuable to owners because they bring home prize money. As they win, they earn more and more prize money. That earning ability makes a horse just like any other income-producing asset. Horse-racing regulatory agencies want winning horses to move on to higher-class races because they want to keep races competitive. Owners are motivated to push their winning horse to compete against better talent because the prizes get bigger as the class of competition gets better.

Horses are constantly *moving up or down in class*, meaning the level of race they compete in is better or worse than their previous race. For example, a horse that last raced in a $25,000 Claiming Race might try a $40,000 Claiming Race the next week. That horse is said to be *moving up in class* because it is participating in a higher-level race.

Rounding into form

Form is a horse's level of physical preparedness to race his best. The quality of recent races and workouts, as well as other factors, such as medication and equipment changes, reveal a horse's level of preparation. The question the form handicapper attempts to answer is simple: Is there any physical evidence that the horse is about to give a performance not in line with his recent racing history and pedigree?

When evaluating the horse's form, a key person to consider is the trainer, the person who oversees the horse's race conditioning. Naturally, statistics are kept on trainers (as they are on jockeys, owners, and anyone else within a mile of the stables), so bettors need to look for trainers with a long-term winning percentage of more than 10 percent.

The *Daily Racing Form* (along with other racing publications) lists recent workouts of each horse. The information usually includes the date, length, and location of the workout, as well as the horse's performance. A horse in form has a steady workout pattern, including one within the last two weeks.

Considering other factors

Trying to capture every single factor affecting the outcome of a horse race is impossible. This chapter provides some of the most important ones for the beginner. You can also find a wealth of information in the *Daily Racing Form* and much of it touches on these handicapping factors:

✔ **Bloodlines:** Horses do a remarkable job of passing along their physical characteristics to their offspring. For horses with little racing experience, you can look up a horse's *sire* (father) and *dam* (mother) to see if he has the genetic makeup of a winner.

✔ **Jockeys:** The best jockeys have more than just physical strength and courage. They have brains, and they know how to get the most out of the horse they're riding. Bettors can find several tables of jockey statistics in race-day publications. Smart gamblers gravitate to consistent winners and avoid jockeys who can't win at a 10 percent clip.

✔ **Surface:** Thoroughbred racing takes place on either dirt or turf (grass), and some horses have a clear preference for one or the other. Precipitation can affect both surfaces adversely, so watch the track conditions and keep an eye out for horses whose past performances indicate sensitivity to less-than-ideal track conditions.

✔ **Medication:** Two common medications for race horses are Lasix (which helps prevent bleeding in the lungs, a common ailment in race horses) and an anti-inflammatory called Butazolidin or Bute. If the horse is taking either med for the first time, your best bet is to stay away.

✔ **Layoffs:** Beware of a horse returning to a live race after a long layoff; it may indicate an injury. A healthy Thoroughbred should be racing an average of once every three weeks. Any vacation greater than six weeks is a red flag to a handicapper, especially if the horse finished in the money (top three places) its last time out.

✔ **Equipment:** Trainers have a barn full of gear for various problems. One example is *blinkers,* which restrict a horse's vision, theoretically improving concentration. Check the *Daily Racing Form* to see if today's race is your horse's first time to wear blinkers. If so, some handicappers would warn you to stay away.

Trip handicapping

If all horses ran smoothly around the track every time they raced, handicappers would only need to know the speed figures. Bettors could just pick the horse with the best speed figures and collect their winnings.

Trip handicapping adjusts speed figures by taking into account how well the horse navigates traffic, avoids contact, and minimizes distance covered in turns. Those factors add up to the horse's *trip.*

For example, horses constantly compete for *position.* As the horses thunder around the track, they sometimes find themselves restricted by other horses. Bad position leaves a jockey with fewer options and can even force a racer wide in a turn, making him cover more ground than the other horses. An experienced trip handicapper adjusts his speed figures to reflect the bad trip. In essence, the trip handicapper makes a note that, with a good trip, this horse would have finished ahead of where it actually did.

If you're not strictly a scientific, numbers-oriented person, try trip handicapping. This strategy is the most subjective of any handicapping method because good or bad trips are impossible to quantify. Nevertheless, trip handicappers swear by their methods, which include looking for evidence that a horse's unusually good or bad recent performance was the result of its trip.

Still feeling lost? Most casinos sell tip sheets from professional handicappers. The publications vary in quality, but most of them are legitimate sources of racing information. If you don't trust the touts, see whether your local newspaper covers your favorite tracks. Most sports sections have a full-time handicapper who gives daily selections. But remember the old adage: You get what you pay for.

Part IV
Taking Casino Gambling to a Different Level

The 5th Wave
By Rich Tennant

"I don't care how many coins you feed that thing, you'll never win! It's a parking meter, Roland, a parking meter!!"

In this part . . .

This part guides you beyond the basics if you're ready to venture outside traditional casino gambling. Chapter 17 covers gambling in online casinos (a burgeoning realm in the world of wagering), with guidelines for staying out of trouble in that murky arena. Chapter 18 speaks to the current craze of tournaments. As the explosion of TV poker commands attention, this chapter shows you that tournament play isn't just for pros.

Chapter 17

Casino Gambling: Online and in the Comfort of Home

Remember on *Star Trek* when they'd beam down a party to the mystery planet? Aliens always seemed to vaporize the guys wearing red shirts, while Kirk and the rest of the crew returned to the *Enterprise* safe and sound. Playing Internet casinos and putting your money at risk can feel like you're beaming down to a strange new world. You may live long and prosper or, well, you may just be wearing a red shirt.

The biggest concern for most players when gambling online is cheating — by the house, another player, or some hacker in Eastern Europe. Even if the games are honest, you hassle with depositing your money and worry about not getting paid. Cloudy legal questions and the increased danger of addiction to Internet gambling also muddy the waters. Don't worry. This chapter covers Internet gambling and helps you decide whether beaming into cyberspace casinos is a risk you want to take.

Mapping the Legal Landscape

The Federal Wire Act of 1961 was enacted as an antiracketeering law aimed at organized crime, but it also implied that gambling over telephone lines is illegal. This edict is the primary reason online casinos can't currently operate from within the United States. But because cyberspace has no border control, *offshore* online casinos can still reach the homes of U.S. gamblers. The hotbed of Internet gambling activity is centered in several Caribbean countries, but a number of other governments around the world have also legalized Internet casinos.

Although the antiquated Wire Act has been the basis for arresting U.S. citizens who operate Internet casinos, debate continues over its relevance to players like you and me and whether it applies to modern communication methods such as wireless Internet. As far as I know, no online bettor has been convicted based on this act. But some states have or are presently enacting laws to make online gambling illegal within their state.

In the meantime, Congress has been debating a proposed regulation, the Internet Gambling Prohibition Act, which would make Internet gambling illegal for American citizens. But, because officials must grapple with enforcing such restrictions, the process has been very slow, and several previous bills attempting to outlaw Internet gambling have died in Congress.

Even though the online player faces little threat of arrest for logging on to an online poker tournament, the situation still poses risk. And the biggest risk is the lack of regulation. Because U.S. laws don't sanction online casinos, the Internet has no gaming commission. As a result, opportunities for fraud and theft are ever present.

Until the government can resolve the legal issues and monitor the industry of online gambling, my advice is to do your homework before taking the plunge. Be sure that online gambling is legal where you live, and carefully check out any gambling Web site before making your first deposit. In this chapter, I show you how.

Understanding How Online Casinos Work

Despite its risks, online gaming is exploding, with yearly revenues topping $10 billion. So, why is online gambling so wildly popular? Plain and simple — the convenience factor. You can gamble from the comfort of your own home or even while sipping a latte at the local coffee shop. Games are available at all hours, and, best of all, you don't need to fly across the country for the privilege of emptying your wallet. (Besides, if you lose your shirt from playing online, just go to your dresser and grab another one!)

Online sites try to pump realism into the games by matching the sights and sounds of the casino. But, if you love the crowded camaraderie at a craps table, playing online may strike you as a poor substitute. On the other hand, if you can teach your dog to give you a high-five when the dealer busts, and if your significant other doesn't mind wandering through the computer room saying "Cocktails? Cocktails?" you can almost match the fun of live gaming without ever leaving home.

So, you're considering taking the plunge? Well, the rules for poker, blackjack, and craps online are pretty much the same as in a bricks-and-mortar casino. But cyberspace does away with card handling and dice tossing — your mouse gets to perform all those Herculean tasks.

This section shows you the essentials of gambling online: practicing, setting up an account, playing the games, and (hopefully) counting your winnings.

Connecting with cyberspace

Internet play is similar to a video poker machine. You have a video interface (your computer monitor) and buttons (on your mouse), and high-tech silicone chips (rather than a real deck of cards) determine the outcome. Just as in video poker, gambling online means that money changes hands. The method of exchange may be slightly different, but your bank account doesn't notice.

In order to gamble online, you need to have access to a computer. To start playing,

1. **Log on the Internet.**

2. **Do one of the following:**

    • **Download gambling software on your own computer.**

    • **Connect directly with the mother ship in cyberspace** (such as with flash or java).

Normally, downloading the casino and saving it to your computer is better; it takes only a few minutes and is totally free. However, if you have dial-up or limited storage space on your hard drive, some casinos offer a *lite* version (a scaled-down version that has only the most popular games).

Downloading software may allow viruses to invade your computer. Be sure you have a good virus protection program before doing any Internet gambling.

Getting up to speed with practice games

Many Internet casinos include features that allow you to practice for free, which is great if you're not familiar with a game before you fork over real cash.

I recommend that even experienced gamblers start off at the free sites because online gambling has a learning curve, meaning you can easily hit the wrong button and accidentally double down on your hard 20, which has happened to me twice. (Can you say *Bust*?)

And there's no disgrace to sticking with free games. Many people are perfectly happy competing for points or pride rather than cash. They're also much safer than cash, given the uncertain legal issues and inherent dangers of online gambling addiction.

Bodog Casino is the best site to test the waters. In addition to playing for free without downloading any software, you don't have to sign up for an account or give an e-mail address, so you can get rolling instantly. And I have even better news: The site has set up a special page for readers of this book (www.bodog.com/blackwood) to help orient you to online play.

Setting up an account

But bluffing with play chips just doesn't cut it for many players. After you're comfortable with online play, you're probably ready to switch to a cash game and play for real money.

After you settle on a casino site (I show you how to pick the best in the next section), the next step is setting up your account. Typically, you provide some information, such as your name, address, and e-mail address. You establish a username and password. (Make sure to record them in a secure place! You need this information to play and get to your money.) However, if you do lose this information, you can usually contact customer service at the casino, and they'll send the username and password to you.

Some sites also let you pick a custom avatar or icon to represent you online. And a few casinos even let you download a personal picture so all of cyber-space can see what you really look like.

Paying to play

For the most part, clicking and dragging makes gambling more convenient and faster than in-casino play, with one major exception — transferring money. Because online gambling has no dealer and your computer doesn't have a handy deposit slot, you need to go through a few online hoops to get your money into play and then get paid when you're done.

You can usually deposit any dollar amount (up to the daily maximum as set by the casino) into your account. After you fund your account, you typically can use that money to play any of the various games throughout the casino.

Deciding how you pay may take some thought because options may be limited. You can send a personal check — if you're patient enough to wait for snail mail to arrive. Or you can send a money order or wire to the casino. But most players prefer other methods.

Putting it on a credit card

Using a credit card to establish your deposit can be a quick and seamless way to go. But beware: Credit cards vary, depending on the bank. Although some banks allow gambling-related transactions, most banks decline them outright. A few banks may turn down the transaction initially, but they ultimately approve it if you call to authorize it.

Despite the credit-card restrictions, whenever there's a buck to be made, someone finds a way to make it happen. Internet casinos sometimes skirt the credit-card prohibitions with this technique: When you make a deposit at a specific online casino, your credit-card statement may show a completely different and seemingly unrelated establishment — Gibraltar Boat Sales, for example.

Paying through a third-party processor

Because credit cards have become increasingly difficult to use for Internet gambling, a new method was developed — using a third-party processor. The industry leader for escorting money from your wallet to your favorite Internet casino is NETELLER. This online account works with electronic fund transfers, bank wires, or credit cards. Firepay is another respected company that serves as a middle man.

Whichever method you use, be conservative about the size of your deposit, especially when you first start out. The temptation to chase your losses online is much greater, and the games are much faster. For example, you can play nearly ten times as many blackjack hands per hour online as in a real casino.

Accessing your winnings

Always keep good records for each site you gamble on, documenting not only your username and password but also any remaining balance in the account. Believe it or not, players routinely leave thousands of dollars at Internet casinos and never come back to claim their funds!

You can usually request to cash out either all or part of the money in your account at any time. The best Internet casinos process your request immediately and cheerfully send the funds within a day. However, some shady sites may take weeks to pay while putting you off with a litany of excuses. As a result, I recommend only playing reputable casinos endorsed by the watchdog groups (check out "Taking the first step: Online watchdogs" later in this chapter).

In most cases, your money will be sent back to you via the same method you deposited. For example, if you funded your account through NETELLER, then the Internet casino uses that same vehicle to return money to you when you cash out. One exception is credit cards. For example, if your initial deposit of $200 was made with a credit card and you doubled your money, the online casino processes your $400 as such: The casino can only pay back $200 to your credit card; the casino has to pay you any winnings via another method, such as check, wire, and so on.

Transferring money to and from the casino is usually free, although some casinos tack on a service charge (especially if you do multiple transactions a month). You may also have to pay bank wire and delivery fees.

You don't need to cash out after every session. If you plan on playing again, leave the money parked in your account. Just don't forget it. One downside to leaving your money in the account: Always having money available for gambling may create unneeded temptations or even worse — the casino holding your life savings may go out of business.

Locating the Best (and Safest) Online Casino Games

Unlike the big boys in Las Vegas or Atlantic City, Internet casinos don't have a gaming commission looking over their shoulder to ensure that all games are on the up and up. Although the vast majority of online casinos are honest, a few unscrupulous operators have cheated customers — either with bogus software that rarely lets you win or by folding up shop after they've taken your deposit.

Taking the first step: Online watchdogs

Choosing which casino to play can be daunting. How can you locate the honest sites and weed out the bad guys? Instead of hacking your way through the jungle, follow the paths paved by other pioneers.

Several watchdog Web sites offer rankings, recommendations, warnings, and tips to maximize your online gambling experience. Check out their message boards in particular. Reading about others' experiences — good and bad — with various sites can be incredibly helpful. Some of the best help sites include

✔ www.thewizardofodds.com

✔ www.gamemasteronline.com

✔ www.casinomeister.com

✔ www.lasvegasadvisor.com

✔ www.rgtonline.com

✔ www.casinocity.com

Fortunately, the vast majority of Internet casinos are safe to play, so it's more important to know which places to avoid. (The watchdog sites cover those sites in their *blacklisted* section.) In fact, I have played at a number of cyber casinos and have been cheated only a few times. In almost every case, I could have avoided that aggravation if I had first visited a watchdog site before depositing any cold cash.

Just as financial planners advise you to diversify your investments, I suggest that you spread your gambling dollars among different casinos to help reduce risk. Even after you've done your homework and homed in on the best sites, divvy your money up among ten or so safe sites, instead of plunking $5,000 on one location.

Sticking to reputable software suppliers

One factor that watchdog sites base their evaluations on is the casino's software. Although there are notable exceptions, most casinos buy their software packages from a trusted outside source. The biggest names in software providers include

✔ Boss Media

✔ Cryptologic

✔ Microgaming

✔ Playtech

✔ Real Time Gaming

Generally, gambling is safer when the casino uses one of these companies for their game software. For more information, www.thewizardofodds.com analyzes all the major software providers for Internet casinos.

Checking out license origin

Another good barometer of integrity is the country where the casino holds a license. For example, a casino originating in Australia or the Isle of Man has a far greater chance of being regulated because of the sterling reputation of its government.

Identifying other signs of a good site

Picking the right Internet casino is critical if you want to enjoy your online gaming experience. I can't begin to tell you how frustrating it is to spend weeks or even months watching the mailbox, hoping some rogue casino finally pays the money it owes you. In addition to using the watchdog Web sites that I mention earlier in this section, you can do a little homework upfront because it pays big dividends later.

Internet game rage

The anonymity of the Internet means you can play poker naked if you want. (Just don't share that information with your online opponents — it may ruin the game for them.) But anonymity also has a dark side. Most online games have chat options, allowing players to type in their thoughts and comments. The fact that they can't see the other players turns some normally meek, well-behaved people into raging bulls at their keyboards, especially in poker. Their mission in life is to point out the mistakes of everyone else at the table, and they caustically attack their opponents, trying to drive them over the edge.

No matter how good you are, a skillful jab in the right place at the wrong time can throw you off your game. Consequently, a thick skin is critical to maintaining your cool and managing your game. One of the best ways to keep your focus is to never stoop to the bully's level. If you're verbally attacked, don't retaliate. Instead, be courteous or employ one of the best features of Internet casinos — the mute button, which silences any player at the table.

Online poker players also tend to bluff more, partially because you can't see their eyes or facial expressions. And the deception involves more than just the cards. The names or pictures of players at your online table may have little in common with the actual person you're competing against. More often than not, *SexyVegasVixen,* who just cleaned you out in Omaha, isn't sexy, nor a vixen, nor is *she* from Nevada.

Here are some of the other factors that are important to check out before logging on to an online casino:

- **Customer service:** The casino site should have 24/7 free tech support, either online or by phone.

- **Prompt payouts:** Make sure the casino is punctual and courteous to winners.

- **Licensing jurisdiction:** Knowing where or whether the casino has a license is helpful.

- **Secure transactions:** With identity theft on the rise, no one wants personal info or credit card numbers floating around in cyberspace. Any reputable Internet casino should ensure that this problem doesn't happen.

- **Independent audits:** Not all sites have this feature, but an independent audit by a known outside auditor can provide peace of mind.

- **Cool graphics:** Although cool graphics don't reflect a game's security, a pretty face sure makes playing more interesting, especially in games where you may be staring at the screen for hours. The background, colors, and bells and whistles can make a big difference.

- **Variety of games:** No site is worth downloading if it doesn't have your favorite game.

Selecting the best games for Internet play

Most Internet casinos offer every game (and even a few new ones) that your local casino has. From blackjack to baccarat, you're sure to find your favorite form of gambling. But some games lend themselves to the Internet more than others. I recommend the following:

Poker: The game's at your house

Internet poker has some undeniable pluses that make it a driving force behind the rapid growth of Internet gambling. First of all, you aren't just competing against a cold, calculating machine. Internet poker rooms simply provide the meeting place for millions of card-playing fanatics around the world to belly up to the table for their favorite game.

Another factor behind this explosion is the tremendous convenience of playing poker at any hour. When the poker bug bites, you don't need to worry about finding enough friends for a game — you just log on. And unlike your freeloading poker pals in the neighborhood, your Internet opponents don't drink all your beer or leave cigarette burns on your card table.

Finishing in the money

Scott Fischman, one of the marquee young names in poker today, feels that online tournaments may be the single most important tool for the development of a poker player. Here are some tips from Scott to help you move up the cash ladder online.

✔ The No. 1 reason online tournaments are such a valuable tool is the sheer volume of available tournaments.

✔ Having 24/7 access to so many tournaments allows players to experiment with their game and test new concepts and styles of play.

✔ Playing online can provide years of experience in a short span of time.

✔ The effect of *stack size* (amount of chips) on betting is extremely crucial in poker tournaments; acquiring the necessary skills online is very easy.

For more about online poker, check out *Winning at Internet Poker For Dummies* by Mark Harlan and Chris Derossi (Wiley).

Video poker: No handles needed

If video poker is your game of choice, you'll love the Internet. Almost every site has a good variety of video poker games available and the interface is nearly identical to playing the real McCoy in a regular casino. Check out Chapter 13 for more on video poker.

Tournaments: Tearing up the tables

I love tournaments and think they're one of the greatest features of online casinos. Because all aspects are automatic (shuffling cards, counting chips, and so on), the game moves at a more rapid and exciting pace than tournaments in real casinos.

If you ever want to try your luck against me in a tournament, you can usually find me playing poker at Bodog Casino (particularly the $100,000 tournament, currently held every Sunday) or blackjack at Global Player Casino (tournaments are currently held every Wednesday). Both of those tournaments often have profitable *overlays,* which means the casino pays back more money than it takes in (see Chapter 18 for more on overlays), making them a great value for your gambling dollar.

Last man standing

Though not totally exclusive to the Internet, Sit and Go (SNG) poker tournaments have blossomed online. Their principle is simple: Rather than compete in a long, full-fledged tournament, you simply sign up (sit down) and wait until your table (six to ten players) is full. Then you play until only one player is holding chips.

SNGs are popular because they appeal to people's love of instant gratification and risk-avoidance; games rarely take more than an hour to crown the champion, and losses can't exceed your initial buy-in. Howard Lederer, popular host of the TV show, *Learn From The Pros*, considers SNGs the perfect training ground, providing valuable final table experience for larger tournaments. Here are some tips from Howard on improving your results in the trendy SNG format.

✔ **Start out conservative.** Initially the *blinds*, the mandatory bet before a hand starts, are small, so the chips to fight over are few. Establishing a tight image early by playing only select hands is a good idea because that may help you steal pots later with weaker hands, when the stakes are higher.

✔ **Play for third place.** The standard prize structure for a ten-player tournament pays 50 percent of the entry fees for first, 30 percent for second, and 20 percent for third place. So if you can survive until the final three, you guarantee yourself a profit.

✔ **Go for the gold.** After you make the top three, shift gears and aggressively play for first place. The difference between third and second is only 10 percent, but finishing first is worth a whopping 30 percent extra.

Taking Advantage of Promos and Giveaways

Your Internet casino definitely doesn't feature an exploding volcano. Nor does it have a wild pirate battle, a roller coaster, or a dolphin habitat. But those extravaganzas don't have the slightest effect on the actual games inside the casino. And if you're there just for the games, you don't miss the sideshow.

The main difference between online and brick-and-mortar casinos is the lower overhead. In addition to all the razzmatazz, online casinos don't have to pay for dealers, pit bosses, slot clerks, or even janitors. So these businesses aren't just cash cows — they're an entire herd worth millions of dollars.

Because online casinos can make so much money, new operators open their virtual doors all the time. Consequently, more than one thousand Internet casinos currently serve the world's gamblers, and they compete fiercely for your business. After you become an online player, you become very popular.

As a common marketing strategy, Internet casinos offer new customers sign-up bonuses, which typically run from 10 to 100 percent of your initial deposit (although they usually have a maximum cap on the bonus). Getting extra cash upfront is a terrific way to stretch your bankroll. And some sites even maintain the gravy train, offering monthly or frequent reload bonuses to keep you coming back for more.

Usually these bonuses are restricted to certain games (sometimes the worst games), but if you have a choice, blackjack and video poker are the best ways to earn the bonus because these two games have very favorable odds. Bodog Casino is the most generous, giving you a bonus on *every* deposit. Obviously this site tops my list of recommended Internet casinos.

Remember the old adage about any deal that looks too good to be true? A number of Internet casinos send e-mails with fantastic bonus offers — too fantastic. If you read the terms and conditions, you discover the headline claims are more than a bit deceptive. In most cases, you must *play through* the deposited amount a certain number of times (15 times, for example) to qualify. And sometimes you can't withdraw the bonus (called a *sticky* bonus), or they make the bonus nearly impossible to claim.

Be careful not to play longer than necessary to claim your bonus. If you're playing a negative expectancy game (check out Chapter 3 for more on negative expectancy games), every extra hand dilutes the value of the bonus. And when you're losing, it's easy to keep playing in a desperate attempt to get even.

Chapter 18

The Wild World of Tournaments

Do you want to add a little spice to your casino-gambling experience? If so, tournaments may be up your alley. Tournament play is a great way to gain big-time experience and hone your skills. Playing in tournaments is a stimulating and energizing experience that successfully combines the glamour of high-stakes gambling with the intoxicating thrill of a sporting event all in a fun environment.

Are you timid and don't think you can tackle tournaments? Well, don't be. Whether your game's poker, blackjack, baccarat, or — yes — even the slots, tournament play is reasonably accessible for all levels of gamblers. You may not be ready for a mega-event like the World Series of Poker, but tournaments come in all shapes and sizes — many with nominal entry fees (some as low as *zero* dollars) and attractive prizes.

What separates tournaments from run-of-the-mill casino gambling? To begin with, you have to beat other players rather than the house, which is fortunately a much easier task. In fact, believe it or not, many casino tournaments even give recreational players an edge. You heard me — you actually may have a better shot of winning a tournament than beating the house in Vegas. You don't have to beat the cards or dice — just your opponents.

Are you interested in trying out a tournament? If so, then read this chapter, where I explain how gambling tournaments operate in general, pointing out some cool features to look for that increase your chances of winning. I give you some tips on how to hang in the competition longer than your opponents. And because tournament poker is the hot flavor of the month, I zoom in on that game in a bit more detail.

Sizing Up Tournaments: Which One Is Right for You?

If you're the type of person who loves competition, then tournaments are just your ticket. And don't worry about being a novice — most tournaments are very player-friendly and easy to understand. But before you play in a tournament (and ideally win), you need to know what you're getting into before you jump in, head first.

Although poker and blackjack are probably the best-known tournament competitions, tournaments in craps, slots, baccarat, Pai Gow poker, video poker, and keno draw good crowds and a loyal following. And even though hot spots such as Las Vegas host the biggest events, casinos all over the country regularly hold tournaments.

The prize money and number of participants in tournaments vary greatly depending on whether the event is a local weekly competition or a huge, heavily advertised extravaganza designed to attract hordes of traffic. Using the example of blackjack and poker, I split these various tournaments into three separate size categories to give you a quick overview. However, if you're considering playing in a tournament, I suggest you start off with the smallest tournament possible.

- ✔ **Mini tournaments:** Small, frequent tournaments, such as a Wednesday-night blackjack tournament, often take place on a regular basis and may draw only a couple dozen players. The entry fees tend to be minimal (typically $5 to $50), and first place rarely pays more than a couple hundred dollars, and the winner is crowned within a few hours.

- ✔ **Medium tournaments:** These events typically take place over a couple of days and consist of multiple rounds of play with more than 100 players. The entry fee is much stiffer than that of mini tournaments (at least $100), but the prize money for the final winner is greater (normally $10,000 to $50,000).

- ✔ **Mega tournaments:** These big dogs offer potentially life-changing prize money for first place ($100,000 and higher). The entry fee is hefty (usually $500 to $10,000), the time commitment is long (up to a week), but the possible reward is huge. (Who can resist savoring the look of envy on your neighbor's face when you return home with $1 million in cold, hard cash?) The prospect of a huge payoff is the reason thousands of hopeful players make the pilgrimage to Las Vegas each year for the World Series of Poker.

The bottom line: Before you even consider playing in a tournament, you need to find the right one for your skill level. For instance, if you're a newer player, you may want to try a mini tournament first because the risk and time commitment is low. Walking away a winner from a tournament isn't the easiest task — even if you're a pretty good player. The prizes are very top heavy, and only a few players take home any cash. (For example, in smaller poker and blackjack tournaments, you must make the final table to get paid at all. In bigger events, you typically have to finish in the top 10 percent to receive any money.)

Betting on the Most Lucrative Tournaments

I used to assume that tournaments were a waste of time. I viewed them as similar to the lottery because their main appeal is the chance to turn a small initial investment into an astronomical sum. Instead of trying to get rich quick, I made my first million the hard way — one chip at a time. I avoided shortcuts and methodically built up my bankroll to higher levels month after month.

I was dead wrong in my assessment of tournaments. They offer some of the best odds in the casino. But before you first start playing in tournaments, you need to find out how to evaluate a tournament to determine its profit potential. After you know that information, you can choose to play in only the most lucrative events.

The best way to evaluate the profit potential of a tournament is to take the total amount of prize money and divide it by the number of entrants (there often is a maximum number of players allowed). In most cases, your *expected value (EV)* is zero. In other words, the tournament returns roughly the same amount of money that it takes in. So if you're an average player, you break even in the long run.

Fortunately, you can dramatically increase your EV in two ways:

✔ Lucrative *overlays,* any gambling situation that gives the bettor an advantage over the house

✔ *Freerolls,* tournaments that have no risk to you

The next two sections analyze overlays and freerolls and look how you can increase your EV.

Taking advantage of overlays

Unfortunately there is no simple way to find out about overlays. They are more frequent online and in smaller events, but few places ever advertise that their tournaments are overlays. Players need to do the math themselves in most cases.

A typical casino game rarely pays back more than 98 percent to its customers, which means you will lose at least $2 for every $100 wagered. But many tournaments return all the entry fees back to the players in prize money, making these events a tremendous value. And some tournaments offer lucrative *overlays,* giving players a return of more than 100 percent on their gambling dollar.

However, even in a tournament with a good overlay, most players end up losing money because the prizes are very top heavy. So what does a return of more than 100 percent mean? A player with average tournament skills is a favorite to win money over the long run, but not necessarily in that individual event. For example, the house has the edge in slots and the return is 98 percent, but the actual amount a player gets back for each $100 bet can be far higher or lower than $98. But over time, $98 is the average.

Overlays happen frequently in tournaments because many casinos either guarantee the prize money or add extra dough to sweeten the pot. Take Bodog Casino for example. Bodog has a weekly poker tournament that guarantees $100,000 in prize money every Sunday. Because the entry fee is $100 per person, Bodog needs at least 1,000 players to sign up to break even (because of the guarantee). Yet this tournament always has less than 1,000 players, which creates a profitable overlay, because if only 600 people sign up, $60,000 goes in, and $100,000 goes out. This extra $40,000 is essentially free money split among the 600 players (EV is determined by dividing the extra money by the total number of players). That translates into a 170 percent return on your money, a number much higher than the 98 percent or less return offered in most casino games.

Finding a freeroll (Who says you can't get a free lunch?)

For the budget minded, the surest way to get an edge is to play in only *freeroll* tournaments. These tournaments are becoming very common in poker and involve absolutely no risk (hence the catchy name). Here's how they work: A casino puts up *all* the prize money and gives you a fixed amount of special tournament chips. There is no entry fee so you can't possibly lose.

Freerolls can be a great way to figure out how tournaments operate without pulling real cash out of your wallet.

Freerolls are especially common on the Internet (see Chapter 17), but many bricks-and-mortar casinos hold occasional freerolls. The trick is determining whether they're worth your time. For example, if a freeroll offered $400 in prize money, but drew 200 players, the EV for each player is a paltry $2 for an event that could take several hours.

Most freerolls are open to anyone. But some tournaments also fall into the category of freerolls. For example, if you're a desired customer, a casino may give you a free entry into one of its private, invitation-only tournaments. These events are closed to the general public. To participate, you must be an established player at the casino.

Entering a Tournament (And Knowing What to Expect)

Are you considering playing in a tournament? If so, then you need to find an appropriate one for your skill level. You can find out about upcoming tournaments in a couple different ways:

- You can subscribe to casino mailing lists, which offer detailed information about different tournaments.
- You can go to comprehensive Web sites, such as www.lasvegasadvisor.com or www.blackjacktournaments.com. They list many upcoming tournaments, from small buy-ins to big-bucks events.

NBA owner scores big

Joe Maloof, one of the owners of the Sacramento Kings, showed that even amateurs can win big in tournaments. He participated in an invitational blackjack tournament at the Barona Casino in San Diego and took $1 million for first place. His victory was dramatic because he came from behind on the last hand and won with a blackjack.

The 41 players invited paid an entry fee of $10,000 for a chance at winning $1 million. So the strong overlay ($590,000) made this tournament one of the best blackjack tournaments in history. But don't call your travel agent to buy a ticket to California quite yet. That tournament isn't an open event, but is restricted to invited premium players. To get on that A list, you must have at least a $100,000 credit line and be a high roller at the tables.

After you pinpoint a tournament you want to enter, signing up is fairly straightforward. The easiest and most direct way to do so is to simply pay the entry fee. To sign up, you can either mail in a check, pay in person, or in some cases, register online or over the phone. These options vary from casino to casino and tournament to tournament, so always read the fine print.

Although most players sign up in advance, in many cases you can still enter on the day of the tournament. However some events require advance registration or only allow a fixed number of players. Also, there are often discounts on the entry fee for "early bird" entries.

This section tells you some important tidbits you need to remember when you're considering or have already entered a tournament.

Eyeing the competition over cocktails

After you enroll in a larger tournament, make sure you attend the welcome reception. During this time, you receive your information packet, which includes the tournament rules and details about your starting time and the location of your table or machine. The tournament director normally speaks at this function and answers your questions. (**Note:** Most mini and medium tournaments don't host welcome receptions so you don't have an opportunity to eye your competition.)

During this reception, make sure you mingle with and meet your opponents. If you're new to the scene, finding a veteran of the circuit to help show you the ropes can be quite helpful. Most tournament players are quite social and are usually willing to share tips to make your first foray into this new world more successful.

Playing with fixed chips

Before the tournament begins, you receive a fixed amount (such as $500) of chips (for table-games tournaments) or credits (for slot machines or video-poker tournaments). In most cases, the chips you use in tournaments equate to *funny money* — they're nonnegotiable and have no real value. The great part is that you can never lose more than your original entry fee.

Playing with a fixed amount of chips can create a totally different dynamic than playing in a nontournament game. If you go to a casino with $500, for example, you're much happier to finish the day with $400 instead of losing it all. But in a tournament, your starting stack of chips is your ammo, and you must view those chips as expendable bullets. By using them aggressively, you're more likely to take the lead in a tournament, so don't hesitate to fire away. (To find out more about being aggressive, check out "Strategizing to Eliminate the Competition," later in this chapter.)

Seating yourself in the tournament section

Typically, casinos hold tournaments in a section set aside especially for the event. Often casinos reprogram slot machines or enhance blackjack rules to give you a greater chance of winning. Casinos assign each table or slot machine a number for the tournament so that you know where to go when your session begins.

Unlike typical casino play, you're usually assigned your seat in a tournament to ensure fairness, because position becomes very important in many tournaments. Most tournaments allow spectators to watch the events, and each round normally lasts an hour or less, so there is ample time for breaks and kibitzing.

Strategizing to Eliminate the Competition

Okay, so you may understand that tournaments offer one of the best deals for your gambling dollar, but deep down do you feel like you have no realistic chance of snagging the big prize? Luck does play a significant role in tournaments, but you don't have to carry a rabbit's foot to win.

This section starts off with some general strategy tips that can greatly improve your chance of success. Then I focus most of this section on the most popular tournament game — poker. Later, I offer some helpful information on other table games and slot and video-poker tournaments.

Incorporating basic strategy for tournament success

You can apply the following general principles to help you rise above your competition in most table-games tournaments (I cover slots and video poker later in this section). A few of these tips originated with gambling wizard Stanford Wong, one of the early pioneers of successful tournament play. Employing these principles can give you an advantage over your opponents — which can translate into a winning track record.

✔ **Go big or go home.** The optimal tournament strategy is to either advance or *bust out,* or lose all your chips, trying. Remember that your chips are like bullets, so don't leave any in your gun when you're behind. (Poker is the exception. Check out the following section, "Soaring over the poker crowd," for the lowdown on poker.)

✔ **Play for the swing.** If you're behind, look for places where you can create a big *swing* to seize the lead. This strategy is especially effective in craps and blackjack tournaments. For example, if the leader bets small near the end of a tournament, push out a large bet in an attempt to close the gap. Or if he bets big, then go with the minimum bet and hope he loses his bet (and most of his lead).

✔ **Go with the flow.** If you're ahead, try to match your opponents' bets. Doing so greatly reduces the chances of your opponents having big swings and catching up to you.

✔ **When in doubt, push it out.** Near the end of tournaments, such as blackjack, medium-sized bets often do little good. They typically don't let you grab the lead — and if you lose, you're left with too few chips to climb back into contention. A better strategy is to *push it all out* — make the biggest possible bet and go for the win.

✔ **Use the matador defense.** Sometimes your best tactic is to simply stay out of the way of aggressive opponents. A common example is in poker tournaments where emotions may fly high as players try to inflict revenge on each other. In such cases, the smartest path is to keep your ego in check (don't seek payback) and quietly move up the money ladder while other players get knocked out.

Now that you know some broad strategies, check out the following sections, where I cover specific strategies for several popular types of casino tournaments, with some practical tips to turn the odds in your favor.

Soaring over the poker crowd

The current star attraction in tournaments is clearly poker, specifically no-limit Texas Hold'em. Because of their skyrocketing popularity, I dedicate a little more space in this chapter to poker tournaments than to other types of tournaments. The appeal of poker is simple — it's a fun game to play, it has almost the perfect balance of skill versus luck, and the bigger tournaments offer fantastic monetary rewards and a chance to be on TV. (For complete details on playing poker, read Chapter 6.)

Because the prize structure for tournaments rewards only the top finishers, even good players can experience long droughts without cashing in. And because poker is more of an art than a mechanical game, you can easily slip into bad habits and start making mistakes.

To help you keep ahead of the other players in a poker tournament, this section gives you important strategies, including how to conserve your chips and scare your opponents.

Conserving (and carrying) your chips forward

In poker tournaments, chip conservation is critical. Poker tournaments follow a *freeze-out* format, which means play isn't restricted to either a certain number of rounds or a fixed time. Play continues until one person has all the chips. Consequently, as other players are knocked out, tables are consolidated, and you and other remaining players move around to new tables, carrying your existing chips with you.

Playing tight in the early rounds

When playing in poker tournaments, you can play your hands in many different styles, but I recommend *playing tight,* especially in the early rounds of a tournament. Playing tight means being extremely selective about which hands you're willing to risk your money on rather than gleefully pushing chips out with any two cards and hoping to get lucky.

Playing tight may not always be the optimal style of play, but it helps keep you out of trouble in the early rounds. That is important because in no-limit tournaments, you can lose all of your chips on any hand.

Creating fear among opponents

You don't need terrifying tattoos on your forehead or a pistol tucked into your belt to scare your opponents. A better tactic (and more likely to keep you out of jail) is to play aggressive poker. When you take the initiative, good things usually happen. Why? People become afraid of you. Fewer players *raise* (increase the bet) in front of you. Others are less likely to try and steal your *blinds* (forced bets before the flop).

The most important benefit of aggression is that it gives you two ways to win:

- ✔ **Check and call:** If you just check and call, the *only* time you rake in the pot is when you have the best hand.

- ✔ **Raise:** A raise doubles your chances of winning. You still win with the best hand, but you also can win if everyone folds — which happens a lot if the table fears you.

Thinning the herd

Isolation is another powerful technique that you can use successfully in poker. You can often *reraise* (raise an additional amount) to drive out other players — thin the herd — in order to play heads-up against one opponent. Your odds increase dramatically when you can isolate one player, especially if he is weak and loose, and you feel you can outplay him after the flop.

Plugging leaks in your game

Whenever I go through a bad run at the tables, I can usually attribute it to one of two reasons: a bad fluctuation where the cards turn cold, or playing too *loose* (playing weak hands). Playing too loose can happen in such little increments that I'm barely aware of doing so. A common scenario is that I start winning consistently and loosen up, getting involved in a few more pots, thinking I can outplay the other opponents at my table. Instead, I usually lose more because of my weaker starting hands.

Always evaluate your style of play in order to identify and to plug any potential *leaks* (holes in your game).

Thinking twice about all-in bets

Think long and hard before calling an *all-in bet,* or putting all your remaining chips in the pot. Dramatically shoving your whole stack without hesitation into the middle may look cool, but stop, take a few deep breaths, count to ten, and carefully evaluate the situation. Things to consider include the following: How strong is your hand? What possible cards does your opponent have? Will you finish in the money if you go out now?

Remember that you've invested some expense (your entry fee) and a considerable amount of time to participate in this tournament and get to this point. Relax and make sure this move is the right one before you shove your chips forward. Rash, impulsive moves may not just bounce you out of the tournament; they may also leave you with regrets for months afterwards.

Bluffing your way to a win

Bluffing separates the men from the boys, the women from the girls. Bluffing is the component that has helped propel poker into a big hit on TV. You have to have guts to hold weak cards and play them so strongly that your opponents fold their winning hands. Two important keys to bluffing are your table position and being able to read your opponents.

You can also keep the following bluffing pointers in mind to elevate your game to the next level:

- ✔ **Don't overbluff.** If you've played only good hands all day, other players are much more likely to believe you if you raise on the river. On the other hand, if you've been caught bluffing more than once already, expect them to call with anything. Bluffing loses effectiveness the more you attempt it.

- ✔ **Don't fidget.** If you start tapping your fingers on the table, rubbing your eyes, nose, and face, and acting like you just drank a 32-ounce double espresso, the other players are going to know you're hiding something. Other players can read your body language, so relax. Stay calm, cool, and collected.

✔ **Wear shades.** The future may be bright (and even the overhead lights), but you aren't wearing sunglasses as a fashion statement. Buy a pair of dark shades to hide your eye movements. Other players can watch your eyes and if you start blinking a lot or your eyes start popping out of your head, they may suspect you're bluffing.

Bluffing has residual benefits. Even when you get caught bluffing and lose, you may change your *table image* (how your opponents view you) in a way that's advantageous to you. For the rest of the tournament, for example, other players are more likely to call you when you raise on your good hands because they remember your foolish failed bluff. So even if your bluff backfires in one game, it can still pay profitable dividends later.

Tabling a win with table tournaments

When playing tournament table games, such as blackjack and craps, just remember one important point: Whoever finishes with the highest total of chips advances from each table. So even if you have a great run, all your "profit" is worthless unless you win your table and advance, which creates some wild and wacky finishes.

Unfortunately, no one-size-fits-all advice applies to every type of game. The tips that help you in blackjack may have no bearing at all in a Pai Gow tournament. With that caveat in mind, the following principles are helpful for craps, blackjack, and Pai Gow tournaments.

✔ **Keep tabs on your opponents' chips.** In most craps, blackjack, and Pai Gow tournaments, in order to advance you must end the round as winner at your table. Consequently, keeping track of your opponents' chip stacks is critical to see where you stand, especially down the stretch. Chip counting is a tough skill to master, but tournament rules do require all chips to be kept on the table in uniform stacks, making the task a little easier.

✔ **Focus on the end play.** Much of the strategy in these tournaments revolves around the *end play,* or the last hand, and the consistent winners are the ones who know exactly how much to bet in order to seize the lead.

✔ **Vote conservative.** At least during the early part of the tournament, adopting a conservative approach is a sound strategy that helps keep you in the game and a shot to win at the end. Watching several other aggressive players flame out early by losing their big bets isn't uncommon. The elimination of any opponent at your table greatly increases your chance for advancing.

✔ **Be the contrarian.** Another approach to use is if everyone around you is timid, be aggressive and try to seize an insurmountable lead. Doing so puts pressure on the competition and forces them out of their comfort zone when they have to start chasing you.

✔ **Be daring.** Many unusual plays that would normally be considered extreme in regular gambling can lead to victory in a tournament setting. For example, blackjack tournaments, which are experiencing a resurgence in popularity, often go down to the final card, which creates some wild and exciting finishes. On the last hand, you may have to hit a hard 18 or double down on a blackjack in order to grab the lead — moves you probably would never make when gambling outside a tournament. (Check out Chapter 7 for more on the specifics of blackjack.)

✔ **Seize the day.** The tournament format usually rewards the brave, so do whatever is necessary to win before the final gun sounds (other than poker, most tournaments have a time limit or fixed number of rounds). In many cases, last place is no worse than second place, so don't worry about busting out early or looking bad. Just remember this mantra: Go big or go home.

✔ **Don't get too attached to your chips.** In regular gambling, you can hang on to your chips or put some away into your purse or pocket for future use. But in tournaments, the chips have no value beyond the round you're playing, and in most cases you can't carry them over into future rounds. So don't get too attached. If you need to make a big bet, go for it.

Maneuvering through slot and video-poker tournaments

Slot tournaments are popular because they retain the fun and competitive elements of a sporting event but require little or no skill. Video poker, on the other hand, does offer some mental challenge. Slot and video-poker tournaments differ from table-games tournaments in several aspects. You start with a fixed amount of credits rather than chips, and play either for a set time (usually 10 to 30 minutes) or for a certain number of spins. The object is to accumulate as many credits as possible, so hitting big jackpots or royal flushes is the ticket to winning.

In slots and other machine games, you typically compete against all other players in that session. For example, 50 players compete in the round, and the overall ten highest scores from that session advance to the next round.

Whenever the tournament format restricts the session to a fixed amount of time, the players who get in the most amount of pulls or spins have the advantage. Here are three strategy tips from the *Las Vegas Advisor* for playing in a "timed" tournament:

- ✔ **Prepare.** Before playing, familiarize yourself with the combinations that produce large payoffs and rest when you hit one. Take care, however, to resume play as soon as the meter stops registering credits. Players who sit for close to a minute without realizing that their machine is ready to play again aren't uncommon.

- ✔ **Play fast.** Stay focused and concentrate on your own play. If you stop in the middle of a round to cheer for someone else who's hit a jackpot, you reduce your own spin total.

- ✔ **Conserve energy.** If you frantically pound the spin button, even when the credits are tallying, you tire and lose spins. Tapping the button lightly is more efficient.

The preceding tips help give you an edge, but the best strategy is to look for tournaments that have overlays (see "Taking advantage of overlays" earlier in this chapter) or other enticements. In addition, many tournaments routinely offer free rooms, hats, T-shirts, or some meals, all of which add extra value to the event.

Part V
The Part of Tens

The 5th Wave   By Rich Tennant

Monte Rio
LEO FLENDER
LIZA
LANCE BURTON

"Heck of a comp, Flender."

In this part . . .

Every *For Dummies* book ends with the famous Part of Tens. Mine includes — drum roll, please — ten cool places to gamble in casinos, ten mistakes to avoid when gambling in a casino, and ten really cool ways to score comps.

Chapter 19

Ten Cool Places to Gamble

*F*rom casino to casino, subtle changes in rules and odds can make a not-so-subtle impact on your gambling outcome, but another factor to consider when deciding *where* to gamble is the destination itself. Of course your selection is limited by gambling laws, but those choices remain diverse and plentiful. Do you like your baccarat near the beach? Or do you prefer slots on the Strip, sizzling with entertainment options? Does a river current stir the appeal of roulette? Or is blackjack on the Boardwalk your idea of a perfect gambling getaway?

Casual gamblers see little difference between casinos, but there can be significant distinctions, especially in nongambling amenities. These subtle differences (in the amenities as well as in the rules and odds) among casinos should play a role in your travel decisions. Consequently, where you gamble is almost as important as choosing what games you play. This chapter gives you ten great places where you can gamble the night away. Some of these locales have better odds than the others, but they're all packed full of fun.

One other distinction to keep in mind: Not all casinos are open 24 hours a day. For example, regulations allow cruise ships to open their casinos only when in international waters. And even then, many close down during the wee hours of the morning. Likewise, some casinos restrict their hours, particularly on riverboats, in small towns, and in foreign locations.

Living Large in Las Vegas

No doubt, Las Vegas is the queen of casino towns. No other gambling capital boasts more glitz and glamour. In Vegas, Lady Luck reigns — or punishes — but always in grand style. Since the days of Bugsy Siegel, when the famous Strip first lit up, Las Vegas has continued to shine, expanding beyond games and lounge acts to a fantasyland for kids and adults alike.

Beyond the slots and table games, visitors can wander a surreal landscape that incorporates the Manhattan skyline (at New York New York) with its very own roller coaster, the Eiffel Tower (Paris Las Vegas), and pirate battles (Treasure Island). Other choices for fun outside the casino include

- ✔ The Bellagio, famous for fountains that blast water high into the air in a choreographed dance to music. Opened in 1998 at a cost of $1.6 billion, it has a Gallery of Fine Art, luxury shops, the Conservatory, and several world-class restaurants.

- ✔ The ritzy Wynn casino, which houses a Ferrari-Maserati dealership, just in case you hit it big.

- ✔ The Venetian, where you can walk around canals and soak in the European elegance. These grounds are so impressive that some American tourists visiting the real city in Italy reportedly said, "Venice is nice, but it's nothing like the real thing back in Las Vegas."

Are you dying to get on the casino floor? Then you may want to take advantage of the ultimate in lodging convenience. Some of the bigger hotels allow check in right at the airport. By the time you get your room key, your luggage has arrived at the carousel.

For everything Vegas, check out *Las Vegas For Dummies* by Mary Herczog (Wiley).

Landing on Boardwalk: Atlantic City

Easy access from major East Coast cities, such as Baltimore, Philadelphia, and New York City, makes Atlantic City, New Jersey appealing. Ever since gambling rejuvenated the dying resort area in the late 1970s, the casinos have been packed.

Donald Trump is big here; his larger-than-life name graces three casinos in this city by the sea. But despite the Donald's broad presence, the marquee casino in town is the Borgata, offering 2,000 contemporary, European-style rooms. When the Borgata opened in 2003, competing Boardwalk casinos took notice of its success and immediately began to upgrade their own properties. The result has been a remarkable revitalization of Atlantic City.

These days this seaside community is seeing a tremendous surge in development, especially along the historic Boardwalk. When you're done offering your monetary sacrifice to the slot gods, check out the Pier at Caesars for some very high-end shops (such as Gucci and Tiffany), or leave the crowds behind for dolphin-watching off the white sands of Brigantine Beach. Another new attraction here is called "The Show" — a dazzling new water extravaganza designed to compete with the spectacular Bellagio Hotel in Las Vegas.

Touring Tahoe and Reno

In my view, Lake Tahoe is the most scenic spot in the United States. The area sparkles with sunny days, a dazzling blue lake, majestic snow-capped mountains, and beautiful alpine forests. My favorite casinos line the South Shore — on the Nevada side of the state line where gambling is legal. They offer a nice blend of entertainment and nightlife that encourages repeat customers.

You can go skiing, mountain biking, boating, and hiking during the day and then hit the local casinos at night. Or, if you want to take a short drive, just about an hour away you can visit Reno — Nevada's "Biggest Little City in the World." Most of the casinos in Reno are smaller than their Las Vegas counterparts, but several make up for their lack of size with a cozier atmosphere. My top recommendation is the Sparks Nugget. This casino is one of the friendliest clubs around, combining top-notch restaurants with loose slots and single-deck blackjack, giving great value to both hungry diners and hopeful gamblers.

Cruising the High Seas

The 1970s TV series *The Love Boat* launched a passion for cruising for mainstream America. Since then, cruises have remained one of the most popular — and affordable — vacation options available. Almost every cruise ship offers a casino, some small and modest, others surprisingly large and sophisticated. Profit from their onboard casinos allows cruise lines to keep the prices for cruise packages reasonable.

Don't have time for a full vacation? How about a short, three-hour cruise — without Gilligan? Several "cruise-to-nowhere" ships (primarily based in Florida) sail out to international waters (just a few miles offshore) to comply with gaming regulations. But you'll think you're in Vegas with the live entertainment, free drinks, and sumptuous buffets. Florida ports are located in Jacksonville, Daytona Beach, Port Canaveral, Hollywood, Key Largo, and the Tampa Bay area, to name a few.

Be aware, however, that at many shipboard casinos, the rules and odds tend to favor the house more than their land-based cousins do — so your chances of winning are diminished.

Fortunately, not all cruise casinos have bad odds. Norwegian Cruise Lines (NCL) offers both generous comps (even free cruises) and fair games to their passengers. I have cruised with NCL seven times and won on every trip. But I'm not sure which was the bigger thrill — filling my pockets with chips or being first in line for the fantastic midnight buffet.

Rolling on the River (or Lake)

Gambling returned to its roots when riverboats were legalized in several states up and down the Mississippi River region in the 1990s. The main recipient of this economic boom was the state of Mississippi, especially Tunica County, which previously held the distinction of being America's poorest county.

Several casinos dot the Gulf Coast along the southern part of Mississippi. This pleasant, sun-drenched area conjures up the region's elegant past and rich history with its mansions and manicured grounds. And, despite the devastating damage caused by Hurricane Katrina, the casino industry is rebuilding and once again welcoming tourists.

You can dismiss any images of Mark Twain and paddleboats because, in some cases, these riverboats never leave the dock and aren't even on the Mississippi River. If you want a more authentic experience, several boats in other states (such as Louisiana) do make short voyages. Always check for sailing times since you can't come and go on these casinos.

This resurgence of gambling hasn't been limited to the South because casinos have popped up all over the Midwest— from the Mississippi and Ohio rivers to Lake Michigan to Iowa. One of the nicer clubs in this region is Resorts Casino and Hotel in East Chicago, Indiana. It has almost 2,000 slot machines and a good selection of table games. The casino boasts having the most video poker progressives and more than a dozen tables of live poker. The Resorts Hotel is upscale and comparable to the finer hotels in downtown Chicago.

Exploring Native American Casinos

In 1987, the United States Supreme Court ruled that tribal lands were sovereign entities where state laws don't apply. This decision sent shock waves through the entire gaming industry as several Native American tribes took immediate steps to establish casinos on their reservations. Previously, casino gambling was confined to Nevada and Atlantic City, but as soon as Pandora's Box opened, gaming spread like wildfire across the country.

Today, more than 400 tribal casinos exist in the United States. Most are sprinkled modestly throughout the states of New York, Minnesota, Michigan, Washington, and Oregon, but the Native American casino presence in two states (California and Connecticut) is so significant that these locations deserve their own section in this chapter (check out the next two sections).

Collectively, the Native American gambling industry is very big business; total revenues at tribal casinos are nearly double that of all the casinos in Nevada combined. After centuries of injustice and broken treaties, Native Americans appear to be making a good economic recovery, one chip at a time.

Some gamblers are reticent to try Indian casinos because these clubs lack a gaming commission or the usual overseers to ensure regulation. My experiences at Native American casinos, however, have always been great. Although they're seldom as glitzy as Vegas casinos, tribal casinos generally have a friendlier, small-town feel to them, and I have never encountered any incidents that even remotely suggest impropriety.

Although times are a-changing, in the past some Indian casinos charged an ante for table games, such as blackjack. This collection fee (typically a dollar or less per hand) dramatically changes the odds and, in most cases, means you should avoid playing at these clubs.

Collecting Chips in Connecticut

Strange as it may sound, the country's third-smallest state is home to two of the world's largest casinos, Foxwoods and Mohegan Sun. These outstanding gambling sites add up to a powerful one-two combination perhaps unrivaled anywhere else.

Foxwoods (tucked away in a wooded rural part of Connecticut) is the biggest casino on the planet. Rising majestically out of a forest, the casino is stunning both inside and out. Slot machines number in the thousands, table games are in the hundreds, and it boasts the mother of all bingo halls. The Mashantucket Pequot Indians, believed to be the wealthiest tribe in the country, operate this behemoth casino, which employs more than 8,000 people and is roughly the size of 30 football fields.

And running a close second, the elaborately designed Mohegan Sun Casino, near Hartford, is home to 6,400 slot machines, 300 table games, 30 shops, and 29 restaurants. Its 1,200-room hotel offers amenities such as a daycare, a spa, and an arcade.

Striking Gold in California

Gambling has exploded in California, now that more than 40 Native American tribes offer some type of gaming activity. With so many superb casinos and gigantic card rooms, residents of Southern California no longer have to commute to Las Vegas to get their gambling fix. Several casinos much closer to home rival the big Nevada casinos in grandeur and amenities.

A perfect example is the Barona Valley Ranch Resort and Casino. This upscale facility near San Diego includes a stylish hotel, a world-class golf course, and a massive 300,000-square-foot casino. Barona gladly takes big action (up to $1,000 on their slot machines and $10,000 on their table games). Its blackjack tables are particularly enticing because the great rules (double down on any two cards and surrender) reduce the house edge to zero in their single-deck blackjack game. For my money, that is the best blackjack game in the country.

In the Los Angeles area, card rooms flourish. Although these aren't full-fledged casinos, the Bicycle and Commerce Casinos are among the world's biggest poker rooms, and both casinos have hosted prestigious World Poker Tour (WPT) events. L.A. has always been a hotbed for poker players, and with the WPT bringing poker into the mainstream, many Hollywood celebrities want in on the game that is sweeping the country.

Palm Springs also offers several charming casinos in the desert. The atmosphere is more casual there, and the almost perpetual sun is a big attraction for visitors, especially during winter months.

Finding Hidden Treasures in the Caribbean

A number of casinos in the Caribbean offer much more than just gambling. These clubs are mostly small and scattered across several islands, including Aruba, Dominican Republic, Puerto Rico, and the Bahamas. In addition to great gaming, they offer the draw of an enticing climate and colorful cultures.

The crown jewel of Caribbean gambling is undoubtedly the Atlantis Casino on Paradise Island in the Bahamas (right across the bridge from Nassau). This spectacular resort is built around an idyllic setting of stunning beaches, beautiful man-made waterfalls and lagoons, and breathtaking architecture throughout the resort. Oh, and by the way, the Atlantis houses the largest casino in the Caribbean.

Most casinos in the Caribbean allow you to gamble in dollars. And because you're in foreign countries (with the exception of Puerto Rico), you don't have to fill out W-2G forms when you win big. (See Chapter 4 for more details about money and taxes.) You're still required to report and pay any taxes on your profits when you return home. Of course, if you hit a *really* big jackpot, you may be tempted to spend the rest of your life on the beach, sipping those trendy drinks with the cute little umbrellas.

Joining the Jet Set

If rubbing shoulders with blue-collar gamblers in Reno or the bus crowd in Atlantic City isn't your style, you may consider heading overseas.

The first foreign casino most people think of is in Monaco. Monaco actually has four casinos total, but the main one (called the Monte Carlo Casino) was built in 1868. Starting with its marble atrium and Ionic columns, the decor and elegance of this venerable casino is markedly different from anything back in the United States, and the clientele is definitely upper crust. But if the posh setting ends up being too formal for your tastes, the area still has many other attractions, such as auto racing, beaches, boating, and a world-famous film festival.

As for the Southern Hemisphere, the place to gamble is at the Crown Casino in Melbourne, Australia. The Crown is the largest casino on the continent and has most games available. Poker's greatest players flock south in January (where it's summer) to play in the Aussie Millions tournament held annually at the Crown.

If you crave action a little closer to home, the Casino Niagara is big, bright, and Vegas-like. It's located near the Rainbow Bridge on the Canadian side. But who wants to spend all day inside the casino when you're at Niagara Falls? Make sure you save time to get drenched on a boat tour, where you can really experience the falls (blue slicker provided), or walk through the tunnels to Journey Behind the Falls (yellow slicker provided), where you can get drenched up close and personal, or take the Spanish aero car (cable car) right over churning, violent rapids. Another highlight is having dinner after dark and enjoying the spectacular light show that illuminates the falls with constantly changing colors.

Chapter 20

Ten (Or So) Common Casino Gambling Mistakes to Avoid

In This Chapter

▶ Relying on luck

▶ Going after losses

Money in a casino is like water in a river: It normally flows in one direction (away from you). Unfortunately, many players speed up this natural process and turn a meandering stream into raging whitewater by foolishly giving the house a larger edge than necessary. The culprits? Playing in bad games, making foolish mistakes, or overestimating their gambling IQs.

Being honest about your own truths and weaknesses isn't easy. Not everyone can be a card shark or an NCAA basketball expert. But the lure of the big win feeds aspirations that are just a little unrealistic. The result: You may have a natural tendency to overrate your own skills and believe you have an edge when you really don't.

Boosting your chance of winning in the casino doesn't require a calculus book or a lucky rabbit's foot. If your expectations are reasonable and you can rein in your emotions, you can avoid many common mistakes that I discuss in this chapter.

Gambling at All

Whenever people ask me for tips or advice on gambling, my stock answer is "Don't gamble." Though my answer is a bit of a joke, I honestly believe most people are better off staying away from casinos. The reason is simple — the overwhelming majority of gamblers lose.

But if you know going into a casino that the odds are stacked against you and that you're unlikely to win, then you can at least be battle ready. For example, acquaint yourself with games with better odds, such as blackjack and video poker. Gambling doesn't have to be about winning big. Even if you know you aren't going to win thousands, you may want to gamble in a casino for the excitement and sheer chance to get a little lucky. I have no problem with that mindset, but just make sure you understand the high cost of your fun.

Failing to Keep Records

Selective amnesia is a contagious disease often contracted by gamblers playing cards or dice in a casino. Sadly, there is no cure. The symptoms are serious; many players remember their big wins and minimize their losses. Consequently, they easily believe that they're ahead overall.

The best way to treat this ailment is by keeping records. Keeping detailed records can help you maintain a proper perspective on your gambling, ensuring that you're honestly aware of the actual amount you have won or lost. A gambling log can help you determine whether it's time to take up a new, less expensive, hobby — like, say, burning dollar bills.

Another good argument for keeping records is that the law requires it. Even if you're not a professional gambler, the IRS expects you to tally your results and report profits to Uncle Sam at the end of the year (see Chapter 4 for more money-management words of advice).

Bouncing Around Like a Pinball

Another helpful trick is to specialize. Rather than bouncing around like a pinball from one casino game to another trying to get lucky, find one (or two) game(s) and become an expert in that field. Knowledge is power inside the casinos walls, so never play in games that you don't understand.

Looking for Luck in All the Wrong Places

Luck is one of the most overused and misunderstood words in the English language. People attribute their big wins in a casino (and in life) to good luck or blame their brutal losses on bad luck. However, a number of factors can cause a gambler to either win or lose in a casino. And luck usually isn't one of them.

Don't confuse superstition with statistics. You didn't lose because you walked under a ladder; you lost because you split sixes against a face card. And your big win had nothing to do with the four-leaf clover you found in your dinner salad. Over time, the decisions you make — combined with the odds of the games you play — ultimately determine your financial bottom line.

So, you still want to improve your luck? Fine. Play only the most favorable games (those with the lowest house edge) and master the correct strategies. You can make your *luck* even better by avoiding bad bets and wrong motives, such as trying to prove how smart you are, playing for thrills, or showing off for your girlfriend.

Giving Up Too Easily

One obstacle that keeps players from becoming experts is that they fear the task. They know some games, such as blackjack, can be beaten, but they think only gifted geeks with photographic memories are able to succeed.

The truth is that anyone with average aptitude and good discipline can master the skills necessary to win. For example, you don't have to remember every card to play a winning game of blackjack (see Chapter 7). And at first glance, you may think the strategy you need to win at video poker (check out Chapter 13) looks overwhelming. But with a little practice on your home computer, you can become proficient enough to break even against the house.

Breaking the Law (of Averages)

Gravity is never suspended in a casino. What goes up must come down, which is why so many players fail to walk away a winner. The odds eventually catch up with even the hottest players and turn sizzling streaks into just another losing day. However, the roller-coaster nature of gambling may cause you to misunderstand the law of averages. For example, after a long cold streak at the craps tables, you may believe that you're due for some good luck and start betting more.

Odds and probability *do* even out in the long run. But in nearly all gambling situations, the past doesn't affect the future. Whether the dice or cards have been running hot or cold makes no difference at all for your next bet. The past is gone. It's history. Don't try to catch up by thinking certain events are due to hit or happen based on past results. This common gambler's fallacy has led many desperate players to ruin. (Check out Chapter 3, which looks more closely at probability and odds.)

Relying on Betting Systems

Finding that *magic bullet* or surefire way to win is the quest of many gamblers. This search often leads to *progressive betting systems,* which are systems that raise or lower your bets after wins or losses. They're surefire all right — a surefire way to lose. (Check out Chapter 3 for more on betting systems.)

Casinos love system players who arrive in town with high hopes and fat wallets. The casino owners are confident because they know that, over the long run, no system sold through a magazine for $99 can take down a billion-dollar casino. You may have small wins in the short term, but no progressive system can mathematically show a profit in the long run.

Being Seduced

Unfortunately, this section has nothing to do with some drop-dead-gorgeous cocktail waitresses wanting to follow you home. Rather, the section heading refers to the seductive nature of gambling, which lures many victims into its web.

Greed is one of the most dangerous emotions in a casino, especially when you're winning. Getting sucked into betting more and wanting bigger wins is all too easy. Be careful not to fall victim to this vicious cycle.

If you win big, get out of the casino and hit the open road. Don't keep playing in a futile quest for an even bigger jackpot.

Another manifestation of casino seduction is *chasing comps,* or trying to attain freebies, such as a free buffet or free show tickets. The prospect of a free lunch has driven many players to gamble far longer and with far more dollars than they normally would have. (Check out Chapter 21 for tips on getting comps.)

Losing It Online

Internet gambling seems to offer the best of both worlds — access to your favorite games without any travel requirement. However, that convenience comes with a potentially high price tag. The biggest danger is that the 24/7 availability of online casinos can quickly spiral out of control for gamblers.

If you aren't disciplined or somewhat compulsive by nature, you should probably avoid gambling. But you should especially stay away from Internet gambling. The temptations are greater, the chips seem less real, and the pitfalls are more numerous.

Taking It to the Limit, One Too Many Times

Many gamblers are tempted to bet more when they're losing in a desperate attempt to get back to even. This strategy is an example of *chasing your losses* or throwing good money after bad. To become successful in the gambling arena, rid your mind of short-term thinking. (For more on money management, see Chapter 4.)

How you're doing for any given session, day, or trip is irrelevant. Instead focus on the big picture. The problem is that few people think that way because today's culture presses you to fixate on the here and now. Although living in the present may be beneficial for other aspects of life, it can be hazardous in gambling. Don't worry about winning every session, day, or trip. Instead concentrate on your overall win/loss results.

Overindulging

A trip to a modern casino is like a visit to a fantasyland. At the biggest clubs everything is over the top and nothing is too outrageous. Unfortunately this mind-set also trickles down to the casino patrons, and many develop an "anything goes" attitude when they gamble. Partying fast may be more fun, but the most successful gamblers are the ones who are slow and steady and always maintain their discipline.

The following are ways some people overindulge and bomb out in casinos:

- They fail to stick to their bankroll and limits (check out Chapter 4).
- They drink while they gamble.
- They try to impress others.
- They play with *scared* money (money they can't afford to lose).
- They gamble when they're tired.

Don't forget to take breaks. Get up, go to the bathroom, get something to eat, take a nap, and relax so that you're sharp when you make that big bet.

Blaming Others

Some people try to blame someone or something else for their problems. This maneuver is especially true in gambling. I don't know how many times I've heard: "I would have won if only . . ." You can pretty much fill in the blanks with:

- ✔ The moron hadn't split his two face cards at the blackjack table.
- ✔ Those stupid casinos didn't cheat.
- ✔ The dealer would learn how to bust.
- ✔ That craps shooter hadn't hit those chips with his dice.
- ✔ Mr. Basketball Star could learn how to make a free throw.

Although bad and sometimes unbelievable events do happen in casinos, the real problem isn't the dealer or the drunk to your left. You need to take a good look in the mirror from time to time and do whatever you can to plug any leaks in your game.

Chapter 21

Ten Ways to Score Comps

*T*he most beautiful sound in any casino is the sound of winning — whether from the clang of slot tokens striking the metal tray after a jackpot or the ear-splitting scream of a craps player who just rolled another seven. But another sound that coaxes smiles from gamblers is that powerful word in the English language — *free!*

Everybody loves getting something for nothing, and the casino comp system is an ingenious way to make you happy, even when you lose. And in the world's casino capitals, opportunities exist to obtain just about any service or coveted merchandise for free. Although most gamblers won't qualify for the VIP treatment of gourmet dinners, limo rides, and penthouse suites, some comps are available for virtually every level of gambler.

Cynics often point out that a *free lunch* is never free and that any comp the casino doles out has a hidden cost to it. That's essentially true, but you can find ways to make the system work for you. This chapter contains ten suggestions that increase your odds of getting back more in comps than you lose in the casino.

The techniques in this chapter primarily refer to table games. The reason is that the rating system in slot machines and in video poker is computerized. Consequently, there is never any debate over how long you've played or how much you've lost. However, rating the play at table games is an inexact science, and that system can create a few interesting possibilities.

Ask and Ye Shall Receive

Go ahead and ask the casino to give you something for free. If you're too shy, the casino can't say *yes*. The person you ask varies, depending on the games you're playing, but normally a pit boss, floor person, or host is the person to approach. You may only qualify for a comp T-shirt or hat, but, hey, it's free and better than returning home empty-handed.

A good place to start your comp career is asking for a free meal. Even modest betting should qualify most gamblers for a free pass to the coffee shop or the buffet. And don't feel guilty asking. You're not a mooch or a beggar. By gambling in their casino, you have earned certain privileges. So don't hesitate in taking advantage of them.

Impressing the Boss with Club Card Mileage

Always use your casino club card, and always ensure that the pit boss is aware of your presence. Your club card is the casino's way of tracking your time and total amount wagered at the tables or slot machines. Most casinos tabulate the total amount of time you gamble, factor in your average bet, and then tabulate those calculations into points. You can use these points for comps (such as meals, shows, rooms, and so on) or, in some cases, converted into cash.

Before you ever play a slot machine or make your first bet, sign up and get a club card. Joining the club at any casino is a simple process and generally only takes a few minutes. (For more information on how to sign up for a card, see Chapter 12.) Another great benefit of becoming a member is that casinos often mail out great deals to active players. These promotions and special offers can really add up, so it's smart to get a card at several different casinos.

Slot machines and video poker have a place to insert your card into the machine. This system conveniently tracks all your play. However, if you're playing table games, make sure to give your card to the dealer or a floor person. If the pit boss doesn't know who you are, then he can't know whom to give the comp to.

Maybe you preferred to sit at the back of class in high school, but now isn't the time to be a wallflower. Don't be invisible. Even short sessions can add up to worthwhile comps over time, so make sure you get credit for every nickel you play.

Finding the Weakest Link

Getting a comp to the buffet while losing a thousand bucks at the roulette wheel is financial suicide (similar to the Pentagon paying $400 for an $8 hammer). A wiser approach is to find the best odds in the house and attack the casino where it's weakest.

Video poker and blackjack are the casino's weakest links. Video poker has far more favorable odds than slot machines and can be a great choice for minimizing your losses and maximizing your comps. Blackjack is easy to master (at least in terms of basic strategy), and the casino has a hard time discerning whether you're a good player or a clueless weekend warrior who relies on hunches for playing decisions. If you stick to basic strategy rather than guessing, receiving more in comps than you lose over the long run is possible because of the slim house edge both in video poker and in blackjack. (Check out Chapter 7 for more info on playing blackjack and Chapter 13 for video poker.)

At some blackjack games, such as the single-deck table at the Barona Casino in San Diego, *no* house edge exists, so you get a small advantage without even knowing how to count cards. Single-deck blackjack with good rules, coupled with generous comps, makes for a powerful package.

Betting More When the Boss Is Looking

Siegfried & Roy weren't the only ones to use the power of illusion to their advantage. If the pit bosses think your average bet is $25 (when it's really closer to $10), then you receive more than twice as many juicy comps during your gambling visits, which can be magically delicious.

Sure, the computers keep track of your casino activity, but they only know what the bosses tell them. And in table games like blackjack, the bosses are often wrong because they don't watch every bet you place — only randomly selected ones.

Because of that loophole, here's a simple, but effective ploy: Make your first bet double or triple your normal bet. When you hand a pit boss or floor person your club card, she often notices the amount of your first bet and writes this number down. Thus, your average bet may be weighted much higher than it really is — which translates into more comps.

Betting Less When the Boss Isn't Looking

Betting less when the pit boss isn't watching you is in the same category as taking out the garbage when the wife is watching. After all, what's the point in doing work if you're not going to get credit for it?

If you're increasing your wagers simply to get the pit boss's attention and earn yourself some comps, then you certainly want to decrease your wagers when she isn't watching. To counter that initial big bet and subsequent big bets you make when the boss has her eye on your game, bet less when the boss isn't around.

Making the Bathroom Your Second Home

The comp meter usually keeps running whether you're playing in the game or not, so take as many breaks as possible. The point is that you want to reduce your financial risk (which increases when you're actively gambling) while you increase your comp potential. Frequent trips to the restroom may seem like a curse to senior citizens — but those breaks can be one of the best techniques for scoring more comps with less financial risk.

Of course, even when your bladder is empty, you can achieve the same end by pursuing other sorts of breaks, such as getting a snack, taking a short walk, observing others, and so on. The bottom line: Try to play as little as possible while you get credit for as much as possible.

Looking Like You're Losing

One way to look like you're losing is by deftly hiding chips every time you play (put them into your pocket or purse). Uncomfortable with being deceptive? Think about sports or other games. Proper strategy in football, poker, or chess is to make moves that fake out your opponents and trick them into misreading you. Trying to score comps is similar; the most successful players aren't afraid to act a little bit or exaggerate their losses.

Greasing the Wheels

A small token of your appreciation to a pit boss goes a long way in getting you an inflated comp rating. There are several ways to do this and most of them don't involve monetary gifts. Casino employees are real people just like us. Their jobs are often very demanding, so kind words, a thank-you card, a sincere compliment, or a letter of praise to their supervisor can create a ton of goodwill. And if hosts or pit bosses like you, it often influences the way they rate your play.

Never Looking a Gift Horse in the Mouth

A good general rule is to never turn down a free comp. The house is bound to remember you as an appreciative guest and perhaps offer you other comps. However, if you're a picky player, the casino likely labels you as *difficult* and — especially if you're not really a high roller — turns the stream of comp gestures off. When the casino offers you a comp, smile broadly and offer your thanks. But if you really can't use or give away that comp, politely ask for a different, but comparable one. For example, if you can't stomach sushi, see if the casino can switch the comp to the Chinese restaurant.

The types of comps you can expect to receive vary greatly, depending on how upscale the casino is. For example, at ritzy clubs on the Vegas Strip, bets of $25 a hand at blackjack may hardly get noticed. But the same action at a riverboat casino may get you a free room, food, and beverage (RFB), while some small casinos (such as cruise ships) may not even offer comps.

Behaving with Courtesy and Respect

Although some people say that sports build character, my experience has taught me that sports *show* your character. The high-stakes drama of a big game strips away the veneers and facades that many people wear, unveiling their real, raw emotions.

Likewise, the pressure-packed arena of casino gambling seems to bring out the worst in many people. Winners can become obnoxious, preening prima donnas. Big losers are transformed into rude whiners who blame everyone around them for their bad luck.

The best approach is to remain friendly and polite, regardless of the cards. Nice guys don't always finish last; sometimes they end up dining on caviar and drinking Dom Perignon. Meanwhile the boorish jerks often wind up with nothing.

Part VI
Appendixes

In this part . . .

This part includes two helpful appendixes that you can use to supplement your casino gambling experience. For example, if someone told you they just crashed out of a tournament because an opponent hit an inside straight on the river, feel free to glance through Appendix A (the glossary), to decipher their intention. In Appendix B, I provide additional helpful resources in case you want to delve deeper in casino gambling, including information about Gamblers Anonymous.

Appendix A

Glossary

action: Total amount of money wagered over a period of time.

active player: In poker, a player who is still playing, or in the *hand*.

all-in: A bet placing all the player's chips in the *pot*.

anchor position: The last seat at a blackjack table, also called *third base*.

ante: In card games, the initial *bet* wagered on a hand; required before play can begin.

any craps: A one-roll dice wager that the next number will be 2, 3, or 12.

American wheel: A roulette wheel that includes a zero and a double zero.

baccarat: A card game where the hand closest to a total of 9 wins. Minibaccarat is identical, only it's played on a smaller table.

bad beat: Losing with a strong hand in poker or a bet in sports that normally would have won.

bankroll: The total amount of money a player sets aside for gambling.

basic strategy: A playing strategy that minimizes the *house edge*.

bet: An amount of money that is risked on the outcome of an event.

betting limits: The minimum and maximum amounts you can wager on a single bet.

Big 6 or **Big 8:** In craps, a bet that a 6 or 8 will be rolled before a 7.

Big Six Wheel: A betting wheel with 54 slots; also called the Wheel of Fortune.

bingo: A game where randomly selected numbers are drawn and players must match the numbers on printed cards. The first person to cover a pattern on a card wins.

blackjack: A card game where the players try to beat the dealer's hand by getting closest to 21 without going over; also, a hand whose first two cards total 21.

blacks: $100 *chips,* typically black in color.

blind bet: In poker, a mandatory bet placed before the cards are dealt.

bluff: A poker betting strategy in which a player with a weak hand *raises* his bet in hopes of making other players drop out.

board: In poker, the *community cards* that are dealt face-up.

bones: Slang for *dice*.

boxman: The supervisor of the craps table.

bullets: A pair of aces in poker.

burn: In card games, to discard the top card or cards from the deck at the beginning of a deal.

bust: In blackjack, any hand that exceeds 21.

button: In poker, a small round disk designating the dealer for each hand.

buy-in: The amount of money required to join a game or the converting of cash into chips at a table game.

C & E bets: In craps, the *hardway bets* of 2, 3, 11, and 12. The C stands for *craps* and the E stands for 11.

cage: The location in a casino where players exchange chips/coins/cash, redeem markers, and set up a credit line.

call: In poker, to match the current bet of one's opponent(s).

caller: In baccarat, the dealer who controls the game; in bingo or keno, the individual running the game and calling the numbers.

card counter: In blackjack, a person who can mentally keep track of which cards have been played.

Caribbean Stud poker: A five-card poker game where all players compete against the house.

carousel: A group of slot machines in a circle or ring.

change booth: A location in the casino that handles coin/cash and slot transactions, but usually not chips. The booth is typically smaller than the cage.

check: A gaming *chip*. Also, a poker term when a player opts not to bet.

checkraise: In poker, when a player first checks, and then decides to raise later in the same betting round.

chemin de fer: (French) A European form of baccarat.

chip: A round gaming token used in place of cash for wagering a bet.

chung: A plastic marker indicating the banker's hand in Pai Gow poker.

claiming race: In horse racing, a race in which all the horses are for sale at a set price.

closing line: In sports betting, the final point spread in the sports book before the game begins.

cold: A player on a losing streak; a slot machine that isn't paying out.

color up: To exchange chips from a smaller denomination to a larger denomination.

columns: In roulette, three betting areas representing 12 numbers each.

combination way ticket: A keno ticket in which two or more groups of numbers are bet different ways, allowing the player to spread money over several combinations.

come bet: A craps bet made after the point has been established. When dice are passed to a new shooter, the first roll is "coming out."

come line: An area on the craps table to place a *come bet*.

come out roll or **coming out:** In craps, the first roll of the dice that establishes the point.

community cards: In poker, the cards face-up in the middle of the table. Any player can use them to make a hand.

comps: Complimentary services given by the casino to players based on their gaming action.

crap out: To throw one of the craps numbers (2, 3 or 12) on the *come out roll*.

craps: A game played with two dice in which a throw of 7 or 11 wins; 2, 3, or 12 loses; and any other number (called a point) must be repeated before a 7 is rolled again.

credit line: Amount of credit extended by a casino to a customer.

croupier: French word for *dealer*.

cut card: A hard plastic card used to cut a deck of cards.

cut the deck: To divide a deck of cards into two parts.

dealer: A casino employee who operates a table game.

dice: A pair of cubes with one to six spots on six sides used by a shooter in a craps game. A single cube is called a **die.**

don't come: A craps bet made after the *come out roll,* betting against the dice.

don't pass: A craps bet made before the *come out roll,* betting with the dice that they won't pass (that a 7 will be rolled before the point number is repeated).

double down: In blackjack, doubling the original bet and receiving one additional card.

double odds: In craps, an odds bet that is twice as large as the original pass or *come bet.* Some casinos allow triple and higher odds bets.

downcard: A card that is dealt face-down.

draw: In draw poker, the second round of cards that replace any cards thrown away or discarded.

Draw button: On a video-poker machine, the button allows the player to draw up to five new cards.

ducks: In poker, a pair of twos.

early position: In poker, to be one of the first players to act in a betting round.

even money bet: A payoff ratio of 1 to 1; that is, you win the same amount you wagered.

European wheel: In roulette, a wheel with a single zero. Also called a *French wheel.*

exacta: In horse racing, a bet in which you pick the first two horses to finish and in the correct order.

exotic: Any sporting-event bet other than a straight bet, such as a *teaser bet.*

eye in the sky: The surveillance video or live monitoring of the gaming area of a casino.

face card: A king, queen, or jack in a deck of cards.

face-down cards: All cards that are dealt down and hidden from view.

face-up cards: All cards that are dealt face up and are visible to everyone.

field bet: A craps bet that the next roll will be 2, 3, 4, 9, 10, 11, or 12.

filly: A female horse no more than 4 years old.

first base: In blackjack, the seat to a dealer's left and the first player to act.

flat betting: Betting the same amount on each wager.

flat top: A slot machine with a fixed-amount jackpot.

floor supervisor: In the casino, a *pit* supervisor who watches the dealers and also reports to the *pit boss.*

flop: In Texas Hold'em poker, the first three community cards dealt face-up in the center of the table.

flush: A poker hand with five cards of the same suit.

fold: In poker, to drop out of play.

four of a kind: Four cards of the same rank.

freeroll tournament: A tournament that offers no risk to the player.

French wheel: See *European wheel.*

full house: In poker, three cards of the same rank plus two cards of another rank.

furlong: In horse racing, 220 yards. Eight furlongs equal one mile.

gelding: A castrated colt.

greens: $25 chips, usually green in color.

gut shot: In poker, to *draw* to an inside straight, as in 2-3-4-6.

hand: The cards held by the dealer or player in a game of cards, or the particular round of a game.

handicapper: A person who analyzes information to predict the outcome of a horse race or sporting event.

hard hand: In blackjack, any hand without an ace, or a hand where aces are counted as 1.

hard-way bet: A craps bet that 4, 6, 8, or 10 will be rolled as an even pair, such as two 5s.

harness racing: A horse race between horses that pace or trot harnessed to sulkies.

high-low split: In some poker games, the pot is split between the best high hand and the best low hand.

high roller: A high-stakes gambler who wagers large sums of money, such as $1,000 a hand at blackjack.

hit: To take another card from the dealer in poker and other card games.

hole card: A dealer's card dealt face-down and not exposed until the end of the round.

horn bet: A one-roll craps bet that a 2, 3, 11, or 12 will be the next roll.

hot: A player on a winning streak; a slot machine that is paying out.

house: The casino.

house edge: The casino's mathematical advantage over the player in any game.

inside straight: Four cards in a hand that needs a middle card to complete it, such as a 4-5-6-8.

insurance: In blackjack, a *side bet* that the dealer has a *natural* (or blackjack) when her upcard is an ace.

jackpot: The highest prize on a slot machine or in keno.

jacks or better: A draw poker game in which a pair of jacks is the lowest possible hand to open the betting.

joker: An extra card in a deck that is sometimes used as a *wild card*.

juice: *Vigorish* or commission charged by the casino on sports bets.

keno: A lotto game in which 20 numbers are drawn from 80. Players select a group of numbers and win based on how many of their numbers match the drawing.

keno runner: The casino employee who picks up your bet and takes it to the keno counter; he also delivers payment for a winning ticket.

late position: For a particular betting round in poker, the player who acts near the end.

Let It Ride: A card game where you try to make the best possible hand with your three cards in conjunction with two *community cards*.

limit poker: A game in which the betting amounts are fixed at each table.

limp in: In poker, to enter the *pot* by *calling* rather than *raising*.

line: The *point spread* on a sporting event.

live blind: The opportunity for a poker player to *raise* his own *blind*, even if no other player raises.

loose: A poker player who plays a lot of hands.

loose slots: A slot machine that pays off liberally.

lowball: A form of poker where the lowest hand wins.

maiden race: A race run with horses that have never won a race.

main pot: The center pot of poker. Any other bets are in *side pots*.

mare: A female horse 5 years old or older.

marker: Casino credit is generally extended to a player by signing a piece of paper called a marker.

minibaccarat: Played on a blackjack-size table, a smaller version of baccarat with less formality and a faster pace.

money line: Betting on a sporting event without a *point spread.*

morning line: In horse racing, the estimate of the win odds for each horse as set by the track's prerace handicap of each race.

muck: The pile of *burn* cards and *folded* hands in poker.

natural: In blackjack, an initial hand consisting of an ace and a 10-value card (also called *blackjack*); in baccarat, an initial hand consisting of 8 or 9 points.

nickels: $5 chips, also called *reds,* typically red in color.

no-limit poker: A game with no restrictions on betting.

nuts: In poker, the best possible hand at any point in the game.

oddsmaker: The person who sets the *line* at a sports book.

odds: A probability ratio used in gambling to reflect the chances of winning.

odds bet: In craps, an additional bet after the point is established.

off: A bet on a craps table that isn't *working,* meaning it isn't at risk with the next roll of the dice.

on: A bet on a craps table that is *working,* meaning it is at risk with the next dice roll.

one-armed bandit: A slang term for a *slot machine.*

opening line: The first official line set by an oddsmaker for a sporting event.

open-ended straight: Four cards to a straight in sequence; 5-6-7-8, for example, in the game of poker.

outside bets: A roulette bet placed on the outside of the table layout. Outside bets include the columns, the dozens, black, red, odd, even, 1 to 18, and 19 to 36.

overlay: Any gambling situation that gives the bettor an advantage over the house.

over/under: A sports bet determined by whether the final score is over or under a specified number.

Pai Gow poker: A game of seven cards where a player must make two separate poker hands — one of five cards and one of two cards.

paint: A *face card.*

pair: Any two cards of the same rank or number value.

parimutuel wagering: A system in which bets are pooled, resulting in odds set by the bettors.

parlay: A sports bet in which two or more events are tied together and must be won in order to win the parlay.

pass bet: In craps, a bet that the dice will *pass,* meaning the established point number will be rolled before a 7 is rolled.

pass line: The area on the craps table where *pass bets* are made.

payline: The line on the slot machine window where the symbols for a winning combination must line up.

payoff: The amount paid for a winning bet.

payout percentage: The percent of each dollar played in a video/slot machine returned to the player.

picture cards: See *face cards.*

pit: The restricted access area inside a cluster of gaming tables where employees work.

pit boss: The person in charge of the tables in a specific gaming area.

place bet: A wager on a horse to finish first or second. Also, a craps bet on a number to be rolled before a 7.

player card: A card that can be inserted into a slot machine or used at gaming tables to accumulate points toward comps, cash, or free gifts.

pocket cards: The two hole cards dealt to every player in Texas Hold'em.

point: In craps, one of six numbers (4, 5, 6, 8, 9, or 10) established on the *come out roll.*

point spread: The method used to even the odds of a particular sporting event; the point difference between the favorite and the underdog as set by the casino.

poker: A card game with many variations and contested against other players.

pot: In poker, the amount of money that accumulates until the winner is determined.

pot limit: In poker, a game in which the maximum bet can't be more than the amount in the pot.

press: Increasing your bet while on a win streak by letting winnings ride.

probability: The likelihood that an event will occur, such as hitting a jackpot once every 500 spins.

progressive slots: A group of slot machines linked together that pool a fraction of each wager into a large jackpot.

proposition bets: Any craps wager made in the center box of the table layout.

puck: A craps table *marker* used to indicate whether a point has been established.

punto banco: European name for the American version of baccarat.

purples: $500 chips, typically purple in color.

purse: In horse racing, the total prize money distributed.

push: A tie between the player and dealer in which no money is won or lost.

put bet: In craps, a *pass line bet* made after the point is established.

quads: In poker, four of a kind.

qualifier: The minimum value a hand must meet in order to play, such as in Caribbean Stud poker or *lowball.*

quinella: In horse racing, a bet in which you pick two horses to finish first and second in either order.

Quarter Horse racing: A race of horses bred specifically to sprint a quarter-mile distance.

quarters: $25 *chips*; also called *greens,* typically green in color.

raise: In poker, to match another player's bet and then increase the amount, forcing other players to also bet more.

rake: In poker, a percentage the casino takes from the *pot* for each hand as a fee.

rank: The value of a poker hand. For example, a player with a flush has a better-ranking hand than a player with a straight.

rating: The casino ranking of players according to how much and how long they gamble. A higher rating helps score *comps.*

reds: $5 *chips,* typically red in color, also called *nickels.*

return percentage: A theoretical measure of slot-machine payouts.

RFB: Complimentary free room, food, and beverage.

riffling: A card-shuffling process.

right bettor: A craps player who bets on the *pass* and *come lines.*

river: The last card dealt.

roll: To toss the dice in craps.

roulette: A game where a ball is spun in a wheel containing 37 or 38 numbered pockets.

royal flush: In poker, an ace-high straight flush, A-K-Q-J-10, of the same suit. It's the best possible hand.

scared money: Any portion of your gambling stake you can't afford to lose.

scratch: Withdrawing a horse from a race for any reason.

session: The time spent gambling in a single sitting.

shill: A casino employee who acts as a customer and starts a table game.

shoe: The box holding six or eight decks of cards from which the cards are dealt.

shooter: The person rolling the dice.

show: In horse racing, a bet on a horse to finish first, second, or third.

showdown: In poker, when all players left at the final round show their hands to determine the winner.

sic-bo: A dice game played on a table layout with three dice and 50 wagers to choose from.

side bet: Many table games offer another bet, the side bet, in addition to the main or primary bet, such as the *insurance bet* in blackjack.

side pot: In poker, a separate *pot* that remaining players can contest.

singleton: In poker, a card that is the only one of its rank.

slot card: See *player card.*

small blind: In poker, the first bet before the cards are dealt.

soft hand: A blackjack hand in which the ace is counted as 11.

spinning reel slots: Slot machines that have mechanical reels with symbols.

split bet: In roulette, a bet on two adjacent numbers. If one of the numbers wins, it pays 17 to 1.

spot: In keno, any number from 1 to 80 that a player selects on the ticket. A 6-spot ticket means six numbers are marked with an X.

sports book: A place within the casino that accepts bets on sporting events.

stacked deck: A deck that has been arranged to give someone an advantage.

stake: An amount of money a player is willing to play (and possibly lose) during a gaming session.

stakes race: The highest purse races in Thoroughbred horse racing.

stand: In card games, to refrain from taking any more cards.

stickman: The craps dealer who moves the dice with a stick and calls the numbers rolled.

stiff: In blackjack, a *hard hand* of 12 through 16, which may bust if hit once.

straight: Poker hand consisting of five consecutive cards not of the same suit.

straight flush: In poker, five consecutive cards of the same suit.

straight-up bet: In roulette, a bet on a single number. If it wins, it pays 35 to 1.

street bet: In roulette, to bet a three-number combination. If one of the numbers wins, it pays 11 to 1.

streets: The card rounds dealt in stud poker. Fifth street, for example, is the fifth round.

stud poker: A poker game in which there is no *draw* and some of each player's cards are exposed.

suit: Any one of the four types of cards: clubs, diamonds, hearts, or spades.

surrender: In blackjack, to give up half your bet before the hand is played.

symbols: The pictures on the reels of a slot machine.

system: A method of wagering to try to get an advantage.

table layout: The markings on a table that tell a player where to place bets.

table limit: The largest or maximum amount allowed for a table bet.

taking odds: In craps, an *odds bet* that pays more than even money on the odds portion of the wager.

teaser bet: A *parlay bet* where you can adjust the point spread by adding points in favor of the teams you're betting on.

Texas Hold'em: Poker game where each player tries to make the best possible hand using their two *pocket* cards along with five *community cards.*

third base: The last seat at a blackjack table.

Thoroughbred racing: A classification for horses whose lineage can be traced back to one of three Arabian stallions in the 18th century.

three of a kind: Three cards of the same value, such as three aces.

toke: A tip or gratuity given to a dealer.

token: A special coin used in place of a real coin to play a slot machine.

tote board: In horse racing, the field information board that shows the totals of bets for win, place, and *show* for the next race.

touch screen: A video slot machine that can be touched by hand to select an object.

tournament: A gaming competition.

trifecta: In horse racing, a bet in which you must pick the first three horses to finish in the correct order.

trips: Three cards of the same *rank.*

true odds: The mathematical odds of something happening. The odds posted in a casino are usually paid at less than true odds.

turn: The fourth *community card* in Texas Hold'em.

twenty-one: Another name for *blackjack.*

two pair: Two cards of the same *rank* and two cards of another *rank.*

underdog: The predicted loser in a sports event or horse race.

unit: The size of a single bet used as a standard of measurement.

upcard: The dealer's card that is dealt face-up.

video slots: Slot machines in which spinning reels are simulated on the video screen.

vigorish: The percentage, fee, or commission, taken by the casino. Sometimes referred to as vig.

VIP: *High rollers* that casinos consider very important players, so they merit special attention and complimentary treatment.

wager: See *bet.*

whale: A super-sized *high roller* who has a credit line of more than $1 million.

wheel: In poker, the best possible low hand: A-2-3-4-5.

wild card: A joker or other card that can be assigned the value of any other card from the deck to complete your hand.

working: In craps, when a bet is *on,* meaning the bet is at risk to win or lose on the next roll.

wrong bettor: In craps, a player who bets on the *don't pass* and *don't come* lines.

Appendix B

Important Resources

*I*f you're ready for the next step — or you're interested in a particular facet of casino gambling, or you just want to hone your skills in a specific game — this appendix is for you. From books and magazines to helpful Web sites, I present some of the best sources in this appendix for furthering your gambling education.

Books

Greater gambling knowledge can only improve your odds in the casinos. Hundreds of books are out there, covering topics from specific games to the world of Internet gambling. Check out these favorites for more information:

- **Blackjack:** *Play Blackjack Like the Pros* by Kevin Blackwood (HarperCollins Publishers)
- **Comps:** *Comp City* by Max Rubin (Huntington Press)
- **Craps:** *Beat the Craps out of the Casinos* by Frank Scoblete (Bonus Books)
- **Horse racing:** *Betting on Horse Racing For Dummies* by Richard Eng (Wiley)
- **Internet gambling:** *Internet Poker For Dummies* by Mark Harlan and Chris Derossi (Wiley)
- **Poker:** *Poker For Dummies* by Richard Harroch and Lou Krieger (Wiley)
- **Slots:** *The Slot Machine Answer Book* by John Grochowski (Bonus Books)
- **Sports betting:** *Sharp Sports Betting* by Stanford Wong (Pi Yee Press)
- **Tournaments:** *Casino Tournament Strategy* by Stanford Wong (Pi Yee Press)
- **Video Poker:** *Video Poker: Optimum Play* by Dan Paymar (ConJelCo)

Magazines

Subscribing to various periodicals is a great way to keep your finger on the pulse of the gaming world. You get up-to-date information on games, casinos, and special events. The following list includes some of my recommendations:

- *All In:* As the new kid on the block, this magazine has quickly become must-reading for serious poker fans. Published monthly, the magazine features plenty of big-name writers and helpful information.

- *Bluff:* This new monthly has exploded onto the scene and is now the best-selling poker magazine available. Each issue features an impressive pedigree of writers who offer their unique perspectives on poker.

- *Card Player:* This biweekly read has long been a favorite of the poker community. An impressive stable of writers packs each issue with powerful information for poker players of all levels. In addition, readers can always get up-to-date information on the booming tournament circuit.

- *Casino Player:* This slick-looking monthly offers extensive coverage of the gambling scene. Each issue has an analysis of nearly every casino game, including tips, strategies, and insider information. The magazine also covers nongaming topics, such as entertainment and dining recommendations in gambling locations.

- *Gambling.com:* This bimonthly magazine focuses on the Internet gambling scene (as if you couldn't have guessed by the name).

- *Las Vegas Advisor:* This superb monthly newsletter gives a no-holds-barred look at the Las Vegas gambling scene. No other periodical provides more practical advice for stretching your gambling budget and finding great deals. The coupons alone are worth the price of the subscription.

- *Midwest Gaming and Travel:* This publication focuses on gambling life and locations in America's Heartland. The magazine features some of the nation's top gambling writers and always has loads of helpful information.

- *Strictly Slots:* This magazine is a must-subscribe for slot lovers. Good writing and quality production make this monthly magazine a winner and a pleasure to read.

Web Sites

Gambling-related Web sites are popping up in cyberspace as fast and as numerous as stars after the Big Bang. Although the immediate accessibility of online information can't be beat, the number of options can be overwhelming. This section includes some of my favorites:

✔ **www.lasvegasadvisor.com:** This Web site is easily my top recommendation. LVA contains helpful information on virtually every topic of interest to gamblers, including tournament schedules, poker forums, upcoming shows, best dining options, and best deals for your next Vegas vacation. You also can sign up for the site's popular *Question of the Day*, which comes by e-mail.

✔ **www.wizardofodds.com:** This outstanding site features the genius of Michael Shackleford, one of the top math minds in the gambling world. Few players are better than Michael at explaining the odds of various casino games and offering practical advice on bets to avoid. This site is particularly good at helping you navigate through the maze of online casinos.

✔ **www.blackjackinstitute.com:** This site is home to MIT Mike, the 2004 World Series of Blackjack champion and one of the best players from the famous MIT blackjack team. The site offers training manuals, DVDs, and seminars to help you elevate your blackjack game to a professional level.

✔ **www.bodog.com/blackwood:** Bodog Casino has put together a special Web page for readers of this book. The site includes articles and tips to orient you to the online gambling world. But the best feature is that Bodog offers free play on several casino games without your having to download or sign up. This venue is a great way to figure out the games without losing your shirt.

✔ **www.blackjackinfo.com:** One of the world's most popular blackjack Web sites has message boards, blogs, and newsletter archives. But the big draw for many players is the basic strategy engine (which calculates the optimal strategy for any set of blackjack conditions) and a free trainer who coaches you in those perfect strategies.

✔ **www.gamemasteronline.com:** This site features tons of material with an emphasis on Internet gaming. GMO offers a number of tips and strategies, including a great section on video poker. A free Poker and Blackjack School helps novices grasp the ropes.

✔ **www.bj21.com:** Gaming guru Stanford Wong has created a great interactive site to keep you on top of the blackjack world. People post their experiences at casinos all over the country.

✔ **www.blackjacktournaments.com:** This site has schedules for most upcoming blackjack tournaments and boards where players can post questions or discuss strategies. Many of the world's top tournament players hang out here, including Ken Smith, who runs the site.

✔ **www.casinocity.com:** This site features a directory of more than 4,000 casinos, weekly gaming news, and an extensive online casino directory.

✔ **www.RGTonline.com:** This site carries plenty of information, including current gambling news, helpful tips and strategies, and various articles.

✔ **www.bjinsider.com:** This online periodical is a great resource for blackjack players. Several experts contribute each month on game conditions for regular and tournament blackjack around the country.

✔ **www.gamblingtimes.com:** This site contains general gambling information, including sections on sports betting and horse racing.

✔ **www.smartgaming.com:** Gaming author Henry Tamburin features gambling books, videos, strategy cards, and software at this Web site.

✔ **www.WPTonline.com:** Home of the incredibly popular World Poker Tour, this site provides information on all its tournaments and the WPT Boot Camp, where you can learn how to play poker from the pros.

✔ **Words of wisdom from the pros:** Some of the world's most successful gamblers host their own Web sites, where tips, tricks, and words of wisdom flow, not to mention visual and audio aids. In fact, each of the following Web sites offers DVD tutorials.

- **www.annieduke.com**

- **www.philhellmuth.com**

- **www.howardlederer.com**

Gamblers Anonymous

I hope I have succeeded in sharing the pleasures of gambling while providing the tools and wisdom to help you balance the thrill of the game with an approach of moderation. Gambling can be a thoroughly enjoyable pastime, especially when you understand a game — and its odds — well enough to play your best.

But, as they say, one man's pleasure can be another man's poison. The casino life can be a high-risk gamble if you don't have a rein on self-control. When gambling gets out of control, *Gamblers Anonymous (GA)* can provide support and guidance. Offering a 12-step recovery plan and a forum for support, this organization has regular meetings in literally hundreds of locations across the United States and Canada. (Cruise ships even offer GA meetings.)

Pay a visit to www.gamblersanonymous.org for more information. A sobering questionnaire helps you gauge whether you have a problem. And if you do, Gamblers Anonymous offers several ways to help you find a solution.

Index

• G •

• H •

• Q •

• R •

• Y •

• Z •

JSINESS, CAREERS & PERSONAL FINANCE

0-7645-5307-0

0-7645-5331-3 *†

Also available:

- Accounting For Dummies †
  0-7645-5314-3
- Business Plans Kit For Dummies †
  0-7645-5365-8
- Cover Letters For Dummies
  0-7645-5224-4
- Frugal Living For Dummies
  0-7645-5403-4
- Leadership For Dummies
  0-7645-5176-0
- Managing For Dummies
  0-7645-1771-6

- Marketing For Dummies
  0-7645-5600-2
- Personal Finance For Dummies *
  0-7645-2590-5
- Project Management For Dummies
  0-7645-5283-X
- Resumes For Dummies †
  0-7645-5471-9
- Selling For Dummies
  0-7645-5363-1
- Small Business Kit For Dummies *†
  0-7645-5093-4

OME & BUSINESS COMPUTER BASICS

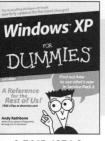

0-7645-4074-2

0-7645-3758-X

Also available:

- ACT! 6 For Dummies
  0-7645-2645-6
- iLife '04 All-in-One Desk Reference
  For Dummies
  0-7645-7347-0
- iPAQ For Dummies
  0-7645-6769-1
- Mac OS X Panther Timesaving
  Techniques For Dummies
  0-7645-5812-9
- Macs For Dummies
  0-7645-5656-8

- Microsoft Money 2004 For Dummies
  0-7645-4195-1
- Office 2003 All-in-One Desk Reference
  For Dummies
  0-7645-3883-7
- Outlook 2003 For Dummies
  0-7645-3759-8
- PCs For Dummies
  0-7645-4074-2
- TiVo For Dummies
  0-7645-6923-6
- Upgrading and Fixing PCs For Dummies
  0-7645-1665-5
- Windows XP Timesaving Techniques
  For Dummies
  0-7645-3748-2

OOD, HOME, GARDEN, HOBBIES, MUSIC & PETS

0-7645-5295-3

0-7645-5232-5

Also available:

- Bass Guitar For Dummies
  0-7645-2487-9
- Diabetes Cookbook For Dummies
  0-7645-5230-9
- Gardening For Dummies *
  0-7645-5130-2
- Guitar For Dummies
  0-7645-5106-X
- Holiday Decorating For Dummies
  0-7645-2570-0
- Home Improvement All-in-One
  For Dummies
  0-7645-5680-0

- Knitting For Dummies
  0-7645-5395-X
- Piano For Dummies
  0-7645-5105-1
- Puppies For Dummies
  0-7645-5255-4
- Scrapbooking For Dummies
  0-7645-7208-3
- Senior Dogs For Dummies
  0-7645-5818-8
- Singing For Dummies
  0-7645-2475-5
- 30-Minute Meals For Dummies
  0-7645-2589-1

TERNET & DIGITAL MEDIA

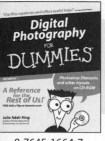

0-7645-1664-7

0-7645-6924-4

Also available:

- 2005 Online Shopping Directory
  For Dummies
  0-7645-7495-7
- CD & DVD Recording For Dummies
  0-7645-5956-7
- eBay For Dummies
  0-7645-5654-1
- Fighting Spam For Dummies
  0-7645-5965-6
- Genealogy Online For Dummies
  0-7645-5964-8
- Google For Dummies
  0-7645-4420-9

- Home Recording For Musicians
  For Dummies
  0-7645-1634-5
- The Internet For Dummies
  0-7645-4173-0
- iPod & iTunes For Dummies
  0-7645-7772-7
- Preventing Identity Theft For Dummies
  0-7645-7336-5
- Pro Tools All-in-One Desk Reference
  For Dummies
  0-7645-5714-9
- Roxio Easy Media Creator For Dummies
  0-7645-7131-1

* Separate Canadian edition also available
† Separate U.K. edition also available

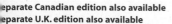

ilable wherever books are sold. For more information or to order direct: U.S. customers visit www.dummies.com or call 1-877-762-2974.
. customers visit www.wileyeurope.com or call 0800 243407. Canadian customers visit www.wiley.ca or call 1-800-567-4797.

 WILEY

SPORTS, FITNESS, PARENTING, RELIGION & SPIRITUALITY

0-7645-5146-9

0-7645-5418-2

Also available:
- Adoption For Dummies
  0-7645-5488-3
- Basketball For Dummies
  0-7645-5248-1
- The Bible For Dummies
  0-7645-5296-1
- Buddhism For Dummies
  0-7645-5359-3
- Catholicism For Dummies
  0-7645-5391-7
- Hockey For Dummies
  0-7645-5228-7

- Judaism For Dummies
  0-7645-5299-6
- Martial Arts For Dummies
  0-7645-5358-5
- Pilates For Dummies
  0-7645-5397-6
- Religion For Dummies
  0-7645-5264-3
- Teaching Kids to Read For Dummies
  0-7645-4043-2
- Weight Training For Dummies
  0-7645-5168-X
- Yoga For Dummies
  0-7645-5117-5

TRAVEL

0-7645-5438-7

0-7645-5453-0

Also available:
- Alaska For Dummies
  0-7645-1761-9
- Arizona For Dummies
  0-7645-6938-4
- Cancún and the Yucatán For Dummies
  0-7645-2437-2
- Cruise Vacations For Dummies
  0-7645-6941-4
- Europe For Dummies
  0-7645-5456-5
- Ireland For Dummies
  0-7645-5455-7

- Las Vegas For Dummies
  0-7645-5448-4
- London For Dummies
  0-7645-4277-X
- New York City For Dummies
  0-7645-6945-7
- Paris For Dummies
  0-7645-5494-8
- RV Vacations For Dummies
  0-7645-5443-3
- Walt Disney World & Orlando For Dummie
  0-7645-6943-0

GRAPHICS, DESIGN & WEB DEVELOPMENT

0-7645-4345-8

0-7645-5589-8

Also available:
- Adobe Acrobat 6 PDF For Dummies
  0-7645-3760-1
- Building a Web Site For Dummies
  0-7645-7144-3
- Dreamweaver MX 2004 For Dummies
  0-7645-4342-3
- FrontPage 2003 For Dummies
  0-7645-3882-9
- HTML 4 For Dummies
  0-7645-1995-6
- Illustrator cs For Dummies
  0-7645-4084-X

- Macromedia Flash MX 2004 For Dummi
  0-7645-4358-X
- Photoshop 7 All-in-One Desk
  Reference For Dummies
  0-7645-1667-1
- Photoshop cs Timesaving Technique:
  For Dummies
  0-7645-6782-9
- PHP 5 For Dummies
  0-7645-4166-8
- PowerPoint 2003 For Dummies
  0-7645-3908-6
- QuarkXPress 6 For Dummies
  0-7645-2593-X

NETWORKING, SECURITY, PROGRAMMING & DATABASES

0-7645-6852-3

0-7645-5784-X

Also available:
- A+ Certification For Dummies
  0-7645-4187-0
- Access 2003 All-in-One Desk
  Reference For Dummies
  0-7645-3988-4
- Beginning Programming For Dummies
  0-7645-4997-9
- C For Dummies
  0-7645-7068-4
- Firewalls For Dummies
  0-7645-4048-3
- Home Networking For Dummies
  0-7645-42796

- Network Security For Dummies
  0-7645-1679-5
- Networking For Dummies
  0-7645-1677-9
- TCP/IP For Dummies
  0-7645-1760-0
- VBA For Dummies
  0-7645-3989-2
- Wireless All In-One Desk Reference
  For Dummies
  0-7645-7496-5
- Wireless Home Networking For Dummi
  0-7645-3910-8